The New Scramble for Africa

THE NEW SCRAMBLE FOR AFRICA

Pádraig Carmody

polity

First published in 2011 by Polity Press

Reprinted 2011, 2012 (twice), 2013

Polity Press
65 Bridge Street
Cambridge CB2 1UR, UK

Polity Press
350 Main Street
Malden, MA 02148, USA

ISBN-13: 978-0-7456-4784-5
ISBN-13: 978-0-7456-4785-2(pb)

A catalogue record for this book is available from the British Library.

Typeset in 10.5 on 12 pt Times NR
by Toppan Best-set Premedia Limited
Printed and bound in the USA by Edwards Brothers, Inc.

For further information on Polity, visit our website: www.politybooks.com

CONTENTS

FIGURES AND TABLES

ACKNOWLEDGEMENTS

Several people have helped in writing this book. First and foremost I would like to express my gratitude to Ian Taylor and Godfrey Hampwaye for allowing me to draw substantially for this book on two articles I co-authored with them (P. Carmody and I. Taylor (2010), 'Flexigemony and force in China's resource diplomacy in Africa', *Geopolitics*, 15, 3, 1–20, and Carmody and G. Hampwaye (2010), 'Inclusive or exclusive globalization: the impacts of Asian-owned businesses in Zambia', *Africa Today*, 56, 3, 84–102). Thanks also to Sarah Smiley and Francis Koti and the referees and editors of *Africa Today* and *Geopolitics* for their comments on those papers. Thanks also are due to Emma Mawdsley and Gerard McCann for their comments on part of chapter 4 which appears in their edited book *India in Africa: Changing Geographies of Power* (Oxford: Fahamu Books, 2010), and for their permission to reproduce material from that chapter here. Thanks are due to Francis Owusu, Howard Stein, Eric Sheppard and Peter Kragelund for comments on sections, and the referees for Polity Press for their incisive comments on the proposal and manuscript, which have substantially improved it. I would also like to thank Louise Knight who suggested this project and David Winters and Leigh Mueller at Polity for helping to bring it to fruition. Thanks also to Sheila McMorrow for producing the map. The support of the National Geographic Waitt Grant Program and the United States National Science Foundation (award number 925151 with Jim Murphy) to undertake fieldwork in Zambia and South Africa is gratefully acknowledged.

ABBREVIATIONS

ABC	Abstain, Be Faithful, Condomize
ACOTA	African Contingency Operations Training and Assistance Programme
ACP	African, Caribbean and Pacific (countries)
AFRICOM	African Command of the United States Department of Defense
AGOA	African Growth and Opportunity Act
AIDS	Acquired Immunodeficiency Syndrome
AU	African Union
BBC	British Broadcasting Corporation
BEE	Black Economic Empowerment
BP	(formerly) British Petroleum
BRICs	Brazil, Russia, India, China
CAR	Central African Republic
CCS	Centre for Chinese Studies
CFA	Communauté Financière Africaine
coltan	colombite-tantalite
CIF	China International Fund
CNN	Cable News Network
CNPC	China National Petroleum Company
CVRD	Companhia Vale do Rio Doce
DFID	Department for International Development (United Kingdom)
DRC	Democratic Republic of Congo
EASSY	East African Submarine Cable
ECOWAS	Economic Community of West African States

EEZ	Exclusive Economic Zone
E-IMET	Enhanced International Military and Education and Training Programme
EPA	Economic Partnership Agreement
EU	European Union
EXIM	Export–Import
FDI	Foreign Direct Investment
FOCAC	Forum on China–Africa Cooperation
FPSOs	floating production, storage and offloading vessels
GDP	Gross Domestic Product
GEDA	Gauteng Economic Development Agency
GPN	global production network
HIV	Human Immunodeficiency Virus
IBSA	India, Brazil, South Africa
ICC	International Criminal Court
IMF	International Monetary Fund
ITEC	Indian Technical and Economic Cooperation
KCM	Koncola Copper Mine
MFEZ	Multi-facility Economic Zone
MNC	Multinational Corporation
MTN	Mobile Telecommunications Networks
NEPAD	New Partnership for African Development
NGOs	Non-Governmental Organizations
NOCs	National Oil Companies
OECD	Organization for Economic Co-operation and Development
ONGC	Oil and Natural Gas Corporation (India)
OPEC	Organization of Petroleum Exporting Countries
PDVSA	Petróleos de Venezuela, SA
PEPFAR	President's Emergency Programme for AIDS Relief
Petrobras	Petróleo Brasileiro SA
PETRONAS	Petroliam Nasional Berhad
PRSP	Poverty Reduction Strategy Paper
RCD	Rally for Congolese Democracy
RoZ	Republic of Zambia
RPF	Rwandan Patriotic Front
SADC	Southern African Development Community
SAP	Structural Adjustment Programme
SAT-3/WASC	South Atlantic 3 / West Africa Submarine Fibre Optic Cable
SEZ	Special Economic Zone
SOEs	state-owned enterprises

SSA	Sub-Saharan Africa
TEAM-9	Techno-Economic Approach to Africa–India Movement
TNCs	Transnational Corporations
UN	United Nations
UNCTAD	United Nations Conference on Trade and Development
VVIP	Very, Very Important Person
WTO	World Trade Organization
ZDA	Zambian Development Agency

RESOURCE MAP OF AFRICA

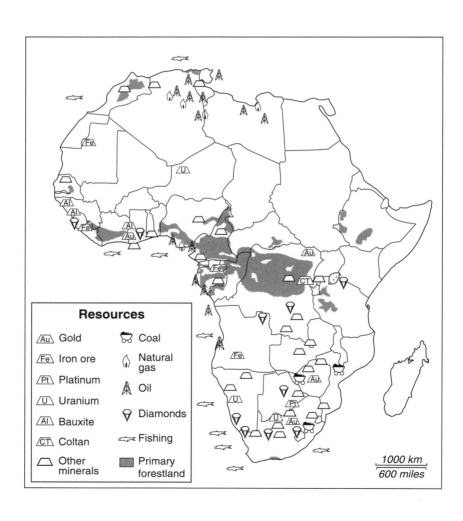

Resources

Au	Gold	Coal	
Fe	Iron ore	Natural gas	
Pt	Platinum	Oil	
U	Uranium	Diamonds	
Al	Bauxite	Fishing	
CT	Coltan	Primary forestland	
Other minerals			

1000 km
600 miles

INTRODUCTION

Africa is 'in play' as never before. (Raine 2009, p. 9, quoting *Final Report of the Africa–China–US Trilateral Dialogue*)

There is now no denying that Africa has become a sought-after continent in a short space of time, thanks to its strategic importance. Today, Africa really matters. (European Union Commissioner for Development, quoted in Holden 2009, p. 128)

Africa has long been held up as a region which has been by-passed by globalization. However, something interesting is afoot in Africa and its relations with the rest of the world. There is now massively increased interest, and investment, in the continent from major world powers. The role of Asian powers in particular is growing rapidly. In some parts of Africa, children now assume that foreigners with light skin are Chinese, rather than European or American (Michel, Beuret and Woods 2009).

Why has Africa suddenly become strategically important for 'great' and emerging powers? Why are Chinese companies now investing heavily on the continent and why do we see on the news weekly about Somali pirates kidnapping sailors or hijacking ships for ransom, and are these issues related? The argument of this book is that they are; that these are features of the deepening process of globalization which has unleashed a new scramble for African resources and, to a lesser extent, markets. This is reconfiguring Africa's economic geography and development, but also reinforcing previous patterns of economy and politics. This book explores the reasons behind the new scramble and its nature and impacts.

African development is defined by the 'paradox of plenty': that is, that it is a very resource-rich continent, but economically poor. Africa is thought to contain 42 per cent of the world's bauxite, 38 per cent of its uranium, 42 per cent of its gold, 73 per cent of its platinum, 88 per cent of its diamonds and around 10 per cent of its oil (Bush 2007). Nonetheless, around half of the population of sub-Saharan Africa (SSA) live on the equivalent of less than US$1.25 a day (World Bank 2010), and despite the fact that Guinea in West Africa contains almost half of the world's bauxite, the raw material for aluminium, its government's budget is only 0.0005 per cent of that of its former colonial master, France (Philips 2007). This is an outcome of the way in which Africa has been integrated into the global economy, which is heavily influenced by its colonial history.

The first scramble for Africa amongst the major European powers was set off in the late nineteenth century by a variety of factors, including English, German and French military rivalry, the need to open new sources of cotton supply as a result of the American civil war, and new markets as a result of the European economic depression (Kennedy 1987; Pakenham 1991; Mamdani 1996). During that era King Leopold II of the Belgians objectified Africa as a 'magnificent cake' which would yield up resources and wealth for Europe.

The rules for the division of Africa amongst the colonial powers were established at the Congress of Berlin, hosted by united Germany's first chancellor Otto von Bismarck in 1884–5 (Pakenham 1991). Having recently fought the Franco-Prussian war, in part to create a united Germany, Bismarck was keen that inter-imperialist rivalry in Africa should not lead to further conflict, as Germany was now 'satiated' in Europe (Joll 1983). The fact Africa was divided in this way is evidenced by the many straight lines forming around a third of African borders, based on geographical lines of latitude and longitude.

The Congress established the rules for the colonial division of Africa based on the principle of 'effective occupation'. Effective occupation was where a European power could claim territory in Africa as its own if it could show that it was in effective control of it: that it had troops and administrators on the ground to rule it. This prevented war, although Britain and France had a military stand-off over Fashoda, in modern-day Sudan, in 1898, which was eventually resolved to Britain's advantage.

While colonial rule was short-lived in Africa – generally less than 100 years – it had profound impacts. Economies were structured to meet the demands of industrializing Europe by producing raw materials. Consequently European prosperity was partly built on the colonization of the continent. This extroversion of Africa, whereby its economy was oriented to meet the needs of other people in other places, continues till today (Amin 1976). The calculus was simple, as illustrated by a children's game.

In the National Famine Memorial in Strokestown House in County Roscommon in Ireland, there is an old board game in one of the children's bedrooms called 'The Colonial Game'. The objective of the game is to import raw materials cheaply and sell expensive manufactured goods back to the colonies. Between 1905 and 1914, 50 per cent of Dahomey's gross domestic product (GDP) was extracted by the French (Manning 1982, cited in Acemoglu, Johnson and Robinson 2001). Unequal trade installed under colonialism is the basis of African poverty today, many would argue, although there are also domestic elites who benefit as the continent has over 100,000 US dollar millionaires (Taylor 2005) and South Africa has 20 US dollar billionaires, many of whom are shareholders in major resource companies (Turok 2008). Some argue that South Africa was an example of 'internal colonialism' (Wolpe 1975).

Resources were central to the first scramble for Africa. For example, the Congress of Berlin granted the Belgian King rights to the Congo, which was held as his personal property and became a major source of rubber for European and American car tyres and also condoms. Indeed, some credit the demographic transition in Europe, in which birth rates fell, to Congolese rubber.

An estimated 10 million people were killed in the Congo during Belgian colonialism in the search for ivory and rubber (Mantz 2008). Refusal to search for and tap rubber under Belgian rule could lead to the loss of a hand or death. This 'plunder economy' continues today (Cramer 2006), with an estimated 3–5 million people killed in the war in the Democratic Republic of Congo (DRC) between 1998 and 2003. As discussed later, conflict this time around was largely about control of the strategic mineral coltan used in new 'heartland' technologies of the information age, such as mobile phones.

The structure of African economies remained largely unchanged in the post-colonial era. Ghana was the first country in sub-Saharan Africa to achieve independence, in 1957. Its first prime minister Kwame Nkrumah wrote, before he was removed from power by a coup, of the dangers of neo-colonialism (Nkrumah 1965). Neo-colonialism is where formal political independence is achieved, but economic control – and hence indirect political power – continues to lie with overseas powers and companies. Tanzania's first independent leader, Julius Nyerere, spoke of 'flag independence' – again, a situation in which real economic control continued to rest with the former colonial powers.

After independence, during the Cold War between the United States and the Soviet Union, Western powers supported 'friendly' anti-communist dictators such as Mobutu Seso Seko in Zaire, who came to power in a coup backed by Belgium and the American Central Intelligence Agency. In the late 1970s Mobutu's Zaire received half of all American aid to Africa (Mantz 2008).

During this time the West did not impose conditions such as democracy or free market reforms on states receiving aid in Africa. However, with the winding down of the Cold War in the 1980s, this changed, and economic and political conditions from Western-dominated financial institutions and donors became the norm. In order to access emergency funds from the World Bank and the International Monetary Fund (IMF) to cope with the effects of the global oil shocks of the 1970s and resultant debt crises, many African countries had already begun to implement free market reforms in the 1980s (Cheru 1989). These economic reforms were to have an unintended effect, however – to open up Africa to trade and investment from rising powers in the East – but they failed to reverse underdevelopment.

There is an extensive literature on the causes of African underdevelopment. This falls into two broad categories: that which blames African elites for their corruption and poor governance (Van De Walle 2001), and that which blames the combined and uneven nature of economic development in the global capitalist system (Bond 2006). A third position has recently emerged and received much media attention. That is, that aid is the primary cause of African underdevelopment (Moyo 2009). It is meant to corrupt political elites, create a dependency culture and distort trade, amongst other defects. The problems with aid are well known (Glennie 2008) and this has led to a variety of responses.

Some corporations, such as the Body Shop, champion 'trade not aid', and the EU now gives 'aid for trade'. However, African trade is booming. Africa's merchandise trade rose from US$217 billion in 1995 to US$986 billion in 2008, but the absolute numbers of people living in poverty in Africa continued to rise (Carmody 2010; United Nations Conference on Trade and Development (UNCTAD) 2010). This is because three-quarters of what Africa exports are unprocessed primary commodities such as oil or copper. This is highly problematic because primary commodities tend to be characterized by very volatile prices and lack of technological dynamism and local economic linkages, and are often subject to looting by political elites. Additionally, many of the biggest companies which exploit African resources are foreign-owned, so the profits flow elsewhere. Is trade, or the current structure of African trade installed under colonialism, one of the primary problems then: producing, rather than reducing, poverty?

In the new scramble there is geo-economic competition between different world economic powers to open up resource access for 'their' companies, in addition to subsidiary motives such as getting access to African markets and seeking diplomatic support in the United Nations. While in the past Europe and North America have dominated trade with Africa, this is now changing. China has now overtaken Japan as the world's second-largest economy after the United States, and its economy is growing rapidly. By some estimates China is already Africa's largest trading partner, though this is still more likely to be the United States.

In China's case, given its 'late start' in accessing African resources, this often involves inducements such as concessional loans, the construction of Special Economic Zones (SEZs), or proxy force, such as the building of arms and tank assembly plants in Sudan and the supply of weapons to Zimbabwe. Which strategy is adopted depends on the nature of existing domestic social relations. Consequently, emerging forms of South–South globalization and investment are sometimes more progressive, and in other cases more regressive, than earlier Northern-centred relations with Africa. Therefore, understanding the differential nature and geography of engagement is key.

In the Chinese case, the emerging form of rule at a distance (Abrahamsen 2000) is a form of 'flexigemony' – discussed later, in which the Chinese state works with and through both authoritarian and democratic states in Africa to ensure resource and market access and diplomatic support, in addition to other objectives. The 'full spectrum approach' – seeking resources, markets and diplomatic support – is also adopted by India, as is discussed later.

While there are many resources that could have been chosen for study for this book, of necessity only a few can be examined in more detail. There are different theories about the etiology of the word 'Africa'. One is that it derives from a Greek word meaning 'without cold', or from a Latin word meaning 'sunny' or 'hot'. There are now elaborate plans to develop solar farms in the Sahara, one of which could supply up to 15 per cent of Europe's power requirements (Salkever 2010). Competition around energy resources is particularly acute given their centrality to the functioning of the global economy. However, as solar mega farms have yet to come to fruition, the focus of this book is on other forms of energy.

As a source of wealth, conflict and poverty, oil congeals the contradictions of globalization. While Africa has had major oil producers for the last half-century, competition around this resource has increased dramatically in the last ten years, partly as a result of the Iraq war. It is examined here, as are uranium and biofuels which are becoming of increasing importance as oil becomes more scarce.

Africa has long produced uranium – for the atom bombs which were dropped on Hiroshima and Nagasaki during the Second World War for example. Biofuels, however, are a new energy resource, with a different geography. While oil is a 'point resource' found at set locations, often coastal or offshore (Le Billon 2008), uranium is found onshore (see resource map on p. xii), and biofuel crops are diffuse resources – and consequently difficult to map – which can sometimes be grown on marginal land. This geography informs patterns of conflict and class formation.

Conflicts around oil and diamonds in Africa are well known and reported in the popular media. However, there are other resource grabs and conflicts which are less well known, but have important implications for African lives and livelihoods. One of these resource grabs involves coltan, a semi-precious metal without which the global informational economy would not function. The extraction of coltan has been associated with war, poverty and environmental despoliation in the DRC.

Timber is a basic input into the global construction and furniture industries and so it too is vitally important to the global economy. Much of the demand for African timber is now coming from China, so that it can be processed and exported as furniture to Europe and the US. Africa is home to major timber reserves, although these are being rapidly depleted. Trees also serve an important carbon sink function vital to global environmental sustainability, particularly in the context of accelerated climate change (Toulmin 2009). Consequently this is also an important resource to examine.

Food, along with water, is the most basic human need. As the global population grows and consumption patterns change, there will also be growing competition around access to food. Given Africa's extensive coastline, fish are a vital source of calories and protein for much of its population, but foreign firms and populations also covet this increasingly scarce resource. Unlike many other resources, fish have a mobile geography, and this is mirrored by the mobility of the extraction equipment which trails them: trawlers and factory ships. Access to fish is also contested and implicated in the rise of Somali piracy, as will be discussed later. The phenomenon of biopiracy or genetic theft of African plants is also discussed.

While the contradiction between the growth of the global economy and the fixed amount of natural resources is fundamentally what has sparked the new scramble for Africa, another contradiction of the globalized market economy also motivates it. The global economy is technologically dynamic and expansive; however, multinational corporations (MNCs) seek out low-cost labour sites for assembly operations to reduce costs and raise profits. Given the low wages paid to Chinese workers, for example, they can often not afford to buy the products, such as iPods, which they produce. Low wages and the high intensity of work were implicated in a rash of suicides at the company that makes iPods in China in 2010.

This mismatch means that surplus profits or capital have to find other outlets, such as asset price inflation in stock markets or housing. Another avenue that global business has been exploring to open up new sources of profit in recent years has been the so-called 'Bottom of the Pyramid' (Prahalad 2005) – the roughly half of the world's population living on less than the equivalent of US$2 a day. While Western companies such as Unilever now produce washing powder in small packets to cater to this market, Indian, Chinese and other companies already manufacture products specifically aimed at this market in their own countries. Africa then represents a sizeable market, with a population approaching a billion people, demanding affordable goods.

Given saturated markets elsewhere, some major Western technology companies also want their systems to become the operating standards so they can capture African markets in the future. In Namibia, Microsoft provided free copies of Windows and computers to go with them, reportedly in part to undercut a non-governmental organization (NGO) which was providing open-source software for free (Patel 2009). This book also examines competition over African markets.

While Africa is being reintegrated into the global economy primarily as a supplier of raw materials, it is too simplistic to present this as simply a rerun of the colonial scramble, for a number of reasons. First, the original scramble was sometimes conducted by what we would now call MNCs, or what were then called concessionary companies, such as the British South Africa Company founded by the English imperialist Cecil Rhodes (Pakenham 1991). They were called concessionary companies because they were granted concessions by their home governments to manage certain overseas territories exclusively.

These concessionary companies were closely linked to home country governments and granted monopoly territorial and exploitation rights. While some companies in the current scramble maintain close ties with their home governments, or in other cases are government-owned, there is no longer exclusive territorial access. Rather, a mixture of companies from different places now invest in the same countries. Additionally, 'partnership capitalism' often characterizes the new arrangements, as MNCs often engage in joint ventures, calling into question the extent to which 'British' and 'Chinese' oil capital, for example, are really distinct social forces.

The second major difference between the first and second scrambles is that African countries are now legally, if not economically, independent, making resource access for MNCs dependent on striking bargains with local elites who serve as gatekeepers. In relation to oil, the Nigerian human rights activist Ken Saro-Wiwa described this as 'the slick alliance' of domestic elites and MNCs (Kashi and Watts 2008). Another way to think of this is as a kind of transnational contract of extroversion, whereby territorial access to resources is granted to MNCs in exchange for a share of resource rents going to local elites (Carmody 2010).

In common with colonialism, the current round of economic restructuring in Africa is, however, reinscribing resource-based economies, and increasing class inequality while simultaneously reducing absolute poverty – as a proportion of the population, if not in absolute numbers of the poor– at least up until the global financial crisis of 2008. Chinese investment in road and rail infrastructure and the revival of the primary sector of the economy (agriculture and mining) present opportunities for growing employment and poverty reduction. However, by reinforcing resource-dependence and reinscribing enclave economies with limited connections to the rest of the national territory, this also risks reinforcing the power of authoritarian states. As resource-based capital accumulation tends to be more conflictual than that in other sectors of the economy, and class inequality increases, new conflicts are emerging on the continent, such as anti-Chinese riots, kidnappings and shootings in previously relatively peaceful Zambia, and also in Ethiopia, for example.

Increased interest in accessing African resources is also driving the militarization of the continent as great powers seek to insure their investments and disrupt potential terrorist threats. The militarization of Africa is proceeding through initiatives such as the new United States African Command (AFRICOM) and the new American military base in Djibouti established in 2003. US military spending in Africa doubled from US$296 million in 1998–2001 to US$597 million in 2002–5 (Yi-Chong 2008). This may further inflame conflict (and resistance) on the continent, although there is evidence that the great powers are also cooperating, through the US–China–Africa trilateral dialogue for example. While the major powers have competing interests over access to specific resources in particular places, they share a common general interest in the continued exportation of African resources, generating incentives for cooperation.

This book examines old and new economic power interest in the current development and exploitation of Africa's resources. It begins in chapter 1 by over-viewing the historical reasons behind the development of resource-based, extractive economies through a focus on current debates about Africa's geography and development. It then moves on to analyse the current increased interest of old and new economic powers in the continent. The geo-economics and political strategies of these powers are assessed, as are the impacts of resource exploitation, through case studies.

Chapter 2 examines old economic power interests and strategies in Africa in recent years. These powers have somewhat different interests, depending on their individual histories and economies. The US, in particular, is dramatically increasing its investment and presence in Africa, partly in response to Chinese resource competition. The United States currently imports three times more oil from Africa than China does, as a result of the African Growth and Opportunity Act (AGOA), developed by the Clinton Administration in 2000, which allows qualifying African countries to export duty-free to the US. Interestingly, over 80 per cent of African exports under AGOA are oil, and American oil interests in the continent are now being securitized or militarized. This chapter describes the US resource strategy in Africa and discusses relations with selected key states.

The European Union (EU) powers and Japan have been playing defensive maintenance and 'catch-up' games with China and the US in Africa in recent years. This chapter also examines the resource interests and strategies of the EU powers in Africa, with a particular focus on Britain and France, the two main former colonial powers. The EU powers have long-standing resource interests in Africa and some argue that the recent aid-related 'humanitarian scramble for Africa' is infused with geopolitical and economic motives. For example the deployment of an EU military 'battlegroup' to Chad, ostensibly for humanitarian reasons, is partly to prevent the government of Chad from being overthrown by pro-Sudanese interests. Sudan is one of China's most important partner countries in Africa, as will be discussed.

The EU's main recent initiative in Africa is 'free trade' Economic Partnership Agreements (EPAs). While among the continents of the world Africa has the smallest economy, in the hypercompetitive environment generated by globalization, there is still competition over access to its markets, and EPAs can be understood in this light. Despite China's dramatically increased presence in Africa, the continent's trade with the EU is still roughly twice what it is with China, and consequently of great importance to African states.

South Africa is both an old and a new economic power. It is old in the sense that it has long had the biggest economy in Africa, although now rivalled by Egypt; and new in that it is only in the last fifteen years that many of the restrictions it had on trade with the rest of the continent were lifted. This chapter also examines the nature and impacts of the re-emergence of South Africa.

China's interests, trade and investments in Africa are growing exponentially. Chapter 3 examines Chinese resource interests and strategies in Africa. From less than US$5 billion in trade between Africa and China in the mid-1990s, the figure for 2009 was over US$100 billion. Imports and exports between China and Africa are roughly balanced, but China's trade with Africa in 2008 was only 8 per cent of its trade with Asia, and consequently it is trade in strategic resources, such as oil, which is most important from a Chinese economic perspective (calculated from National Bureau of Statistics of China 2010). Through comparative case studies of Sudan and Zambia, this chapter, co-authored with Ian Taylor, explores the impacts of Chinese interests on governance in these countries.

A variety of other new economic powers are also dramatically increasing their economic presences on the continent – particularly Brazil, Russia and India (along with China, these are commonly known as the 'BRICs'). Chapter 4 explores the reasons behind this rapid growth in trade and investment and the logic behind and impacts of other new economic power engagements, with a particular focus on India.

The subsequent chapters undertake case studies of particular sectors and commodities, and report on primary research on Asian-owned companies in the Southern African country of Zambia. Zambia is important as the third-largest recipient of Chinese investment in Africa, by some estimates, and the site of China's first operational SEZ on the continent.

Chapter 5 examines external economic interest in West African and Sahelian oil. Oil is the primary fuel for the global economy and economic growth, and supply problems in the Middle East, as a result of the war in Iraq, have made West African oil a resource of particular interest to the major powers. Africa contains about 7 per cent of known global oil reserves, and West African oil tends to be 'light and sweet' with a low sulphur content, suitable for burning in cars. West

African and Chadian oil also does not have to pass through the 'choke point' – where it could potentially be disrupted – of the Suez Canal and, because of its greater proximity, shipping time to the East Coast of the US and Western Europe is reduced.

China is also a growing presence in oil production, and Angola is now, in some years, China's largest single supplier of oil. This chapter explores the nature of oil competition between the great powers in West Africa and the impacts on people's livelihoods and governance. While much has been written about Nigerian oil, and also Sudan, less is known about newer oil producers such as Angola and Equatorial Guinea which have had the fastest-growing economies in the world in recent years, and consequently the discussion focuses on them.

As a result of the small size of its economy, Africa is often presented as being largely irrelevant to the broader global economy. However, its minerals are of enormous economic and strategic importance, making it centrally vital (Moseley and Gray 2008). Chapter 6 examines competition and conflict over the key strategic minerals of uranium and coltan. Much of the literature on resource competition in Africa to date has focused on oil; however, its increasing scarcity, and also global climate change, are prompting governments around the world to turn to nuclear energy as an alternative.

Uranium is the key raw material in nuclear energy production and Africa holds 18 per cent of the world's known recoverable uranium resources. There is already substantial competition around access to this resource on the continent, with Russia an important emerging player. Active prospecting is being undertaken in thirty-one countries, and uranium mining has been associated with pollution and violent conflict in Niger over the distribution of rents. This chapter reviews this industry in Africa, with a focus on the Sahel, or the region bordering the Sahara, in particular.

Coltan is an abbreviation for colombite-tantalite from which the precious metals colombium and tantalum are extracted. Tantalum is twice as dense as steel and can capture and release an electrical charge, which makes it vital for capacitors in portable miniaturized electronic equipment such as mobile phones. Of known global tantalite reserves, 9 per cent are found in the DRC. Before the new major power scramble for Africa, there was a regional scramble for coltan, which helped to fuel the civil war in the DRC from 1998 to 2003 and involved eight African militaries at its height. Chapter 6 also explores this.

While most of the literature has focused on external power interest in Africa's non-renewable mineral resources, there is also increasing competition over living renewable resources. Chapter 7 explores this and the related issue of land. The current deforestation process in Mozambique is locally referred to as the 'Chinese takeaway'. Old-growth timber is in high demand around the world and is a principal raw material in the furniture industry. The value of Tanzania's timber exports increased by 1,400 per cent from 1997 to 2005, and sometimes a single tree may be worth tens of thousands of dollars. Harvesting has also sometimes been associated with conflict, to which large corporate conglomerates may contribute through their purchases. An estimated 70 per cent of Gabon's timber is exported illegally to China, and the figure rises to 90 per cent in the case of Equatorial Guinea. There have also been reactions against this, however, such as the government of Gabon's suspension of logging in nature reserves in 2002, although enforcement has been lax. This chapter explores the scramble for Africa's timber and its environmental impacts.

China's consumption of fish may treble by 2025. A reported 90 per cent of abalone shellfish have now been fished out in Southern Africa in recent years, and a Chinese ship is reported to have docked in Mozambique with 4 tons of shark fins, leading to accusations of resource colonialism. Since the collapse of the Somali state in the early 1990s, its waters have also been plundered by foreign business interests. Indeed, the current wave of piracy in Somalia began with boardings of overseas fishing vessels to discourage them from entering the country's territorial waters illegally. The world's largest trawler, formerly known as *Atlantic Dawn*, has also been operating off the West African coast. This chapter explores the 'fish rush' around Africa's coast as well.

Given predicted worldwide energy shortages in the coming decades, another area of world economic power interest in Africa is in the production of crops for biofuels. In 2007, the Brazilian President, Lula da Silva, undertook a tour of Africa during which he particularly promoted these. Prior to that, the Nigerian National Petroleum Corporation had signed an agreement with the Brazilian state-owned energy company, Petrobras, to import ethanol and develop its production in Nigeria. Biofuels are highly controversial in Africa because they may take land away from food-crop production, and in some cases are actually produced with staple food crops such as cassava. Asian and other companies are also now buying land for food production in Africa.

China is now the world's largest consumer of copper and has shown particular interest in this metal given its strategic importance to its economy. Zambia is a major copper producer and now the third-largest recipient of Chinese foreign direct investment (FDI) in Africa. Consequently Zambia is a key state for China in its resource strategy in Africa. While the focus of previous chapters is on resources, chapter 8, co-authored with Godfrey Hampwaye, focuses on markets and examines the nature and impacts of Chinese and Indian investment, in Zambia in particular.

The final chapter explores the prospects for African development in the context of the new scramble. The last scramble for Africa in the nineteenth century was provoked by a particular conjuncture of events. The new scramble for Africa has both similarities with, and differences from, the previous scramble. Formal colonialism is gone and Africa no longer serves as a major market, at least not for the older industrial powers. However, it is arguably now one of the most important arenas in which global power politics is played out. Just as the original scramble for Africa did not result in open conflict between the great powers, this is likely to be the case today, as their economies are increasingly interwoven as a result of processes of globalization. However, there are a number of proxy conflicts on the continent – in the Chad–Sudan borderlands, for example.

This final chapter assesses the likely impacts of the new scramble on African economic development, resource conflicts, and whether or not there are more cooperative institutional arrangements which could result in 'win-win' games for the continent and the great powers. Unfavourable raw material contracts have recently been renegotiated by a number of African governments. Greater coordination amongst these governments to ensure the best returns from their resources, and their ability to 'sow' these rents for industrial transformation, will be key to the continent's renaissance. Consequently, the nature of the African state remains central to the continent's (under)development.

1 THE NEW SCRAMBLE, GEOGRAPHY AND DEVELOPMENT

State weakness invites external exploitation and much of Africa represents a power vacuum that predatory outsiders are only too anxious to
fill as they search for resources in an ever more competitive world.
(Arnold 2009, p. 9)

As the global economy continues to grow, while natural resources
remain fixed, there is an imperative for industrial and industrializing
countries to open up new long-term sources of raw material supply.
The rise of China is particularly significant in this regard, given its
voracious demand, as are the other so-called 'Asian Driver' economies
such as India and other regional middle powers such as Brazil. China's
economic growth over the last thirty years has been phenomenal,
averaging 10 per cent a year. This gives a doubling time of seven years
and the move from it being an oil exporter to an oil importer in the
mid-1990s gave rise to the need for China to source this commodity
around the world.

As noted earlier, there are substantial differences between the first
scramble for Africa in the nineteenth century and the current one.
According to Satgar (2009, p. 37) 'the nature of rivalry today is not
inter-imperialist but global. This is observable on the African continent in various sectors as transnational capital scrambles to capture
resources to meet the needs of global capitalism.' However, transnational corporations' (TNCs') home country governments also play an
increasingly important role in support of 'their' companies, and major
powers have interests in Africa outside of direct economic ones as well,
particularly in relation to security.

Talk of the 'new scramble for Africa' may serve to reinforce images of Africans as passive and powerless, which are now very far from accurate, particularly as regards government leaders who are finding their power strengthened (Perrot and Malaquais 2009). African governments now act as gatekeepers for resources and often hold shares in companies undertaking their exploitation. Consequently, access to resources is now based on bargaining relationships, rather than the brute force that characterized the colonial period. This is leading to novel reconfigurations of politics, power and the economic geography of the continent, although there are still similarities with the first scramble.

According to Okeke (2008, p. 194), 'just like the first scramble, the second scramble is clearly more beneficial to the main actors – that is, the private foreign corporations and their home governments – than to African governments and people'. However, as will be discussed below, the rewards for African elites can be very substantial, even if the proportionate rewards to international corporations are bigger in certain cases. Thus the current relations must be characterized as post-imperial ones, in which national elites have substantial power in their bargaining with external actors (Becker and Sklar 1999). The extent to which this new configuration will lead to substantial poverty reduction on the continent, however, remains an open question

The paradox of plenty, or 'resource curse' – that Africa is mineral-rich, but the poorest and most conflicted continent in the world – was noted earlier. Africa has about 30 per cent of the world's mineral reserves, including 90 per cent of the world's platinum and 40 per cent of its gold (Southall 2009). However, these resources have typically only benefited elites in Africa in partnership with foreign interests and external powers. Resource scarcity is leading to deepening levels of investment and interconnection of Africa with the global economy: a new period of evolution in the globalization of the continent. The scale of increased economic interconnection or globalization between Africa and elsewhere can be demonstrated by a simple graph of exports from Africa to some of the world's major economic powers (figure 1.1). The vast majority of increased exports to the United States are of oil. What does the increasing globalization of the continent mean for its peoples?

Globalization is often defined as increased interconnectedness between places. The creation of a global economy characterized by 'network trade' – whereby components from around the world go into final products – 'deep integration' – whereby different countries harmonize their laws and regulations in relation to trade and investment – and increased information exchange is often presented in mainstream

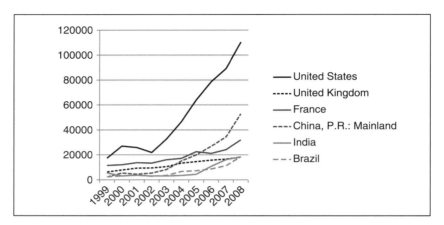

Figure 1.1   Imports from Africa in millions of US dollars (including cost, insurance and freight)
Source: IMF (2009)

accounts as a benign phenomenon which enables the 'connection of the disconnected' in the developing world. However, social and economic networks are not 'flat' but structured by hierarchy as the actors involved have different types and levels of power. Consequently, both growth and uneven development continue to shape the evolution of the global economy and of Africa. The new scramble for Africa represents a deepening of the process of globalization on the continent, which is reshaping its geography. Recently, however, the process of economic globalization has undergone a setback.

According to the IMF, the global economy contracted by 0.8 per cent in 2009. Nonetheless, that year the Economist Intelligence Unit had predicted that SSA would be home to seven of the top ten fastest-growing economies in the world, as oil importers such as Malawi benefited from favourable movements in the terms of trade as the price of oil fell. As it turned out, these predictions were not generally realized, although Malawi was one of the world's top fifteen fastest-growing economies in the world that year.

As a whole SSA had an economic growth rate of 5.6 per cent in 2008. This fell to 1.6 per cent in 2009, and the IMF predicted growth for the sub-continent of 4.3 per cent in 2010. However, economic growth is likely to return to high levels in the medium to long term as global resource scarcity becomes more acute. However, the nature and quality of this growth is important. As this book will show, it is based primarily on investment and trade in raw materials and mineral exploitation and exports, and as a result risks reinscribing Africa's previous unfavourable relations with the international system.

More than half of the population of SSA live on less than the equivalent of what a dollar a day would buy in the United States. Recently there has been a substantial debate about the causes of African underdevelopment, with some ascribing it to Africa's 'natural geographic disadvantages'. However, the deepening of the process of globalization on the continent is reconfiguring its socio-economic geography and linking it more closely to other places. In order to understand the nature of African underdevelopment and how it is being reconfigured by globalization, it is worthwhile examining the relationship between geography and development.

Geography and Development in Africa

In the last 25 years, we find that the bottom half of world income earners seems to have gained something in relation to the top half...but the bottom 10 per cent have lost seriously in comparison to the top 10 per cent. (Sutcliffe 2007, p. 71)

At the root of Africa's impoverishment, in our view, lies its extraordinarily disadvantageous geography, which has helped to shape the nature of African societies and Africa's interactions with the rest of the world. (Bloom and Sachs 1998, p. 4)

The most well-known recent explanations for Africa's underdevelopment are linked to its physical geography. For some, Africa is a victim of its geography, with many landlocked countries, far from world markets and with a particularly dangerous type of mosquito. For the well-known Oxford economist Paul Collier, and Jeffrey Sachs in his earlier work, internal geography or site characteristics are most important. Africa is 'cursed' by its resources, and by many countries having 'bad neighbours'. According to Jeffrey Sachs (2008, p. 50), 'The challenge now is that extreme poverty is concentrated in the toughest places: landlocked, tropical, drought-prone, malaria-ridden, and off the world's main trade routes. It is no accident that today's poorest places have been the last to catch the wave of globalisation. They have the most difficulty in getting on the ladder of development.'

In this reading, Africa is by-passed by globalization because: 'when the preconditions of basic infrastructure (roads, power and ports) and human capital (health and education) are in place, markets are powerful engines of development. Without these preconditions, markets can cruelly bypass large parts of the world, leaving them impoverished and suffering without respite' (Sachs 2005, p. 3). For Jeffrey Sachs the free market of a 'laissez faire' (literally 'let do') approach to African development is a 'murderous' one and there needs to be massive public investment so that Africa can take advantage of the opportunities of globalization (Sachs 2010). The levelling effects of the global free market are countered by 'natural' geographic disadvantages which can be overcome by infrastructural and other public goods investments, some of which may now be provided by China in particular.

For Paul Collier (2009), Africa is cursed by its resources and many countries are situated in 'bad neighbourhoods'. These themes have also been taken up in the recent 2009 *World Development Report, Reshaping Economic Geography*. A central theme of this report is that there is a need to integrate Africa more fully into the global economy through a reduction of 'distance' from world markets.

What these influential accounts share is an emphasis on what geographers call first nature geography – or the natural geography of coastlines, mountains and physical distance (Sheppard 2011). While not denying that landlocked states may face particular challenges, these accounts neglect the way in which 'distance' from world markets has been created. Why is Chicago central while Kigali, the capital of Rwanda, is peripheral to global flows of investment and trade? Only by taking a historical approach which examines the interactions between the past and the present can we understand the ongoing construction of African underdevelopment (Cox 1987).

Some recent mainstream approaches to African development have been critiqued as environmentally deterministic and lacking historical perspective. While more recent work by some mainstream economists now analyses the social construction and political economy of the resource curse, 'bad neighbourhoods' and the environment (Humphreys, Sachs and Stiglitz 2007), this is where mainstream work is generally weakest.

Geography, particularly socio-economic geography, is largely socially constructed, rather than being a natural artefact. While it may be uneconomic to grow bananas in Britain, it does not follow that steel should not be made in Senegal or Singapore. Resource dependency and lack of value addition in Africa are central to the continent's underdevelopment.

In the economics literature there has been a substantial debate about whether it is institutions or geography which most determine (Africa's) economic development. However, this misses an important point – institutions are geography. According to noted political theorist Raymond Duvall, institutions are structured sets of practices informed by shared sets of meanings and understandings. These practices occur in particular places and hence create socio-economic geographies. Consequently, rather than the resource curse being a 'natural' condition, it can be conceptualized as a mode of governance which involves coordination between domestic and transnational elites to secure access to resource revenues or rents. Because of the inequality and exclusion associated with this bargain, instability and conflict arise in Africa and elsewhere.

While the developed world, in general, experienced continued economic growth from 1980 to 2000, average incomes in SSA, despite its rich resources, declined by about 15 per cent (Weisbrot, Baker and Rosnick 2007). The manifest failure of Africa to develop economically despite the implementation of market-led reforms across the continent has led to a new focus in mainstream work on the 'new' economic geography to explain the continent's underdevelopment. This 'new economic geography' often uses sophisticated mathematical models, but its core ideas can be easily explained, and, while they seem intuitive, they are misleading.

Paul Krugman won a Nobel prize in 2008 for his work on how economies of scale, whereby bigger factories are more efficient, can lead to uneven development (Krugman 1991), a fact long known to economic geographers, whereas Jared Diamond, a biologist, in his work has argued that initial environmental conditions explain developmental divergence across continents (Diamond 1997). These two strands of work have recently been brought together by other economists and development institutions to explain Africa's general developmental failure. However, this chapter argues that current explanations for African underdevelopment by some economists and the World Bank have a number of critical flaws, as they are largely ahistorical and neglect the global politics of power and inequality. Through an examination of these issues, the nature of uneven development and African underdevelopment can be illuminated.

The Inequality of Geography or the Geography of Inequality?

There is no agreed-upon definition of what constitutes geography as a discipline, or perspective. For non-geographers the term is often synonymous with physical geography – the ways in which physical features are shaped and located and the impacts that these have on human settlements and patterns of economic activity. However, for geographers what is more important in determining developmental patterns is the way in which the relationships between places – or social agents embedded in them – are constructed. This is not to discount the importance of agro-ecological conditions, for example, but acknowledges these are, partially, human artefacts.

In the post-independence period, more autonomous economic strategies were tried in Africa. Western allies such as Mobutu in Zaire effectively nationalized much of the formal sector of the economy, and the West, through the World Bank for example, was willing to support Tanzania's – ultimately failed – strategy of socialist transformation, as long as the country remained politically non-aligned. Development strategies of the time were heavily influenced by ideas about 'delinking' from an exploitative global economy. However, with the end of the Cold War, such experiments were no longer tolerated. In future the market, and the market alone, would determine the prices for Africa's exports, unless of course these were also influenced by European and American subsidies for their own agricultural products, such as cotton and sugar.

During the 1980s and 1990s much of the Third World undertook programmes of economic restructuring sponsored by the World Bank and the IMF, both of which are headquartered in Washington, DC, and controlled by their largest stake- or share-holders, the rich industrial countries – particularly the United States, which is the only country to hold veto power in both institutions.

These 'structural adjustment programmes' (SAPs) promoted by the World Bank and IMF centred on liberalization, privatization and state cut-backs or retrenchment. African countries which undertook them generally eliminated so-called 'quantitative restrictions' on imports, drastically reduced import tariffs, opened their economies to foreign investment and privatized many state-owned industries. Indeed it was these SAPs which set the stage for the new scramble for Africa by opening up what had often been relatively closed economies (Kragelund 2009). SAPs were meant to (re)integrate Africa into the global economy.

Structural adjustment was notably unsuccessful in achieving its ostensible objectives of economic diversification (Bloom and Sachs 1998) and poverty alleviation (Cheru 2002) however. It turned out that simply 'getting the policies right' would not deliver improvements in living standards, although there was also substantial debate about the extent to which these policies were faithfully implemented by often corrupt political elites in Africa (Van de Walle 2001).

The widely acknowledged failure of programmes of economic liberalization in Africa generated a host of different explanations, ranging from the supposedly unique political structures of African societies to a lack of social capital or social ties between individuals and communities (Carmody 2007). As noted above, however, recently the general failure of economic development in Africa has been presented as a result of its geography, and how this interacts with the continent's politics. In some of these readings 'natural' geographic disadvantages have isolated Africa from the positive effects of economic globalization, while its primordialist identities have corrupted its politics in an interacting vicious circle.

The recent annual *World Development Report* of the World Bank (2009), which is the world's leading development institution and think tank, pays particular attention to geography, especially ideas about first and second nature geography. While first nature geography refers to physical geography, 'second nature emphasizes the gains from proximity' as firms cluster (Kanbur and Venables 2007, p. 204). Clustering reduces transaction costs between related and supporting firms. It allows pools of skilled labour to develop, and knowledge on best practices to be transferred between firms. In its report, however, the World Bank also emphasizes that Africa was affected by the colonial experience, particularly the Congress of Berlin.

According to the *World Development Report* (2009, p. 283), 'For Sub-Saharan Africa, the Berlin conference was just the last in a long line of what geographers have termed "formative disasters", unfavorably altering the human, physical, and political geography of the continent, creating continentwide problems of low density, long distances, and divided countries.' However, while there were extensive ecological transformations, such as the development of plantations, associated with colonialism, the physical geography of the continent was not substantially altered. Perhaps more interesting is the admission that colonialism is responsible for 'low density' in Africa.

In the World Bank definition, 'density refers to the economic mass per unit of land area, or the geographic compactness of economic activity. It is shorthand for the level of output produced – and thus the income generated – per unit of land area' (p. 49). How did the legacy of colonialism affect post-colonial development?

The World Bank's report suggests, in places, that it is the colonial division of Africa which is at the root of the continent's current problems, a proposition around which there is substantial agreement.

However, in other parts of the same report it is argued that it is 'first-nature geography' or the physical characteristics of a place which largely determines its developmental potential in the first instance, as this kick-starts a process of cumulative causation – or a kind of snow-ball effect – leading to developmental divergence. This idea of cumulative climatic causation is similar to ideas in the new geographical economics about economies of scale (Krugman 1991). This idea is itself economical; it doesn't deal with the messiness of politics, for example, and can potentially be seen as an attempt to constitute a new 'common sense' or hegemony – 'Africa is poor because it has bad geography.'

In this reading, Europe had certain climatic and physical geographic characteristics which put it at an initial advantage when compared to Africa. While this may be true, these two accounts (colonialism vs first nature geography) are somewhat at odds with each other. Was it Africa's physical geography or its forcible conquest and subjugation which laid the basis for subsequent developmental underperformance, or a combination of the two? The World Bank leaves out the way in which economic power was politically expressed through colonialism.

Before the rise of Dutch dominance in the sixteenth century, China was the world's leading economic power, a position to which it now aspires again. After the sixteenth century it then fell into impoverishment and later civil war, largely as a result of external intervention, including the global war for drugs fought by the British to open up the country to the opium trade (Stavrianos 1981). The British wanted to open up China to Indian opium so that India could pay for British textiles.[1]

In India under colonial rule the British cut off weavers' thumbs to prevent competition with their textiles (Lipietz 1987). It is difficult to see how these policies of underdevelopment have anything to do with 'first nature' geography, except in as much as the mixed farming systems of Europe enabled agricultural surplus to be invested in industry and the development of military capability. Rather, the history of imperialism shaped current development patterns. While US Secretary of State Hillary Clinton recently encouraged Africans to 'get over'[2] colonialism, as Lambert (2008, p. 321) puts it: 'we cannot dismiss what occurred in the past as things that just happened "a long time ago" because these things have fundamentally shaped the globalized world in which we live today'. Of particular interest here is how they have shaped African political and economic systems – with important implications for how the new scramble for Africa is being conducted and its developmental impacts.

If previous modes of African integration into the global political economy were detrimental – 'a rapacious trade *in men* [slavery] was then replaced by a plundering of the continent for minerals [colonialism]' (World Bank, 2009, p. 283 – emphasis added) – it would logically follow that care should be taken in analysing whether or not there is a developmental mode of integration into the global economy for Africa. However, this is absent in the World Bank analysis which endorses the open door or free market approach, which allows unrestricted access to the continent's resources.

Some scholars have noted that there is a strong correlation between current low per capita income and European extractive institutions established in colonies that could not be settled (Acemoglu, Johnson and Robinson 2001). As a result of colonialism and its socio-economic disruptions, previously relatively rich areas, such as those of the Aztec and Inca empires, are now amongst the poorest on the planet (Woods 2004). However, the World Bank simply advocates unmediated integration into the global economy, although it is not clear how this differs in essence from colonialism economically, except that, rather than national overseas capitals, such as British or French big business, having a *chasse gardée* ('private hunting grounds' in the French terminology), Africa is to be open to largely unregulated investment by global capital.

The policy prescription of unmediated integration – to connect the 'unconnected' 'Dark Continent' – is all the more surprising given the acknowledgement earlier in the World Bank report of globally combined and uneven development. For example it is argued that 'globalization and liberalization may rearrange production within countries, leaving people concentrated in places no longer favored by markets' (World Bank 2009, p. 230). This does not sit well with the mainstay of conventional trade theory: the theory of comparative advantage, developed by David Ricardo, which argues that all places are favoured by markets as it allows them to specialize in those areas in which they are relatively most efficient.

'Across provinces, nations and the world, development comes in waves and leaves behind a bumpy economic landscape – prosperity in some places and poverty in others' (World Bank 2009, p. 8). In this quote the World Bank acknowledges the contradictory nature of capitalist development and the ways in which wealth and poverty are co-produced. However, in a sleight of hand this statement is qualified with the rider that 'geographic differences in living standards diverge before converging, faster at the local scale and slower as geography exercises its influence' (p. 8). Thus a spatial problem (uneven development) becomes presented as a temporal one of modernization (the poor have to wait to catch up) (Graham 2011). However, this argument is contradicted again later in the report as it is argued that 'with the right mix of policy actions, even countries in parts of the world that have been left far behind can overcome their geographic disadvantage' (p. 30).

This is a curious form of reasoning. It posits development as a race in which some lead and others lag. However, colonialism opened markets around the world enabling economies of scale to be realized in the colonizing countries. Can (under)developing countries now compete, particularly under a liberal economic regime which institutionalizes the advantages of first movers over late comers through productivity differentials as a result of economies of scale, and uneven technological capabilities? The implication is that they can, but the reason they have not done so to date is because these countries have poor policies and politics. The implicit argument is that if they had had better policies in place, they would have caught up. Thus geography and politics become conflated and thereby distract attention from the failure of orthodox economics. But this neglects the fact that most of the countries of the 'bottom billion' (Collier 2007) have been implementing the policies of unmediated integration promoted by the Washington-based international financial institutions for the last few decades. For example, average tariff rates in SSA are now around 10 per cent, making it one of the most open regions in the world to trade – if not *the* most open (Lines 2008). In contrast, up until the 1990s China's average tariff rate was 30 per cent (Chang 2008).

The *World Development Report* is replete with references to 'harsh' and 'good geography' as if these are natural artefacts rather than social constructions. However, African boundaries are products of European colonialism which explains why many countries are landlocked. As Lines (2008, p. 33) puts it: 'unlike British rule in India, [Africa] was divided into dozens of colonies and protectorates, each of them separately administered even when two neighbours were controlled by the same European state'.

If the pattern of state formation had been different, rather than following a logic of divide and rule, many territories might have been bigger, like India, and more likely to have had sea access. The fact that India was a single large territory enabled some of its companies, such as the multinational giants Tata and Mittal, to achieve economies of scale and subsequently invest in Africa. In reality the production of poverty has less to do with physical geography and more to do with current policies of integration. As a well-known former World Bank economist puts it, 'the poor in developing countries are often better off when their governments ignore the policy advice of the IMF and the World Bank' (Easterly 2000, quoted in Jomo and Baudot 2007, p. xx), as their programmes try to reduce wages, to enhance competitiveness, and thereby raise the profit share of total income in order to increase investment (Lensink 1996).

In other places the *World Development Report* offers other explanations for the failures of economic liberalization. In a nod to the structural power of global business it notes:

> capital can go where it wants to, even if it does not always go where people would wish it would. Indeed, recent comparisons of the marginal product of capital between high-income and lower-income countries show little evidence of friction preventing the flow of capital to poor countries. Instead, the lower capital ratios in poor countries are explained by lower efficiency and a lack of complementary factors [such as infrastructure]. (World Bank 2009, p. 149)

While there is truth in this explanation, it implicitly posits a division between the internal and the external as the effective withholding of global business investment (other than in natural resources) in Africa is presented as a result of internal inefficiencies and lack of skilled labour and infrastructure. However, this neglects the way in which the 'internal' has been historically constructed through Africa's extroverted economic relationships. Poor infrastructure, for example, is in part an outcome of the political economy of plunder from colonialism to corruption (Cramer 2006). While there is mention of remittances in the World Bank report, the fact that 40 per cent of Africa's private wealth is held offshore is not noted (Collier 2007). Distance does not seem to have been a problem for Africa's offshore transnational investors. Is it the particular mode of globalization in Africa then which is the problem, rather than a lack of globalization?

Echoing the work of Ohmae (1995), the World Bank argues that 'today's developing countries, as latecomers, face a stark choice: stay divided and lose ground, or become winners without borders' (World Bank 2009, p. 262). Earlier on in the report it is noted – contrary to the assertions of the *New York Times* columnist Thomas Friedmann – that the 'world is not flat' or an even playing field. Again these statements sit somewhat uneasily with each other. Consequently, the logical contortions of the *World Development Report* offer us little guidance on this as it seeks to evade the central problematic: the way in which extractive and exploitative patterns of globalization have been constructed in Africa to the benefit of world powers, TNCs and local elites (Bond 2006). Indeed these contortions may be strategic as 'increasingly it appears that the inconsistencies and omissions in the Report are not incidental but effectively constitute a strategy to draw in academics and practitioners into broadening circles of engagement year after year' (Marginaganti, Sheppard and Zhang 2009, p. 45).

Making Distance: The Construction of Markets and Commodity 'Chains'

The 2009 *World Development Report* notes the highly uneven nature of global development, largely as a result of internal (factory-based) and external (clustering between firms) economies of scale. For example, half of the world economic product comes from 1.5 per cent of the world's land area. However, the solution presented in the report is deeper unmediated integration into the global economy. In the foreword it is noted that 'a billion people, living in the poorest and most isolated nations, mostly in SSA and South and Central Asia, survive on less than two per cent of the world's wealth' (Zoellick 2009, p. xiii). As noted earlier, it is also acknowledged that most of the now developed countries industrialized through policies of 'infant' industry promotion and protection, and yet the prescription offered by the report is further liberalization. It is difficult to see how this advice can be justified.

In the report the creation of centres of mass capital accumulation such as Tokyo or New York is presented as the outcome of internal processes. However, this is an impoverished conception of geography which neglects the way in which these places grew on the basis of internal (New York) and external (Tokyo) colonialism and how the power relations which were politically and militarily inscribed during these encounters laid the basis for future growth. Indeed New York is known as 'The Empire State', although this American empire was an internal one, in the first instance, before becoming globalized (Smith 2005). The spatial concentration of capital is a function of both 'economic' processes such as positive externalities and spillovers, for example an existing pool of skilled workers attracting new firms to set up, and political-economic power and military force which can be used to open up markets around the world for production complexes based in the powerful countries.

In the *World Development Report*, distance is identified as a primary reason for underdevelopment. In particular, distance from major world markets in the developed world is identified as a major constraint on economic development in Africa and other less developed regions. The central idea is that, as a result of its geography, Africa suffers from a 'proximity gap' (Naude 2009). The solution presented is to reduce distance through investment in infrastructure and through economic liberalization – such as tariff reductions, for example – to make borders 'thinner'. The problematic of underdevelopment then is presented as lack of contact between the First and Third Worlds, although – somewhat surprisingly – the role of China and other rising powers is ignored.

Underlying this idea of the proximity gap is the idea of development as being promoted through a process of 'contagious diffusion' ('development is contagious' (World Bank 2009, p. 118)), in which it spreads from more to less developed regions, provided that 'artificial barriers' to trade and other economic flows of investment and remittances are eliminated or minimized. Implicit in this is the idea of 'distance decay': that development is reduced the further away from world markets a country is. There would appear to be some empirical support for this argument.

Eastern Europe and North Africa are able to take advantage of their proximity to Western Europe to sell their products more easily there, compared to SSA for example, and thereby also to attract 'market-serving' FDI. Consequently, they have higher per capita incomes than much of SSA. However, it does not follow that by reducing trade and other barriers to investment, SSA will 'naturally' catch up with these more developed regions. On the contrary there is a (dys)functional global division of labour in place, promoted through policies of economic liberalization, which largely consigns SSA to the position of primary commodity exporter, as manufacturing there cannot compete with production complexes and developmental macro-economic regimes – in China, in particular (Kaplinsky, McCormick et al. 2006). Likewise, foreign investment in manufacturing is not unlimited, so there is what economists call a fallacy of investment composition at play as well. Attracting foreign investment is a zero sum game: one place will get it, another will not. Consequently, globalization is more like an electrical current than a wave, whereby some places are more plugged in to flows of investment and trade.

Global investment is limited by market size – as, consequently, is the international division of labour. It may be possible for African countries to attract a higher proportion of global FDI, but this has proven exceptionally difficult outside of the resource sector as a result of socially constructed distance, small domestic and regional markets and political instability associated with economic stagnation. The problematic of African development has been largely that domestic manufacturing was underdeveloped and that distance from major markets and the other problems noted above have served as a disincentive to FDI in manufacturing and services.

Distance is at first glance a straightforward concept. It can be measured in miles or kilometres. However, in terms of economic development, distance is more complex. It is linked to time and to money. Poor infrastructure will lengthen the cost and time of transporting commodities and intermediate goods. In a world increasingly characterized by 'network trade' (Broadman and Isik 2007) and 'just-in-time' inventory and delivery systems, so that companies do not have to keep inventories of spare parts, poor infrastructure has a particularly detrimental effect.

Extension of delivery times also increases the length of time in which capital is dormant or tied up in intermediate goods or in shipping, increasing turnover times and consequently reducing profitability. 'Virtual distance' is also increased by the need for export permits and administrative delays in obtaining these. In the Sahelian (border of the Sahara) country of Chad, six documents are required for exports, which take an average of seventy-eight days to obtain (World Bank 2007, in World Bank 2009, p. 189). This makes the export of perishable agricultural products particularly challenging. Such bureaucracy is functional for a minority political and administrative elite in the sense that it provides opportunities for corruption.

Infrastructure is, however, only one part of a successful production complex. Simply building it does not mean that they (foreign investors) will come, as the poor history of Export Processing Zones in Africa has shown. Rather, poor infrastructure is a symptom of underdevelopment: a reflection of limited tax revenues and sometimes poor administrative capacity. These are in turn a function of lack of investment, which is itself an outcome of underdevelopment: as Jeffrey Sachs rightly calls it, a 'poverty trap'.

Paul Collier identifies additional developmental traps in Africa, such as the 'conflict trap' and the 'resource trap'. However, the question is: how are these traps socially constructed? Are they to do with a lack of social surplus which can be invested or with the extraction of social surplus (exploitation), or a combination of the two? In other words, is it distance from markets (Africa's 'proximity trap', as the World Bank would have it (2009, p. 293)) or the spatially specific and embedded nature of markets – which creates 'remoteness' – which is the problem?

Markets are institutions in which property rights change hands. There are now elaborate rules which regulate markets in many parts of the world, as codified in contract law for example. In the mainstream economic literature, markets are presented as benign institutions where willing sellers meet willing buyers. However, this neglects the differential power positions of market participants and the way in which markets have historically been constructed through the use of force, both in Britain during the enclosure – or landgrab – movement in the fourteenth to eighteenth centuries, and later on a worldwide scale through colonialism. Much of the world's property initially changed hands through violent force, which gave structure to subsequent economic force. If someone is landless and unemployed, the level of choice or agency they bring to the labour market is highly constrained, particularly in poor countries (Standing 2002). It is then essential to understand geographic differences in markets.

In a recent paper Jeffrey Sachs (2003) implies that state failure and more protectionist economic policies are linked. Quoting the State Failure Task Force (1999), he argues that state failure is related to 'openness of the economy, in that more economic linkages with the rest of the world diminish the chances of state failure' (p. 28). However, the economies which are the most linked into global markets in terms of absolute volumes of cross-border trade and investment are those with the most diversified economies, which are often home to major multinational companies, and this does not necessarily equate to openness. African countries are much more dependent on trade than European countries or the US, as a proportion of their economies, and the region has the lowest tariff rates in the world.

As noted earlier, the World Bank (2008) now acknowledges that most now developed countries incubated their industries behind protectionist barriers before exposing them to global market competition. For example, the electronics division of mobile-phone-producing giant Nokia lost money for seventeen years, during which time it had to be subsidized (Chang 2008). The most successful countries at poverty reduction recently – China in particular – have gradually liberalized based on judgements about the competitive strength of the economy, and have eschewed the 'big bang' (everything at once) approach to liberalization favoured by the World Bank and the IMF in Africa (Arestis and Caner 2009). Indeed much of the poverty reduction in China took place during earlier stages of economic reform when the new Township and Village Enterprises, rather than foreign investment, were driving growth (Breslin 2007).

In Africa the commodification or marketization of labour was introduced through land dispossession and hut and poll taxes. As is well understood by political economists, underdevelopment was socially constructed (Rodney 1972). Africa under colonialism was to be a producer of raw materials rather than manufactured goods. Negative movement in the terms of trade against primary commodities, as their prices fell and those of manufactures rose, and the lack of technological development and spillovers associated with them ensured immiseration and consequent small domestic, and 'distance' from world, markets, rather than Africa being a 'world market' itself. 'Distance' in the World Bank schema, then, serves to disguise the processes of underdevelopment. Given this legacy, recent economic openness is implicated in the generation of poverty, as the following examples demonstrate.

As a result of economic liberalization, 97 per cent of poultry in Ghana is now imported, as compared to only 10 per cent twenty years ago, for example (Glennie 2008). These chicken imports are heavily subsidized by the EU and have dramatically displaced domestic production, affecting about 400,000 farmers (Lee 2009) – an example of structural destruction, rather than adjustment. These processes also operate outside of Africa. As large retailers have cut prices for bananas to increase market share, for example, cost pressures have been transmitted down the line, so that plantation workers' wages in Costa Rica fell from US$12–15 a day in 2000 to US$7–8 a day in 2003 (Lines 2008). Poverty and power are then intimately related.

The Political Economy of Inequality, Poverty and Conflict in Africa

As will be discussed later in more detail, the new scramble for Africa is implicated in the development of certain conflicts. Increasing inequality is also implicated in conflict and 'national' inequality is structured by the way in which places have been incorporated and reincorporated into the global economy. For example, in Nigeria it is estimated that 80 per cent of the hundreds of billions of dollars of oil revenue which have been derived in that country has accrued to only 1 per cent of the population (Watts 2006). This pattern of income distribution is a product of the way in which Nigeria has been incorporated into the global economy, as most of the oil produced there is extracted by foreign companies and exported.

The Nigerian elite have benefited, while the majority of the population have got poorer. This then generates incentives for the elite, in partnership with transnational oil companies, to retain the status quo, while those who are excluded want either to replace the existing elite or to achieve a fairer distribution of resources – generating incentives for system maintenance, reform or subversion for different social actors.

This unequal integration has, in turn, generated wide-scale violence and social conflict. As noted earlier, the resource curse then is actually a mode of governance for many resource-dependent economies based on a transnational contract of extroversion, or outward orientation, between domestically based elites and TNCs, and the global powers in whose territories many of them are headquartered (Carmody 2009a). Resource conflict may spill over borders, particularly as neighbouring territories are more likely to have similar socio-economic structures, creating regional conflict complexes – 'bad neighbourhoods' in Paul Collier's schema. Poverty, inequality and conflict are, then, interrelated.

Africa has the highest level of consumption inequality in the world (White and Killick 2001), and probably the most conflicted region in the world over the last decade has been the Great Lakes region of Central Africa. As in Nigeria, this conflict is to do with the particular mode of integration centred on natural resource extraction. The presence of the strategic mineral coltan, discussed in more detail later, has contributed to the conflict there (see Nest and Grignon 2006). Consequently, rather than isolation, it is precisely demand from, and the particular form of connection to, world markets which has fomented conflict over this resource.

In their mathematical economic work, Collier (2007, 2009) and his team have associated natural resource wealth with conflict. Some resources are inherently more 'lootable' than others: arable diamonds, which are found in the soil layer, being a prime example. However, while diamonds may provide the resource to facilitate conflict, they do not by themselves spark it (Le Billon 2008). Rather, in poor societies, grievances often take shape or coalesce around inequality and poverty. Poverty and conflict are also linked to corruption, which may also generate resistance.

According to Paul Collier, development is largely voluntarist: 'with hard work, thrift and intelligence, a society can gradually climb out of poverty' (Collier 2007, p. 5) – that is, if people have innate intelligence (apparently some societies have it and others do not) and (implicitly) adopt the Protestant work ethic, then they can prosper. However, 'local' characteristics are often 'globally' constructed. For example, the history of corruption is associated with colonialism in Zambia, where the indigenous colonial administrative class (the Boma class) sought to emulate the lifestyle of the colonial bourgeoisie and to generate its own resources, through corruption, for business development (Chipungu 1992). This legacy has had long-lasting impacts on African governance.

There are two types of corruption: grand and petty. Grand corruption, sometimes known as vertical corruption because it often involves payments from big business to political elites to award resource or other contracts, attracts the most media attention (de Sardan 1999). However, there is also substantial horizontal, small-scale, petty or day-to-day corruption in many African countries, where nurses have to be paid to allow patients to get appointments with doctors, for example. The two also interact, as poor salaries in the police and judiciary mean they are open to corruption and consequently are highly unlikely to keep politicians accountable. It is important not to overgeneralize, however, as some African countries, such as Botswana, score better on corruption perception indices than some countries in Europe. Arguably, Chinese methods, whereby loans for infrastructure often have as a condition that contracts go to Chinese companies, may reduce opportunities for corruption (Brautigam 2009). Thus the new scramble for Africa is altering patterns of governance and economy on the continent.

It is to this scramble that we now turn. While much of the world's media has focused attention on China's rising role in Africa, the old economic powers remain dominant there, for the moment, economically if not politically. The next chapter explores old economic power interests on the continent.

2 OLD ECONOMIC POWER INTERESTS AND STRATEGIES IN AFRICA

Mr. President ... I believe you intend to put an end to the British Empire. All your ideas on the post war world demonstrate it. But, in spite of it all, we know that you are our only hope. And you know that we know it. You know that without the United States, Her Majesty's Empire cannot last. (Winston Churchill to Franklin D. Roosevelt, quoted in Yepe 2008)

The British Empire in Africa at one point stretched continuously, in Cecil Rhodes' famous phrase, from 'Cairo to the Cape' of Good Hope in South Africa. However, with the end of the Second World War, global leadership moved decisively to the United States. Britain was virtually bankrupt and became economically dependent on the US for loans. It was in this context that the so-called 'special relationship' between Britain and the United States was forged.

This relationship was special in the sense that one former hegemonic power cast its lot in with the ascendant hegemon and essentially transferred many of its interests to it. Particularly after decolonization, the focus of British attention in foreign policy was 'East of Suez' and on maintaining and deepening its relationship with the United States. In part to counteract the fear of Soviet domination, the British were willing to let the Americans take the lead on Western foreign and security policy. The underlying idea was that by being able to influence the Americans, the British would be able to 'punch above their weight' and thereby retain influence in international affairs.

In the post-imperial era, Africa's other major colonial power, France, took a different course, seeking to build European integration as a counterweight to American power. In order to retain influence at the United Nations General Assembly and maintain its claim to great power status, France nurtured close relations with its former African colonies to offset the Anglo-American 'special relationship' (Clapham 1996). France has long pursued a policy of 'FrançAfrique', which meant keeping close ties to former colonies in Africa. Extensive economic and political relationships were maintained and deepened. In practice this meant backing friendly dictators to hold on to France's *chasse gardée*, or private economic hunting ground on the continent. France underwrote the Communauté Financière Africaine (CFA) currency union in West Africa for example, linking it to the French franc. Total, the French oil company, remains the biggest in Africa, and up until recently the majority of Air France's profits came from Africa (Schraeder 2000).

During the Cold War the United States took an active interest in Africa, often supporting military dictators such as the infamous Joseph Mobutu in Zaire, who is thought to have plundered billions of dollars from that country and oversaw its economic ruin. On a visit to Washington, US President Nixon even claimed that the US could learn about economic management from Mobutu (Meredith 2005). As Zaire's economy crumbled and public servants' salaries collapsed, Mobutu had exhorted them to 'steal a little, in a nice way' to survive. With the end of the Cold War such blatant and destructive autocrats were no longer supported and US President George Herbert Walker Bush declared a 'new world order' in which American power would be unchallenged. This power was demonstrated against Iraq in the First Gulf War (1990–1).

In Africa the test case was Somalia, where American troops were sent to restore order, after that state collapsed into anarchy in 1991, under the United Nations-authorized 'Operation Restore Hope'. However, when American Special Forces were killed and dragged through the streets of Mogadishu, given the lack of identifiable strategic interests in Somalia, American forces were withdrawn by the new Clinton Administration. During much of the 1990s the Western powers adopted a policy of malign neglect towards Africa, given the small size of its economy. The one exception was South Africa where UK investments were estimated at £24 billion (Porteous 2008).

The experience of Somalia made the US very wary of direct intervention in Africa. The influential 'Powell Doctrine', named for the then Commander of the Joint Chiefs of Staff in the US, argued that America should only become militarily engaged where its vital national security interests were threatened (Powell 1992). Sadly the genocide in Rwanda did not meet that criterion, with tragic results, condemning the Great Lakes region to at least a decade and a half of conflict (Prunier 2009). When President Clinton visited Rwanda in 1998 to present a statuette of the genocide to the Rwandan President, he never left the airport and the engines on Air Force One were kept running (PBS 1999).

Subsequent American policy was strongly to support the new Tutsi-led Rwandan government both militarily and economically, which was to bring it into conflict with France. According to Tom Porteous (2008, p. 29), 'for the rest of the 1990s, the United States and the UK preferred to secure their interests, sometimes in competition with the French and often at the expense of long-term stability, through local African proxies', such as Paul Kagame's Rwandan Patriotic Front (RPF).

American motives for supporting the new RPF government were driven by guilt over the failure to prevent the Rwandan genocide of 1994, a desire to try to stabilize Central Africa and strategic economic considerations. During his 1998 visit to Africa, President Clinton hailed a new breed of African leaders who, he argued, would bring stability to the continent. These were all leaders of formerly war-wracked states (Uganda, Rwanda, Eritrea and Ethiopia) who purportedly were democratic reformers and supported free market economies. With the end of the Cold War, the US made efforts to promote market opening around the world, including Africa, and consequently these leaders were supported. As the US Assistant Secretary of State for African Affairs said in Gabon in 1995 in a direct challenge to the policy of the *chasse gardée*, 'The African market is open to everyone... We must accept free and fair competition, equality between all actors' (quoted in Schraeder 2000, p. 326). This prompted the French Minister of Cooperation to acknowledge that the French government was holding meetings on how best to 'defend' its interests in Africa against the United States.

According to Africa expert Peter Schraeder, 'from the perspective of most French policymakers, the RPF's military victory in 1994 constituted the first time that a francophone country had "fallen" to Anglo-Saxon influence... According to this culturally inspired theory, Central Africa could become a "Trojan Horse" projecting Anglo-Saxon influence throughout the remainder of francophone Africa' (2000, p. 332). In 2008, in the context of increasingly tense relations, French was replaced by English as one of the official languages in Rwanda.[1] But while there is some competition between the US and France, there is also extensive security cooperation. For example, a joint intelligence centre was set up in Paris in 2002 and relations have become much closer since Nicolas Sarkozy came to power (Kennan 2009). Partly in order to counter the 'Chinese threat', Western interests in Africa have become more closely aligned – but still distinct as explored below. Western interests in Africa centre on resources, markets, security and humanitarianism, with a frequent blurring between categories.

Britain in Africa: Markets, Development and Security

> Even before 9/11, al Qaeda had bases in Africa...They still do, hiding in places where they can go undisturbed by weak governments, planning their next attacks which could be anywhere in the world, including Africa. (Tony Blair, quoted in *Mail and Guardian*, 7 October 2004, in Burr, Jensen and Stepputat 2007, p. 9)

Britain has extensive economic, military, political and cultural engagements in Africa as a result of its colonial history on the continent. For example, Britain maintains a permanent military presence in Kenya, where troops are routinely sent for training. South Africa is by far Britain's largest trading partner on the continent and British investment is substantial there. Tony Blair enjoyed a close relationship with the former South African President Thabo Mbeki, and together they came up with the idea for the New Partnership for African Development, discussed in more detail later (Porteous 2008).

While Africa was low on Britain's foreign policy agenda during the years of Conservative Party rule from the late 1970s onwards, this changed with the election of Tony Blair in 1997. Blair was a Prime Minister 'on a mission'. As former Foreign and Commonwealth Office official Tom Porteous puts it, Blair 'led Britain back into Africa in a manner that was self-consciously interventionist and neo-imperialist, albeit justified in terms of partnership with African leaders and humanitarianism' (2008, p. 5).

International development was an area of particular interest for the New Labour government of 1997 and it quickly established a new ministry – the Department for International Development (DFID) – led by Clare Short. Tony Blair arguably had some emotional attachment to the continent as his father had taught law at a university in Sierra Leone. Some argue that this was central to the British military intervention to stop the civil war in that country in 2000, although in reality this evolved from the initial operation to evacuate EU nationals. When the British commander encountered weak resistance he pushed for the country to be 'pacified'.

This intervention was in line with the thinking of Blair's influential foreign policy advisor, Robert Cooper, who argued that there was a need to use 'rougher methods' from an 'earlier era' to contain the dangers of failed states. This was acceptable because, according to Cooper, 'foreigners are different' (Cooper 2003). In some cases foreigners would feel the effects of Britain's military and its aid programme, combining, in Cooper's schema, force with legitimacy. This martial philosophy would be displayed again by Blair during the Iraq and Afghanistan invasions. The creation of DFID also had other motivations, however, as it helped to maintain within the New Labour coalition older-style, internationalist leftists. Clare Short reportedly told her officials in DFID that they could be as radical as they liked as the Foreign and Commonwealth Office did not care about their operations.

With the creation of DFID Britain explicitly untied its aid from its commercial interests, although these would still impinge. When the Tanzanian government wanted to buy a top-of-the-line military radar system – that it arguably did not require – from British Aerospace Engineering (BAe), the Secretary for International Development questioned whether this was a wise use of money. The World Bank had criticized the system as 'too expensive and not adequate for civil aviation' (quoted in Arnold 2009, p. 102). The project was to be funded by a loan from Barclays for US$40 m and would supposedly enable Tanzania to charge airlines engaged in over-flights of Tanzanian airspace between US$3 and US$5 m a year. However, Clare Short was eventually overruled by Tony Blair and the sale went ahead. British jobs (and re-election) were more important than 'good governance' in Tanzania. This outcome could have been foreseen, despite World Bank, NGO and cabinet disapproval. Writing in BAe's magazine in 1997 before coming to power, Tony Blair said 'winning exports is vital to the long-term success of Britain's defence industry. A Labour government will work with the industry to win export orders' (quoted in the Campaign Against Arms Trade 2003, p. 3).

Arms design and manufacture is one area in which British manufacturing still has a competitive advantage. Under an agreement with the US, British arms manufacturers are now treated as if they are US companies by the US government for procurement purposes (Chossudovsky 2002). While the African market for high-tech products and arms may be relatively small, it is still worth having, particularly as, with the end of the Cold War, Western and other powers sought new markets for arms exports.

In 2006 China became the world's largest exporter of small arms, which it sometimes swaps for oil or mining concessions (Michel, Beuret and Woods 2009). While China is often criticized over its arms sales to abhorrent African regimes such as Sudan and Zimbabwe, and for selling arms to both sides during the Ethio–Eritrean war, arms sales from Britain to Africa quadrupled during Tony Blair's premiership (Southall 2009), increasing 'arms pollution' on the continent. In fact, from 1999 to 2004, Britain earned £1 billion from its arms exports to the continent (Grimmett 2009). In 2000 the British government even granted an export licence to BAe to supply spare parts for Zimbabwean Hawk jets.

Zimbabwe was at the time engaged in a war in the DRC. When questioned as to why the licence had been granted, it was argued that if these spare part exports had not been allowed it would have damaged BAe's reputation internationally. This philosophy was in contrast to that of Clare Short who argued in 2002 that 'whilst successive governments have promoted arms sales, I think that it belongs in a world of the past' (quoted in Campaign Against Arms Trade 2003, p. 2).

Britain is also the world's second-largest service exporter, and British aid to Africa has sometimes been tied to the privatization of water utilities, which British companies such as Thames Water could bid on and run (Curtis 2009). In Tanzania British taxpayers' money was used to produce a video promoting water privatization, which subsequently had to be reversed by the government because of its disastrous effect.

Tony Blair became increasingly concerned with Africa in the wake of the 11 September 2001 attacks in the United States, famously declaring at the British Labour Party Conference in October of that year that Africa was 'a scar on the conscience of the world'. While his concern with the fate of the continent was undoubtedly genuine, it was heightened by security concerns around failed states in Africa, as the 9/11 attacks were planned from Afghanistan. It also served an instrumental function as increased aid for Africa would serve to 'humanize' the other axis of British and American foreign policy – the so-called 'war on terror' (Abrahamsen 2005). For example, according to Tom Porteous (2008, p. 23), in Rwanda the overriding consideration for DFID was that Kagame was performing well in helping the department to achieve its development targets. He was, according to DFID's research, doing a good job in reducing poverty, in increasing girls' access to education, in improving the health infrastructure in rural areas, etc. This trumped all other considerations, including human rights and regional stability. There were other motives as well. Tony Blair's Secretary for Trade spoke of fighting 'terror with trade' (Curtis 2009).

While he was Premier, Tony Blair, on the advice of the Irish musician and campaigner Bob Geldof, established a Commission for Africa composed of various political and business 'luminaries' from around the world. This produced some interesting insights, but the main policy proposal to come out of it was to double aid for Africa to enable it to break out of its 'poverty trap' (Commission for Africa 2005). However, some were sceptical of the Commission for Africa report and the actions taken at the subsequent Gleneagles Summit of the Group of 7 rich industrial countries.

According to Mark Malloch Brown, who was then Chief of Staff for the UN Secretary-General and later joined the new British Prime Minister Gordon Brown's government as a Minister for Africa, Asia and the United Nations, 'there will be a lot of smokescreen and buckets of G8 paint thrown over old aid' (quoted in Arnold 2009, p. 16). A more damaging criticism of the report was that there was no 'recognition that the rich world's lifestyle and rapacious use of Africa's resources had created, and continues to create, unsustainable economies on the subcontinent in the first place. The loud and clear message is: Africa is at fault and Africa has to change with our help' (Hoogvelt 2005, p. 597, quoted in Lee 2006, p. 310). However, there are fears that the influence of China may prevent this. The Chinese, however, are not afraid of flexing their muscles with Britain.

When Jack Straw, the then British Foreign Secretary, compared what the Chinese are doing in Africa today to what the British did during the nineteenth century – building infrastructure and opening mines ('welcome to the new colonists', he declared) – the Chinese government refused meetings with their British counterparts on Africa for over a year as a way of showing displeasure: he had hit a raw nerve (Dowden 2009).

French Interests: From Neo-colonialism to Rapprochement with the US

Africa without France is like a car without a driver. France without Africa is like a car without fuel. (Omar Bongo, former President of Gabon, quoted in Yates 2009, p. 206)

It is not really possible to find satisfactory criteria for distinguishing between countries requiring aid for development and countries in which cooperation based on influence should operate. (C. Josselin, French Minister for Cooperation, quoted in Massey and May 2009, p. 215)

France also has extensive economic, military and political links in Africa dating from the colonial era. As noted earlier, the close politico-economic links between France and its former colonies gave rise to an imagined space of 'FrançAfrique'. This was expressed through the linking of former colonies' currencies in West Africa to the French franc and through the presence and maintenance of French military bases on the continent. Despite Nicolas Sarkozy's protestations, Africa is still important to the French economy as it accounts for about a twentieth of French exports (Schraeder 2000; Arnold 2009). Over half of Total's daily oil production on the continent comes from outside of 'Francophone' Africa, from Nigeria and Angola (Massey and May 2009).[2]

France, along with other major powers, has a sorry history of supporting compliant African dictators. The French President Giscard d'Estaing even attended the obscene coronation of 'Emperor' Bokasa in the Central African Republic in 1977. The diamonds, crown, etc., for this event had been imported from France at a cost of US$22 million, while the country had only 260 miles of paved road and poverty was rife. The French footed most of the bill for this event (Meredith 2005). In response to criticism from overseas, the French Minister for Cooperation argued that those who objected had racist inclinations as they did not protest at the ceremonies surrounding the English royal family, for example. Africa policy at that time and subsequently was under the *Cellule Africaine* or 'African cell' in the French President's office: a measure of the importance attached to the relationship (Michel, Beuret and Woods 2009).

The long-time architect of French Africa policy, who served under a number of presidents, Jacques Foccart, boasted that France could decide who was in power in its former colonies in Africa. Given the fact that it intervened militarily several times to put down coups during his tenure, this was not an idle boast. For example in 1990 the French were reportedly unhappy with the gross human rights violations under the Habré regime in Chad and encouraged the rebellion by the Mouvement Patriotique du Salut, which was led by a former army commander, Idriss Déby. Despite Déby's own chequered human rights record, France has continued to support him against rebellions, some of which have been led by his own nephews and uncle.

Since coming to power in 2007, the new French President Nicolas Sarkozy has sought to reposition France's relationship with the United States, with implications for Africa. Rather than adopting an oppositional position to the 'hyper-power', as previous French leaders had, he has brought France back into the North Atlantic Treaty Organization's integrated command, for example, and was fêted in Washington by the Bush Administration. His 'socialist' Foreign Minister, Bernard Kouchner, has also declared that FrançAfrique is dead. However, the facts on the ground would seem to suggest otherwise. As there is not the space to delve in detail into France's manifold relations with African countries, the subsequent discussion will focus on Chad, where the French recently sent troops as part of a EU peacekeeping force.

France has been progressively reducing its military presence in Africa from 1997 onwards. In part this may be based on economic calculations. Nicolas Sarkozy has declared that 'France's economy does not need Africa' (quoted in Michel, Beuret and Woods 2009, p. 202). Partly this calculation is because so much French electricity, around three-quarters, comes from nuclear power, so African oil is not as strategically important to France as to other powers. It may also have a geopolitical element – to promote the idea that France can consequently be guided by disinterested humanitarianism on the continent.

Further base reductions in Africa were announced in 2008, but France also opened a new military base in the United Arab Emirates on the Straits of Hormuz, through which half of the world's oil supply transited in 2009. However, France still maintains 60,000 troops in Africa, by far the largest external military presence on the continent (Diop 2010).

Sarkozy has realigned French military policy generally towards anti-terrorism and cooperation with the US. Indeed, as the French military presence in Africa is reduced, the American one is increasing and the French are making space for the Americans on the continent. The American military base in Djibouti, Camp Lemmonier, is a former base of the French Foreign Legion, although the French continue to maintain another base nearby in that country. Nonetheless, France continues to provide active military support for African allies, such as President Déby in Chad.

France does not now have major economic interests in Chad, although there are French companies invested in cotton, sugar, electricity, water and other sectors. While France is Chad's main source of imports, the United States now takes much of its exports (around a third – mostly oil). However, the World Bank and American oil companies, and the Malaysian national oil company PETRONAS, do have substantial interests in the Chad–Cameroon pipeline which was opened in 2003 at a cost of US$3.5 billion, making it the largest ever private sector construction project in Africa. Villagers in the way of the pipeline were asked to choose from items such as ploughs or bicycles in exchange for the loss of their land and were asked to sign agreements that they would not make any future claims against ExxonMobil, the largest investor (Ghazvinian 2007).

The size of the resource extraction facilities being constructed in the new scramble is sometimes breathtaking. The ExxonMobil facility in Kome, Chad, produces six times more electricity than the entire rest of the country, and a squatter camp known as 'Quartier Attend', or 'Waiting Town', has grown up around it as people settle there in the – mostly vain – hope of finding jobs. One industry in which there is work, however, is the sex industry, which has grown quickly in the Quartier Attend.

The Chad–Cameroon oil pipeline was initially to have involvement by the French oil company Elf, but it withdrew after a thirty-month consultation process, convinced that the controversy over the project's environmental and social impacts made it not worthwhile participating (Massey and May 2009). As it turned out, the project was highly controversial for other reasons, as the Chadian government used part of the signing bonus from oil companies to buy arms, and the lure of oil revenue has undoubtedly contributed to the motivations of different rebel groups (for a fuller discussion, see Carmody 2010). Even the World Bank, which co-funded the project, admitted that it was likely to aggravate political tensions by raising the stakes associated with holding state power.

The Chinese had previously opened an oil pipeline in neighbouring Sudan in 1999 to ship oil from the south to Port Sudan on the coast. This pipeline is guarded by 5,000 Chinese 'private defence contractors' and terminates at the al-Bashair 2 terminal in Port Sudan (Michel, Beuret and Woods 2009). Sudan is the only country in Africa where the Chinese have been allowed to develop their own oil facilities, and in between these two pipelines lies a geopolitical fracture zone or shatterbelt, in Darfur and Western Chad, where external powers support different governments and rebel factions.

In the initial agreement Chad was only to receive a 12.5 per cent royalty payment on the oil, in addition to corporate income tax and some small pipeline and other fees. The government of Chad subsequently rewrote the Petroleum Law governing allocation of revenues from the project, which were meant to be directed to 'poverty reduction', because 'slavish adherence to the model would mean that N'Djamena was supposed to be building schools and clinics whilst Khartoum was diverting funds for the overthrow of the government. At this point Sudan was able to outspend Chad militarily by 50 to one' (Junger 2007, cited in Massey and May 2009, p. 224). After the law was rewritten, Déby's government purchased new assault helicopters, which are very effective against rebels crossing desert in 'technicals' – often Toyota Land Cruisers fitted with heavy machine guns.

As France's economic interests in Chad have now been eclipsed by those of the United States, French troops initially remained neutral when rebels crossed the desert from Sudan to attack the Chadian capital N'Djamena in 2008. But when it looked like Déby might fall the French provided ammunition and military intelligence and also – crucially, in terms of denying the rebels strategic advantage – held the airport (Massey and May 2009). In a previous attack French fighter jets had fired over the heads of the advancing rebel column to 'express' the French government's position.

The Toyota vehicles captured after one rebel attack on Chad were reportedly bought by a Chinese oil company (*Journal du Dimanche*, 23 April 2006, cited in Massey and May 2009), and there were even reports that the rebel column had stopped at a Chinese oil facility to refuel (Junger 2007, cited in Michel, Beuret and Woods 2009). Later in 2006, Déby recognized Beijing over Taiwan, and this opened the door for subsequent Chinese oil investment in Chad.

In 2008 the EU deployed a 'battlegroup' to Chad under the auspices of the United Nations. This was subsequently 'reflagged' as a UN operation. The French-led UN peacekeeping force in Chad is ostensibly to protect refugees from neighbouring Sudan but, according to Professor Gérard Prunier (quoted in Storey 2008, p. 12), 'Idriss Déby is hanging on to power by the skin of his teeth but he is likely to hang on only as long as Paris and Brussels continue to support him under some kind of pseudo humanitarian face-saving dispensation.' Thus France is now in the unusual position of serving as a protector of American interests in Africa, at least in this instance, in arguably the same way as Britain is. These informal – and more formal – kinds of political integration have led some to speak of the development of a 'global state' (Shaw 2000), with a Western core.

European Union Interests in Africa: Globalizing Markets

The EU is not a traditional state actor. Manuel Castells refers to it as a 'network state' (Castells 1998). It has some of the features and institutions of a state, such as a common currency[3] and a parliament, and also some of the attributes of sovereignty, in that the European Court of Justice now has superiority over national law. It is also continuing to deepen its integration through the formulation of a common European defence and security policy – as evidenced by the deployment of the EU battlegroup to Chad – and is now the world's largest overseas aid donor. It uses its international aid to try to enhance its structural power – or ability to set the rules of the game – to shape domestic policy regimes in recipient states to bolster European economic and political power (Holden 2009).

As noted above, the major former colonial powers have retained substantial economic and political interests in Africa and the EU has inherited some of these. The EU also has a distinctive agenda which is informed by the collective interests of its member states. For example, the so-called 'Lisbon agenda' of the EU aimed to make Europe the most 'competitive, knowledge-based economy in the world' by 2010, although it still lags behind the US and Japan in technological innovation. Nonetheless, to advance in the field of economic competition it is engaged in market opening around the world, including in Africa. Given its history, Germany, which was until recently the world's largest exporter, often prefers to work through the EU to achieve this objective.

In 2005, the so-called 'year of Africa', when the Gleneagles Summit of the Group of 7 was held in Scotland and agreed substantial debt relief for Africa, the EU adopted its Africa strategy.[4] This is the first single-policy document to provide an overall reference plan for all EU cooperation with the continent. The strategy is structured around eight thematic areas including Peace and Security, Trade, Regional Integration and Infrastructure, and Climate Change. One of the principles on which the strategy is meant to be based is 'equal partnership' (European Commission 2005) but, given the vast power differences between the EU and Africa, this is an impossibility. Such rhetoric performs a useful function in serving to disguise these power differentials, however.

The EU's relations with Africa used to be structured under the Lomé Conventions, whereby Europe agreed to trade preferences for the African, Caribbean and Pacific (ACP) countries which were its former colonies. However, these preferences were judged not to be compatible with the World Trade Organization agreement after the United States petitioned against them, and, after an interim arrangement expired, the EU has been negotiating EPAs with different regional groupings in Africa (Asche and Engel 2008). The EU would like the signatories to these EPAs to open 80 per cent of all trade in goods to free trade with the Union after a transitional period of fifteen years (Schieg 2008).

Regional integration efforts in Africa, such as the Economic Community of West African States (ECOWAS), were meant to strengthen member states' collective bargaining power with the developed countries. However, Patrick Holden (2009) notes that they are now being used as vehicles to penetrate Africa more deeply through EPAs. A European Commission official noted that 'the overall objective of the EU was to force Africa to rationalize the [regional economic] integration process' (quoted in Lee 2009, p. 97), but it could be argued that the fact that the EU carved Africa up into four blocs of countries with which it would negotiate EPAs is reminiscent of the bordering practices of the Congress of Berlin. Margaret Lee (2009) argues EPAs represent an effort to 'divide and rule'. However, this imposition of externally sponsored regionalism is likely to be rightly resisted and to fail, and the President of Senegal and South African officials have noted publicly that, with China's and other powers' increased presence, Africa has other choices outside of Europe for trade and investment (Keet 2010).

Nicolas Sarkozy lent his support to those African countries which opposed EPAs, arguing that 'he was in favour of globalization but not the despoliation of countries that had nothing left' (quoted in *New York Times*, 9 December 2007, cited in Lee 2009, p. 103). This may in part have been playing to a domestic constituency, as France seeks to maintain the EU's protectionist economic regime for agriculture. However, Germany is very interested in opening markets around the world, as indeed are most other EU members.

Officials from the European Commission and EU member states note that the ACP as a proportion of European trade fell continuously under the Lomé Conventions, despite the granting of non-reciprocal preferences. Consequently, the then EU Trade Commissioner Peter Mandelson argued that the EU was pushing EPAs for the ACP countries' own good. According to him, 'the EPAs should be seen as a positive lever to work on some of these wider policy issues – not because these issues are important to Europe, primarily, but because they are fundamental for economic and human development' (Mandelson 2005, quoted in Jonne 2008, p. 1940).

There has been much disagreement about the developmental impacts of EPAs. At a meeting in Dublin, Ireland, to discuss the issue, the Namibian ambassador to the EU noted that he signed the interim EPA under duress and that the strategic promotion of certain exports, such as the hoodia plant, with which Namibia has had some success, would be outlawed under the EPA. ACP countries are essentially being forced to sign these agreements, however, for fear of losing preferential access to the EU market. One study by the British Overseas Development Institute found that, if EPAs were not signed, 267 products would face tariff increases of over 10 per cent of their value. Taking 2006 as a base year, it was estimated that taxes on Namibia's agricultural exports would be €45.15 m and meat exports would face tariff increases of up to 132 per cent. As EU taxation of Namibia's beef exports into the EU, without an EPA, would have been equal to around 80 per cent of their value, they would likely have ceased (Overseas Development Institute 2007, cited in Meyn 2008).

The European Commission official at this event in Dublin noted that, while the economic evidence was ambiguous in relation to free trade and economic development, EPAs were going ahead in any event: to paraphrase Margaret Thatcher, 'there was no alternative', at least as far as the European Commission was concerned. Some might consider this a startling display of arrogance. Reading between the lines this attitude could be summed up as: 'We are not sure what this will do to your economy and society but we know it is good for us, and we have the money and power, so it is going ahead' – so much for 'partnership' and 'equality'.

On the other hand, as noted earlier, the EU has been dumping agricultural produce on Africa. In Senegal almost half of all chicken farms have gone out of business as a result of a 1,000 per cent increase in imports of poultry from the EU (*Business Report*, 18 October 2004, cited in Lee 2009). These chicken imports are heavily subsidized by the EU and have dramatically displaced domestic production. Although exports from the EU that are subsidized are meant to be excluded from liberalization under EPAs, according to an official in the Directorate-General of Trade in the EU: 'We are not dumping poultry parts in Africa. The parts exported to Africa are parts not meant for consumption here. They would not be fed to animals...parts that would be dumped in the sea' (quoted in Lee 2009, p. 83). This statement is reminiscent of the famous quote from Larry Summers, currently a cabinet member in the Obama Administration in the United States and former President of Harvard University, that Africa was 'under polluted' because people had such low life expectancy there and would likely be dead before the effects of deadly pollutants and carcinogens could take effect (quoted in Shiva 2000).

EPAs represent a form of 'deep integration' into the global economy whereby free market policy reforms are locked in by binding regulations (Meyn 2008), to the advantage of European exporters. As noted earlier, average tariff rates in SSA are now around 10 per cent, making it one of the most open regions in the world to trade – if not *the* most open (Lines 2008): 'One might even wonder why the European Union makes so much ado of eliminating the remaining 10 per cent' (Asche 2008, p. 91). However, in a context of hyper-competition, with the rise of new industrial producers such as China and India, a margin of 10 per cent can make a substantial difference. As Milner, Morrissey and Zgovu (2008, p. 58) note, 'there is...potential for reciprocity to substantially change the composition of African countries' trade, with switching of sources away from other regional and world suppliers to the EU, especially in manufactures'.

Given the size of its economy and the scale of European investment there, South Africa is particularly important to the EU. The EU accounts for 66 per cent of FDI in that country (Arnold 2009) and has also negotiated a free trade agreement with South Africa. South Africa has also signed a strategic partnership with the Union, which means that there will be regular political dialogues and summits.

Within the eighteen months approaching the signing of this free trade agreement two-thirds of the dairy processing sector in South Africa had been bought up by European TNCs such as Danone and Parmalat (Goodison 2007, cited in Lee 2009). Given its economic weight, other powers and companies use South Africa as an entry point to the rest of Africa, raising the issue in some people's minds of whether South Africa is a Trojan horse for European and broader Western interests on the continent.

While markets are central to EU engagement in Africa, the Common Security and Defence Policy means that the EU can now send military deployments to Africa, with the agreement of member states. However, it is the United States which has the most extensive military cooperation agreements with African governments, described below.

United States Interests in Africa: Oil (and) Security

According to the so-called 'Cheney Report' (2001), named for the then US Vice-President and former oil executive, by 2020 US domestic oil production would supply less than 30 per cent of the country's needs (Kennan 2009). The US is heavily dependent on Saudi oil, but that country's major fields, which were discovered in the 1950s and 1960s, are producing an average of 8 per cent less oil per year. On the other hand, the US government estimates that one of every five new barrels of oil coming on-stream to the global economy will now come from the Gulf of Guinea in West Africa. Consequently, United States interests in Africa are increasingly structured by interlinked concerns over energy and security.

The United States brings substantial hard-power advantages to its negotiations with African states, as it is the world's single largest economy and now the largest aid donor to Africa. It has not been shy of using this power. For example, while Enron and the corruption of that company are often associated with the Bush Administration in the United States, the previous Clinton Administration also aggressively promoted this company overseas. For example, the Mozambique government had offers from South African and Argentine companies to develop the Pande offshore gas fields in the mid-1990s. However, according to the Minister of Natural Resources, 'there were outright threats to withhold development funds if we didn't sign (the deal with Enron) and sign soon... Enron was forever playing games with us and the embassy was forever threatening to withdraw aid' (quoted in Arnold 2009, p. 31). Aid is still used to promote economic or political advantage as the United States recently withheld Economic Support Funds from the six African countries that refused to grant US citizens immunity from extradition to the International Criminal Court (ICC) (Copson 2007), which the United States has not signed up to, although waivers were subsequently granted as the US obtained for its citizens an exemption from the ICC's jurisdiction from the UN Security Council.

Increased US interest in Africa was evident during the latter years of the Clinton Administration. This was driven by a variety of imperatives: guilt about failure to act over the Rwandan genocide and increased US strategic interests in accessing African markets and resources. These found expression in AGOA, which President Clinton felt was the 'best thing' he did for Africa.[5]

AGOA was adopted in 2000 and is a programme which allows duty-free access to the American market for exports from qualifying African countries. It was controversial initially because it required some of the more developed African countries to source their inputs, such as textiles for clothing, either domestically, or from the United States, rather than from low-cost producers such as China. While some argued that this was discriminatory and a hidden method of boosting American exports (Tabb 2001), according to President Clinton this was an attempt to put a human face on globalization as half of the world's population was not benefiting from the phenomenon (Clinton 2004).

Contrary to its general espousal of free trade, the United States has certainly used mercantilist measures in its foreign economic policy. The website of the United States Agency for International Development notes, for example, that one of its roles is to promote American interests. However, the provision relating to sourcing of inputs in AGOA was later relaxed, because the amount of clothing being exported to the United States has remained small as the vast majority of what enters the United States duty free under AGOA is oil. While AGOA has promoted some economic diversification (Odularu 2008), in 2001, its first full year, exports from SSA to the US actually declined, and 83 per cent of eligible exports are in the energy sector, largely Nigerian oil (African Development Bank 2003, p. 197).

AGOA fits within a broader context of market opening pursued aggressively by the first Bush and Clinton Administrations with the end of the Cold War. The former United States Trade Representative under George Bush Sr, Carla Hills, once advocated that the United States should pry open countries with a crowbar 'so that our private sector can take advantage of them' (quoted in Dunkley 2004, p. 220). This attitude also extended to Africa when in 1996 the then Commerce Secretary of the United States, Ron Brown, said that 'from now on the United States is not going to give away African markets to the old colonial powers' (quoted in Holslag 2007, cited in Okeke 2008, p. 197). Indeed, the Commerce Department had described Africa as 'the last frontier' for its business community.

AGOA was associated with labour abuses in certain cases, although this cannot be blamed on the Act itself, but on the context of globalization of which it is a part. In 2001–2, a Malaysian company, Ramatex, opened a textile factory in Namibia to take advantage of AGOA. The Namibian government had given substantial subsidies in order to attract the investment, but to minimize costs and raise profits the company employed hundreds of workers from Bangladesh, brought in by labour brokers illegally. When the workers went out on strike in

2003 against unfair and exploitative labour practices, the factory closed: 'Like under colonial rule, workers who revolt against their inhuman conditions are simply deported to their "homelands". Previously back to Ovamboland [in Namibia], now back to Bangladesh, China or the Philippines' (Jauch 2004, cited in Melber 2009, p. 67). This story shows one of the worst sides of contemporary economic globalization: a poor country subsidizing a transnational company to the tune of US$40 million to import 'disposable people' illegally, exploit them, and then make them unemployed.

The Clinton Administration also stepped up security cooperation with African states after the bombing by Al-Qaeda of the American embassies in Tanzania and Kenya in 1998. After the débâcle in Somalia at the beginning of the decade, the Americans had favoured a policy of political *laissez faire* towards Africa: refusing to intervene, and actively blocking United Nations intervention, during the Rwandan genocide, for example. However, after the embassy bombings, security considerations came to the fore again, although American policymakers were, particularly after the experience in Somalia, keen to avoid American military casualties. Consequently the Americans set up the African Crisis Response Initiative to train and equip African militaries to respond to regional crises. The name of this programme was later changed to the somewhat less threatening and more nondescript title of the African Contingency Operations Training and Assistance Programme (ACOTA) by the new Bush Administration, which also introduced a special Pan-Sahel Initiative (later renamed the Trans-Sahara Counter-Terrorism Initiative).

Much of the training of African troops under the ACOTA programme was undertaken by Military Professional Resources International, which is a private military contractor (Ghazvinian 2007). ACOTA was then absorbed into the Global Peace Operations Initiative which was launched by President Bush in 2004. This initiative aimed to train and equip 75,000 peacekeeping troops around the world by 2010, with a focus on Africa (Copson 2007).

Under these security programmes, 'surplus' weapons are sometimes donated by the United States to friendly African governments. The US gave surplus Coast Guard ships to the Nigerian navy, for example (Copson 2007). Nigeria, which is the largest oil producer in Africa, has also received the most military aid from the US for arms purchases (Yi-Chong 2008). But the militarization of relations with African governments has strengthened unaccountable African elites who have been the source of much conflict and destabilization in Africa in the first place (Porteous 2008).

On coming to power, George W. Bush declared that Africa didn't fit into US national strategic interests: a somewhat surprising statement, given the previous embassy bombings. These were obviously not given serious consideration at the time, as most of the casualties were locals rather than Americans. However, the calculus changed with the events of 11 September.

In the build-up to the invasion of Iraq in 2003, the United States became particularly keen to diversify its oil supplies away from the turbulent Middle East. In 2002 the US Assistant Secretary of State with responsibility for Africa noted that: 'oil and gas is [sic] one natural resource that Africa does have. And what we would like to see is Africa use those resources, and we are very interested in helping African governments use those resources and prioritize how they might build on a successful national resource economy' (Katzensteiner 2002) – although these are very rare around the world. Indeed, the Bush Administration declared that African oil is 'now of national strategic interest' to the US, given that the United States is likely to import two out of every three barrels of its oil by 2020 (Servant 2003).

Whereas it takes about six weeks for oil from the Persian Gulf to reach the US, it takes only two weeks from West Africa (Ruppert 2005) and avoids potential supply disruption through the Suez Canal and Sumed pipeline (USEIA, n.d.). West African oil is 'light and sweet', with low sulphur content, particularly suitable for burning in cars. Around 17 per cent of US oil imports currently originate in West and Central Africa; and major new investments are being undertaken in Nigeria, Angola, São Tomé and Equatorial Guinea. Nigeria is currently the fifth-largest crude oil exporter to the US, and Angola is sixth. In 2005 the US imported more oil from Africa than it did from the Middle East (Arnold 2009).

There are now direct weekly flights from Texas to Equatorial Guinea, which for much of the 2000s had the world's fastest-growing economy (CBS 2003). It has a population of half a million people, but US oil firms have invested more than US$5 billion there. According to Human Rights Watch, continued human rights abuses have not deterred US investment, and it is geo-strategically attractive to the US because it is non-Muslim and not part of the Organization of the Petroleum Exporting Countries (OPEC). The size of oil revenues is a state secret, but in the first year of its contract with ExxonMobil, Equatorial Guinea got to keep only 12 per cent of its oil revenues (Klein 2005).

While Equatorial Guinea is now a major supplier of oil to the United States, there has also been tension. The Clinton Administration had closed the embassy in Malabo after the US ambassador was threatened by a government minister. However, given the importance of opening up new oil supplies, the Bush Administration reopened it, and the long-term Equato-Guinean dictator, Obiang, was invited to the United States to meet Secretary of State Condoleezza Rice, who declared that he was a 'good friend' to the United States. The Bush Administration even thoughtfully gave back hundreds of millions of dollars salted away by Obiang in Riggs Bank in Washington, DC, a US Congressional investigation notwithstanding. Some of this money had arrived in million-dollar shrink-wrapped bundles (Maass 2009).

In part this handover of money may have been to mend fences after Spanish, British and American intelligence agencies reportedly got wind of a coup plot to depose Obiang, funded and planned partly by Lady Margaret Thatcher's son Mark, who was convicted of involvement in the plot in South Africa (Roberts 2006). After that Obiang turned towards China, calling that country Equatorial Guinea's most important development partner and signing contracts with Chinese companies to build a new capital, Malabo II. Most Equato-Guinean oil now goes to China (Waters and Koppel 2009).

Consequently the United States is now very accommodating and the new scramble has resulted in renewed support for authoritarian governments. The American army show up to honour Obiang at military parades in Equatorial Guinea (Maass 2009). In fact the United States Agency for International Development even takes money off the Equato-Guinean government to deliver health and educational programmes in the country (Copson 2007). Despite having one of the world's highest per capita incomes, the country does not have a single bookshop, and some of the American oil company compounds are in the Texas, rather than the Equato-Guinean, area phone code. Little wonder that oil platforms are known in West Africa as 'mosquitoes'. They extract oil, but bring problems with them.

The Bush Administration also for the first time set up a US military base in Africa, in Djibouti, and funded counter-terrorism cooperation with African militaries. While only 3 per cent of American humanitarian aid was distributed through the US Department of Defense in the late 1990s, from 1998 to 2008 the average rose to 22 per cent. Indeed, the Bush Administration went as far as setting up a new Africa Command in the Pentagon (AFRICOM), which has been highly controversial, and no African country, save perhaps Liberia, was willing to host it. Liberia's infrastructure was, however, reportedly too poor and, as a result, it was rejected by the United States as a location (Michel, Beuret and Woods 2009). Consequently, it is currently run out of US military bases in Europe. However, this may be advantageous to the United States, which wants to keep its military 'footprint' in Africa as light as possible. For example, rather than having many permanent military bases there, it seeks a lily-pad structure whereby weapons are stored and facilities provided to United States troops by African countries with which it has military agreements, should they be needed. The goal is to make the American military presence real, but so light that it appears not to be there (Carmody 2007). The US base in Diego Garcia in the Indian Ocean, which is leased from Britain, also holds stockpiles of tanks and other military hardware which could equip up to 20,000 American troops (Arnold 2009).

Increased military cooperation was driven by the fact that 'Washington had come to realize that Africa – with its vast natural resources, rising population, and unexplored markets, coupled with internal instability, rampant disease and terrorism – demands special attention' (Kfir 2008, p. 110). AFRICOM fitted with the Bush Administration's militaristic approach to the 'resolution' of foreign policy problems. However, unlike other United States military commands, AFRICOM is staffed by personnel not only from the Department of Defense, but also from the State Department and the United States Agency for International Development.

AFRICOM serves a number of US interests: combating terrorism, securing natural resource supplies, containing armed conflict, reducing crime and responding to growing Chinese influence (McFate 2008). United States National Security Strategy identified Africa as a high priority in order to bring 'ungoverned spaces' under governments' territorial control (Ploch 2007, cited in Rupiya and Southall 2009, and commanders from the Pentagon noted that the setting up of AFRICOM was to 'meet the challenge of China' (quoted in Campbell 2008, p. 15).

In addition to brandishing the stick of military escalation, President Bush also sought to humanize the 'war on terror' through dramatically increasing funding for HIV/AIDS prevention and treatment through the President's Emergency Plan for AIDS Relief (PEPFAR). The Administration also had an eye to resource access. Commenting on the dramatic increases in aid to Africa under the Bush Administration, a Republican Congressman noted 'this is something Republicans normally don't do, but what drove this change in policy was very much the events of September 11th [after which] our traditional sources of oil are not as secure as we once thought they were' (Royce 2002, quoted in Yi-Chong 2008, p. 22).

The United States is now the leading provider of aid to Africa (Copson 2007), causing some commentators to argue that the 'humanitarian scramble for Africa' is linked to the scramble for the continent's natural resources (Lee 2006). Tom Porteous (2008, p. 138) concurs:

> In Africa's unstable regions UK and US decision-makers were engaged, under the guise of partnership with African governments in a quasi neo-imperialist project in which the quest to secure trade, investment and energy interests was tied up with grandiose plans to bring about stability through political transformation and state-building. But as in Iraq and Afghanistan, neither the UK nor the United States had the drive, the commitment and the self-belief that their colonial forebears could bring to the task.

Perhaps this was just as well.

Increased American aid also served domestic political purposes in the US as it was popular with Evangelical Christians (Patterson 2006) and this may have been important in explaining the funding pattern.[6] While malaria kills roughly a million Africans annually and is the leading cause of under-five mortality, 93 per cent of PEPFAR funding went to AIDS in the fiscal years 2004 and 2005, despite the fact the programme was also meant to deal with other diseases (Copson 2005, cited in Patterson 2006). Congressional amendments authorizing the PEPFAR legislation earmarked a third of the money for programmes that promoted abstinence and remaining faithful to one partner, although many campaigners in Africa have seriously questioned the effectiveness of these approaches, and indeed some have argued that they are likely to worsen the AIDS crisis. There is already evidence that this has been the case in Uganda.

Uganda is often noted as the first African country successfully to control and reduce the AIDS epidemic. There is some debate as to how this was achieved, with more rapid economic growth and poverty reduction undoubtedly playing an important part. However, the government also adopted a determined approach based on Abstinence, Being faithful and Condomizing (known as 'ABC'). However, when the Bush Administration came to power in the United States, with the support of the Ugandan first lady Janet Museveni, abstinence assumed far greater importance in government policy. At times this resulted in stockpiles of millions of condoms not being released and the HIV incidence rate, or number of new infections, increasing (see Carmody and Elder 2008).

Surprisingly, the Obama Administration has largely maintained Bush's policies in Africa as the containment of Sudan and the elimination of potential terrorist threats remain top priorities, as does fighting piracy off the coast of Somalia, discussed later. While his Assistant Secretary of State for African Affairs highlights the importance of 'good governance' for African development (speech to the African Studies Association, New Orleans, November 2009), in the most recent Nigerian elections when the (literally) short-lived President Yar-Adua came to power, there was less than 20 per cent of the required number of ballot papers and these were mostly distributed to governing-party strongholds (Hattingh 2007). Nonetheless, military cooperation with the United States continues, with the US still providing military training to Nigeria – on how to repel attackers from oil platforms, for example. Additionally, President Obama has refrained from outright criticism of Nigeria as 10–12 per cent of US oil imports come from the Niger Delta, which has been beset with conflict (Arnold 2009). The new Nigerian President, Goodluck Jonathan, met Obama in Washington in 2010.

US interests in Africa will continue to be dictated by the twin and interlinked concerns of oil and security and the continent will also play an increasingly important role in the global struggle for political influence between the United States and China. The Obama Administration is attempting to reassert the United States' 'soft power' – whereby allies are won through persuasion and affinity rather than force (Nye 2004) – around the world, in the wake of the damage done to it by the Bush Administration. However, many African leaders are only democrats at a rhetorical level. In the poorest countries in the world, a sitting President has a seemingly amazing 88 per cent chance of re-election, as compared to only a 45 per cent chance of an incumbent government retaining power in the rich countries of the Organization for Economic Co-operation and Development (OECD) (Collier 2009). Thus, in its relations with Africa, the United States continues to deal with the autocratic leaders of resource-rich countries, while preaching democracy, whereas the Chinese maintain no such illusions or contradictions in their policies, discussed later.

Japanese Interests in Africa

Since the Second World War, Japan has closely aligned its foreign policy with that of the United States. However, it is increasing its engagement in Africa, and in 2008 Japan announced that it would double its aid to Africa during the next five years. Japan has had an active interest in Africa, particularly as a result of the fact that it was, until recently, the world's second-largest economy, and has a paucity of domestic industrial resources. The website of the Japan Oil, Gas and Metals National Corporation notes: 'JOGMEC integrates the functions of the former Japan National Oil Corporation, which was in charge of securing a stable supply of oil and natural gas, and the former Metal Mining Agency of Japan, which was in charge of ensuring a stable supply of nonferrous metal and mineral resources and implementing mine pollution control measures.' Japan has had oil interests in Angola since 1986 (Vines et al. 2009).

Like the Chinese, and now the Indians, Japan holds periodic summits with African leaders. It has established a Tokyo International Conference on African Development, in partnership with the United Nations, which is held periodically. The next conference will be held in 2013.

The Japanese have, however, sought to distinguish themselves from previous Western approaches to aid by emphasizing the importance of country ownership and the fact that policies must be tailored to individual circumstances, rather than adopting a 'one size fits all' approach. This is similar in orientation to the Chinese approach, in which economic and political goals are thought to be best achieved through persuasion, rather than force.

While Japanese resource companies continue to work actively in Africa, they have not had the same prominence as others and the Japanese government has lost influence relative to the Chinese government on the continent – as most others have, as well. Another country which has arguably had a substantial governance impact and has major and growing economic interests in Africa is internal to the continent: South Africa.

South African Interests in Africa: Minerals, Mobiles and Marketizing Governance

South Africa is both an old and a new economic power in Africa. Old in that it has long had the biggest economy in SSA, and that its companies have been a dominant force in the Southern African region; and new in the sense that its companies and its government have emerged from economic sanctions and enforced isolation as a result of the abolition of the system of apartheid or racial segregation roughly fifteen years ago. In 2006 South African trade with the rest of Africa was about a third that of China's with the rest of Africa (Daniel and Bhengu 2009).

South Africa accounts for about 80 per cent of the economy of the Southern African Development Community (SADC), which, with thirteen countries (Adebajo, Adedeji and Landsberg 2007) and a population of around only 50 million people, accounts for over a third of SSA's economy and fully three-quarters of all electricity generation on the sub-continent. Less than a fifth of the population of Africa has access to electricity (Clarke 2008), and South Africa, Egypt and Nigeria together generate three-quarters of the continent's electricity, meaning that much of it is literally a 'dark continent' at night, as evidenced by satellite photos. Of Africa's top 500 companies, 54 per cent are South African, as are 19 of the top 20 (*Africa Report*, April–May 2008, cited in Daniel and Bhengu 2009), and these are major players in Sub-Saharan African economies.

Under the system of racial segregation and discrimination in force until 1994 – apartheid – South Africa was subject to a variety of sanctions and constraints which inhibited its companies from investing overseas. However, with the winding down of apartheid and the loosening of capital controls, South African companies began to invest extensively in SSA. Such was the scale of this investment rush that the *New York Times* labelled this as a 'new scramble for Africa', although in this case it was 'internally' driven in the first instance. Rather than being externally imposed through World Bank programmes, this was an example of globalization from the inside out as South African conglomerates expanded into the rest of Africa (see Carmody 2007). The regional expansion of South African companies was meant to be a piece of the strategy to drive an economic renaissance, first in South Africa and then in the region more generally.

South African companies have rapidly expanded their presence throughout the African continent. Sub-Saharan Africa was an attractive investment ground for South African companies because they were generally too small to compete in the developed world (Hudson 2007). The main areas of South African outward investment into Africa were in infrastructure (27 per cent in 2000–3), mining (22 per cent) and oil, gas and petroleum (18 per cent) (Daniel and Lutchman 2006, cited in Southall and Comninos 2009). By 2002 major South African companies such as AngloGold Ashanti and Mobile Telecommunications Networks (MTN) were deriving more than half of their profits from their African activities (UNCTAD 2005).

In terms of trade, while South African manufactures were not, for the most part, globally competitive after the end of apartheid, given sanctions and the particular economic incentive structures that prevailed prior to economic liberalization, they were competitive in the region. Indeed South Africa has enjoyed a massive and consistent trade surplus with its neighbours, with a ratio of exports to imports of six to one in its favour (Landsberg and Kornegay 1999, cited in Landsberg 2002) – although this has recently fallen to two to one, perhaps partly because of re-exports from South Africa of African natural resources to Asia and elsewhere. Copper cathodes produced in the Chinese-operated SEZ in Zambia are exported to China through Africa's busiest port, Durban in South Africa, for example (interview at SEZ, Chambishi, August 2009).

In 2002 the South African Department of Foreign Affairs argued that 'the current most important issues with regard to the Central African Region are conflict resolution, promotion of peace and stability and good governance and reconstruction and development' (quoted in Landsberg 2002, p. 169). The other main priority, it argued, was the expansion of economic and trade relations with the region. According to the head of the local economic development unit of eThekwini municipality in South Africa, 'our own market doesn't have the numbers to put us in a competitive position' in manufacturing, and South Africa can't compete with low-cost producers internationally (interview, 21 July 2010, Durban). Consequently the focus is on developing manufacturing for the regional market – the 'Sub-Sahara'. According to him, the New Partnership for African Development (NEPAD) which South Africa has promoted heavily has infrastructural projects such as roads and railways which will allow more access to SSA.

Political stability would in turn, it was felt, facilitate commerce. However, as will be discussed later, the existing types of economic engagement in the Great Lakes region may have facilitated or fomented conflict. Extensive resource extraction and political stability have proven to be seemingly incompatible in many countries in Africa. A United Nations Report to the General Assembly cited twelve South African companies which may have been involved in the looting of minerals during the war in the DRC (Hudson 2007).

By 2004, South African companies were allowed to invest up to 2 billion rand per project in Africa (approximately US$300 million), which was still, however, only half what they were allowed to invest outside of Africa. Nonetheless, this represented a dramatic increase from 1997 when they were only allowed to invest 50 million rand (UNCTAD 2005, cited in Miller, Oloyede and Saunders 2008). South African investment in the thirteen countries of the SADC was almost a billion dollars a year between 1994 and 2004, and the country ranked as one of the top three sources of FDI in ten of those countries

(UNCTAD 2005, cited in Schroeder 2008). According to the Chief Executive of South African Breweries-Miller: 'if there were more of Africa, we would invest in it' (quoted in Anonymous 2005, in Schroeder 2008).

South African investments range across sectors from mining and retailing to manufacturing. For example, in 2007, the South African canning company Nampak announced that it was investing US$100 million in a plant in Luanda, Angola, for the local and export markets (Daniel and Bhengu 2009), and in Tanzania alone there are over 150 South African companies active, where many locals regard them with disdain, and some boycott them, as they are 'white' and colonially associated. One Tanzanian pastoralist activist noted, 'we now live in the United States of South Africa' (quoted in Schroeder 2008, p. 24). By 2005 only 8 of the biggest 100 companies quoted on the Johannesburg stock exchange did not have operations in Africa (Hudson 2007).

Between 1992 and 2007 it was neighbouring Mozambique which attracted the most South African foreign investment: 34 per cent (Daniel and Bhengu 2009). Some major investments with South African involvement are the Mozambique Aluminium Processing plant, Mozal – which is a several-billion-dollar investment – and the Illovo and Tongaat-Huletts sugar plantations. The latter company spent over US$100 million acquiring more land for its plantations.

The South African government has actively encouraged regional expansion by its companies, sometimes in partnership with the state-owned Industrial Development Corporation which has invested in sixty projects in twenty-one countries. The expansion of South African mobile phone companies internationally is interesting because it has sometimes been spearheaded by indigenous entrepreneurs.

Africa has the highest proportion of mobile telephone users out of total telephone users of anywhere in the world, as fixed-line communication is not used much (International Telecommunication Union 2007, cited in Sanchez 2008). According to Southall and Comninos (2009), mobile telephony is one of the few areas in which indigenous capitalist participation has been significant in Africa. They see this as resulting from a confluence of factors, particularly: the exploitation of market opportunity by a number of indigenous entrepreneurs, backed by state, multinational and private capital; the generally dreadful state of fixed-line communications on the continent, which allowed for rapid penetration of mobile phones; liberalization and privatization of the telephony market; and, finally, rapid advances in telecommunications technology.

MTN is the largest mobile telephone operator in Africa, with a subscriber base of over 48 million in 2007, with operations in twenty-one countries in Africa and the Middle East in 2006 (Southall and Comninos 2009). In 2003/4, MTN Nigeria's profits surpassed those of MTN South Africa (Hudson 2007), and by 2007 it had a subscriber base of 16.5 million in that country, which represented 43 per cent of the Nigerian mobile telephone subscriber base (Daniel and Bhengu 2009). Econet, another mobile phone company based in South Africa, is also active in Nigeria. Thus, while the formal economy of SSA, excluding South Africa, is around the same size as that of Belgium or Texas, it can be of major importance to specific large companies (Lockwood 2005), exacerbating uneven development. According to Nobel Laureate Joseph Stiglitz, because these companies repatriate their profits to South Africa, they are 'mining' poorer countries of their money.[7]

MTN is an interesting company because it was a product of the government of South Africa's Black Economic Empowerment (BEE) initiative, which sought to redress the historical exclusion of people of indigenous origin from business. The chairperson of MTN is Phuthuma Freedom Nhleko, who is also a director of another BEE company, Johnnic Holdings, and also of older South African companies such as Old Mutual and Nedbank.

MTN now employs over 6,000 people and operates in more than twenty countries, mostly in Africa but also in Cyprus and the Middle East (Monama 2009). There are relatively few successful South African multinational companies, but in 2007 MTN announced that it planned to purchase the Dubai-based company Investcom, for US$5.5 billion (Daniel and Bhengu 2009). It was able to use its regional growth in Africa as a springboard to globalization. However, whether this success can be replicated is increasingly open to question. South African negotiators of a free trade agreement with the United States are highly concerned that unregulated competition from US firms would undermine the BEE programme in South Africa (Copson 2007), although this has arguably mainly benefited a few hundred, largely politically connected, individuals (see Ponte and van Sittert 2007).

The massively increased presence of South African companies and trade in SSA has been highly contentious in other countries. For example, some in the Zimbabwean business community have accused South Africa of deliberately trying to deindustrialize the Zimbabwean economy (Landsberg 2002). Many formal retailers in Africa also find themselves under increasing pressure, from South African supermarkets in particular, which also tend to source their supplies from South

Africa. For example, the major South African retailer with operations across Africa and also now in India, Shoprite, by the early 2000s reportedly contributed 2 billion rand to South Africa's exports (Naidu and Lutchman 2005, cited in Miller, Oloyede and Saunders 2008). This has given rise to fears over South African neo-colonialism in the region. In a little over ten years after the fall of apartheid, South African companies acquired controlling stakes in Tanzania's national brewery, airline and largest banking chain (Schroeder 2008). In Kenya there was a so-called 'beer war' between South African Breweries and Kenya's national brewery, which ended when the two agreed to grant each other effective near-monopolies in Tanzania and Kenya, respectively.

In some cases locals have been displaced to make way for South African businesses. For example, in Tanzania hundreds of small-scale gemstone miners were forcibly removed from a tanzanite mining site in 1997 to make way for South African investors. Tanzanite is a precious stone only found in Tanzania, and the main company which mines it there now is trying to get people to buy it to celebrate births, in the same way as diamonds are associated with engagements. Thus, depending on where you are positioned in the commodity supply chain, the same commodity can have very different meanings – joy over family expansion or displacement and loss of livelihood.

Some academics also refer to the 'Malling of Africa', as a result of the fact that many of the shopping malls being built around Africa are being built by South African companies. Often these are highly exclusionary and controlled spaces. For example, in Zambia, where South African companies control 39 per cent of the retail sector (Zambia Investment Centre, cited in Miller, Nel and Hampwaye 2008), some of the shopping malls are guarded by police with AK47 assault rifles.

There have also been more positive effects from South African investment. In many cases the sale of former state-owned enterprises to South African companies has reinvigorated them, as in the Zambian dairy industry, for example (Kenny and Mather 2008). In some cases South African companies, like Chinese ones, have taken opportunistic advantage of economic and political crises in other countries to invest and purchase assets at bargain-basement prices. For example, the South African Impala Platinum Company has invested in Zimbabwe.

The platinum mine in which it invested was opened in the mid-1990s by the Australian miner BHP (Broken Hill Proprietary), cost US$200–250 million to build, and exceeded the total FDI in Zimbabwe since independence several times over (Gibbon 1996). But BHP shut it down in 1999 because of difficulties with equipment, manpower and unstable geological conditions (Economist Intelligence Unit, 2005). It was subsequently sold to Zimplats in 2000 for a 'nominal amount' (Zimplats n.d.). Despite the political turmoil in that country, South African investment in Zimbabwe rose in 2001 (Palloti 2004).

Zimplats is 83 per cent owned by the South African Impala holdings – the holding company for South African Impala Platinum (Implats) Ltd. Some members of the board of directors of Implats, such as Khotso Mokhele and Thandi Orleyn, 'straddle' both public and private sectors, being President of the South African National Research Foundation and a member of the board of the South African Reserve Bank, respectively. However, most of the board are 'white'. Zimplats made an operating profit of US$25.4 million in the quarter to 30 June 2006 and was planning to invest US$2.5 billion in Zimbabwe in the subsequent ten years (*The Herald*, 2006).

Despite Zimbabwe's deepening economic crisis, Zimplats recorded a profit of over US$100 million in 2007, which was more than double its 2006 profits (Daniel and Bhengu 2009). Shockingly, domestic ownership of the Zimbabwean economy is now at 1960s levels. Thus, while Robert Mugabe trumpeted his nationalist credentials as a way of trying to stay in power, the economy has been largely sold off to foreigners. Consequently, Zimbabwe's crisis may be very profitable for South African business in the medium to long term, with it getting substantial assets like this almost for free. Also, there are still opportunities for Zimbabwe's political elites domestically, such as the major diamond find in Marange, where hundreds of informal miners were murdered by the army to assert state control in 2008 (Moore and Mawowa 2010).[8]

There has also been South African cooperation with other 'rogue regimes'. Despite the development of syn-fuel technology to convert coal to oil under apartheid in South Africa – which is now being exported to China – South Africa is dependent on importing about 98 per cent of its oil needs (Hudson 2007), with around a quarter of this figure coming from Africa. The national oil company PetroSA has an agreement with the Sudanese state oil company, Sudapest, for example. Therefore, just like China, or indeed – some would argue – the United States, 'when it comes to South Africa's economic relations, it now seems that anything goes – or rather if it is oil any government will do' (Hudson 2007, p. 143). This is in contrast to the ethical foreign policy which Nelson Mandela sought to pursue during his administration, although this was also of course tempered by *realpolitik*.

Energy also provides other investment opportunities. The South African state-owned power generation company, Eskom, which generates over 90 per cent of South Africa's electricity, is active in thirty-one countries in Africa (Southall and Comninos 2009), and the biggest potential investment is in the Grand Inga project in the DRC: the biggest hydroelectric project in the world, twice as big in terms of generating capacity as the controversial Three Gorges Dam project in China. When and if it is developed, it is projected to generate sufficient power for the entire continent of Africa and to be able to export power to the Middle East and Europe.

Large dam projects such as these are controversial because they often displace significant numbers of people, submerge local ecologies, serve as breeding grounds for malaria and water-borne diseases, and are sometimes subject to mismanagement. In Lesotho, the Katse dam was constructed on unsuitable geology, meaning that there are periodic earthquakes. The amounts of water behind large dam walls, sometimes in the millions of tonnes, are so significant that geophysicists can measure their impacts in the altered spinning of the earth (Rich 1994).

While some have argued that South Africa serves a 'sub-imperial' role in Africa (Bond and Zapiro 2006), as a gateway for Western interests, others argue that it is attempting to be a regional hegemon in its own right. However, given its own economic problems, it has found being a regional hegemon difficult, although under Nelson Mandela it did intervene militarily in Lesotho and has made extensive arms purchases. In part, these arms purchases may have been made to facilitate large commissions being paid. A former associate of the current President of South Africa, Jacob Zuma, was imprisoned because of this (Mangcu 2009).

A hegemon must 'use its domestic market to stabilise the larger continental economy and it must be able to resist domestic pressures to look out only for its citizens' own interests' (Grieco and Ikenberry 2003, p. 112, quoted in Schoeman 2007, p. 104). Thabo Mbeki, the former President of South Africa, attempted to gain acceptance of South African leadership in the region and to further its companies' expansion in Africa, without the economic resources to back it up, through the idea of African Renaissance and, in particular, NEPAD: what has been called 'hegemony on a shoestring'.

NEPAD was in essence a bargain between the rich countries and Africa, whereby African governments would agree to peer review of their governance by an eminent persons group in exchange for more trade, aid and investment from the West. However, this attempt to balance internal African and external power interests on the continent had its own contradictions. When South Africa was the only African government to condemn the human rights abuses of Sani Abacha, the Nigerian military dictator in the 1990s, it showed itself to be out of step with other African leaders, who value regime survival above almost everything else, given the economic benefits which flow from it. This explains why Mandela's successor, Thabo Mbeki, adopted a 'softly, softly' approach towards Robert Mugabe, and other African autocrats, despite NEPAD. This approach has been continued by his successor Jacob Zuma.

South African regional dominance is, however, under pressure from the increasing Asian presence in Africa. For example, 'exports to Africa as a percentage of total exports have barely changed since 1998 (at around 13–14 percent). Exports to SADC states have actually *declined* to around 10 percent of South Africa's total exports. As these figures suggest, industrialized South Africa faces potential competitive pressures from the industrialized East that are unlike those of Africa's primary producers' (Martin 2008, p. 129).

According to the head of economic development in eThekwini, China had previously had a 'devastating' impact on the textile and clothing industries in South Africa itself, and this was now beginning to be seen in other manufacturing sub-sectors, such as furniture.[9] Martyn Davies, Director at the Centre for Chinese Studies at the University of Stellenbosch, argues that 'what is naturally South Africa's regional commercial space is fast becoming China's' (quoted in Lee 2006, p. 322). It is to an examination of China's interests and strategies in Africa that we now turn.

3 CHINESE INTERESTS AND STRATEGIES IN AFRICA [WITH IAN TAYLOR]

The twenty-first century is the century for China to lead the world. And when you are leading the world, we want to be close behind you. When you are going to the moon we don't want to be left behind. (Nigerian President Olusegun Obasanjo speaking to Chinese President Hu Jintau, Nigeria, 2006, quoted in Michel, Beuret and Woods 2009, p. 11)

Before we get carried away about Chinese investment it is worth noting that the entire stock of Chinese FDI in Africa in 2005 was just one-tenth of the flow of new FDI from the United Kingdom into Africa the previous year. (Glennerster 2009, p. 115)

The previous chapter dealt with old economic power interests in Africa, but it is new economic powers' emergence on the continent which has attracted the most media attention in recent years, particularly that of China.

One of the most significant events in the last few decades globally has been the rise of China. The Chinese economy has grown by approximately 10 per cent a year, on average, for the last thirty years, since Deng Xiaoping began the process of economic liberalization. The scale of economic transformation in China is vast.

Between 1978 and 2005 China's 'trade volume increased by 70 times, the share in world trade increased from 0.8 per cent to 7.7' (Min Zhao 2006, p. 4). The country overtook the United States in 2002 as the single biggest recipient of FDI (Breslin 2007) and already produces half of the world's clothing and footwear and most of its computers (Leonard 2008). Chinese cotton imports rose 175-fold from 2001 to 2004 (Bello 2009). Unbelievably, one factory in Shunde in the Pearl

River Delta, by itself, makes 40 per cent of the world's microwaves (Kaplinsky 2005).

Given the fact that China has a population of over a billion people, economic growth on this scale was likely to have massive resource implications, for Africa in particular. As Beijing has moved from being an exporter of raw materials and minerals to a large-scale importer, it now consumes one-third of global steel output, 40 per cent of cement and 26 per cent of the world's copper. In the early 2000s the Chinese government formalized its 'go global' or 'go out' strategy, which encourages companies to invest overseas through tax incentives and loans to source natural resources, and to offshore less technologically sophisticated processes to enable China to move up the value chain, amongst other objectives (Brautigam 2009).[1]

From 2000 to 2003 China accounted for the vast majority of increased global demand for aluminium (76 per cent), steel (95 per cent), nickel (99 per cent) and copper (100 per cent) (Kaplinsky 2005). For oil, the figure is around 40 per cent. Already by 2003 China was taking over a third of African iron ore exports (Mayer and Fajarnes 2005). Crucially, China's trade with developing countries grew 88 per cent faster than its trade with developed ones between 1999 and 2003 (Eisenman, Heginbotham and Mitchell 2007). However, there has been relatively little critical, analytical and systematic case-study based work which has analysed the governance implications of this phenomenon. This chapter – partly co-authored with Professor Ian Taylor of the University of St Andrews – which is based on numerous periods of fieldwork, seeks to examine Sino-African relations and address this gap.

'Going Out' with China: The Impacts of Dual Economic Reform on Sino-African Relations

While China was growing, much of Africa experienced economic stagnation in the post-independence era. There is a substantial academic debate about why this is the case; however, the human costs were staggering. The DRC's real income per head fell from US$2,469 in 1975 to just US$705 in 2004 (United Nations Development Programme 2006). The scale of economic contraction was also associated with outbreaks of conflict, as has been well documented. However, the 2000s were different for much of Africa as most of the continent experienced rapid economic growth. Even with the global economic slowdown, Africa was home to four of the top ten fastest-growing economies in the world in 2008 (Angola, Ethiopia, Rwanda and Equatorial Guinea) (United States Central Intelligence Agency 2009).

As the global economy recovered in 2010, the number of fast-growing African countries increased again, largely as result of Asian demand for resources. According to some sources China is now already, as of 2009, Africa's biggest trading partner (*African Business* 2009; van Dijk 2009) – although it is still likely to be the United States. While the rapid growth of Brazilian and US exports to Africa is shown in figure 3.1, it is the Chinese growth which is particularly spectacular and noteworthy. Thus, Chinese interests in African markets are also increasing, and there are other motives in addition to resource access.

Van Dijk (2009, pp. 11–12) astutely argues that there are eight different objectives behind the Chinese presence in Africa. These are to:

assure the supply of raw materials for China, including agricultural products;
create a market for Chinese products and services;
obtain land for agricultural purposes;
channel migration of Chinese people to Africa;

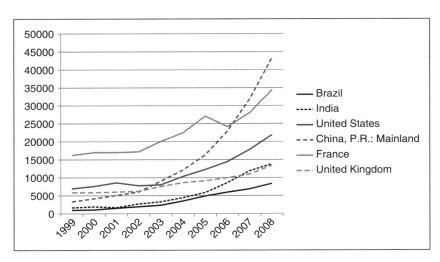

Figure 3.1   Exports to Africa in millions of US dollars (including cost, insurance and freight)
Source: IMF (2009)

gain diplomatic support from African countries;
present an alternative to the Western development model;
provide an alternative to Western development cooperation; and
emphasize China's status as a superpower.

Given the country's growth, the Chinese are anxious to secure access to resource supplies. In China itself, ten out of the eleven biggest oil fields have already passed their peak production, and 31 per cent of the country's oil imports come from Africa, particularly Angola, which is now its biggest supplier (Arnold 2009). In the United States this has prompted concern that China is trying to 'lock up' barrels of oil at source, thereby restricting supply onto the global market. According to the US Council on Foreign Relations, 'China seeks not only to gain access to resources, but also to control resource production and distribution, perhaps positioning itself for priority access to these resources as they become scarcer' (Lake et al. 2006, p. 53). Others note, however, that if China's national oil companies in Africa did not ship some of their supply directly to China, this oil would have to be sourced on the world market, further constricting supply (Downs 2007). China has also expressed desire to become independent of prices for metals set on the London Metal Exchange as well, and has pursued this by signing long-term purchase contracts (*Purchasing* 14 June 2007, cited in Prichard 2009).

Chinese engagement in Africa has been controversial. As the Chinese Communist Party redefined the basis for legitimizing its rule as economic growth and stability, this has meant that, in its relations with African states, it has adopted a largely 'no questions asked' policy towards partner states on the continent, raising widespread governance concerns.

Labour relations at Chinese companies in Africa have also been highly controversial. For example, in 2005 forty-nine workers were killed in an explosion at a Chinese-owned explosives factory in Zambia, which produced dynamite for a major Chinese-owned mine there. There have also been strikes, shootings and kidnappings of Chinese managers in the Zambian Copperbelt over wages and often poor working conditions. In one Chinese-owned mine in Zambia, workers were reportedly sent down the mine shaft to work without any safety equipment whatsoever, in their jeans and T-shirts. Are these safety lapses just a way to cut corners and make more money, or is there a policy basis for them? This chapter argues that these practices should be understood in relation to the dual process of economic reform in both China and Africa.

The labour practices alluded to above can be explained by reference to the primacy of economic development in Chinese Communist Party ideology. According to the Chinese President in 1987, China would have to go through: 'An extremely long primary stage so that it can achieve the industrialization and commercialization, socialization and modernization of production that other countries have secured through capitalistic means' (quoted in Breslin 2007, p. 51). The terminology is important in this quote. Karl Marx talked about an original or primary type of accumulation in the transition from feudalism to capitalism in England, where the labour market was created through the process of land dispossession called enclosure. There was extreme violence associated with the enclosure of common lands through force to enable the gentry class to build their land holdings. The well-known geographer David Harvey has argued that these processes of 'accumulation by dispossession' continue today (Harvey 2003).

The Chinese President's language of the 'primary stage' should be read in this light: that economic development may be dangerous, brutal and violent, but that it should proceed nonetheless. Indeed, some in China speak of an 'enclosure movement' there currently, as 'every week newspapers and websites carry stories of party bigwigs carving up and plundering the nation's assets under the cover of privatization' (Leonard 2008, p. 38).

Labour practices in China have been very controversial domestically and 'China exports the capitalism it knows' (Alden 2007). This is a globalized capitalism, where cost-down pricing, which forces suppliers to reduce prices to major buyers such as Wal-Mart every year, is forcing Chinese managers to cut corners and break labour laws (Kaplinsky 2005; Breslin 2007). Consequently Shaun Breslin argues that Chinese power is itself dependent on the power of TNCs in the global political economy, a feature and outcome of economic globalization. If an illustration of this power were needed, a shocking statistic is that Wal-Mart's sales are bigger than the entire economy of SSA (Stiglitz 2006).

Another interesting feature of the reform process in China is that the 'iron rice bowl', or the idea of guaranteed employment for life, was punctured, with unemployment actually increasing in that country despite its rapid economic growth (Yardley 2004). So while Chinese companies have gone out around the world looking for resources to fuel the country's continued rapid economic growth, there has also been an imperative and a push to encourage emigration from China as unemployment there has risen.

Other aspects of China's internal reform process have had implications for Africa. The fact that China attracts so much of the world's FDI makes it a competitor in that area with Africa, although, given current politico-economic conditions on much of the continent, it is doubtful that Africa would attract much FDI in manufacturing anyway.

Chinese manufacturing wages are, incredibly, only around 3 per cent of those in the US, and a quarter of those in Mexico and Brazil (Banister 2005, cited in Breslin 2007). In most foreign-owned factories in the Pearl River Delta, one of China's main manufacturing regions, the minimum wage was US$54 a month in 2004, and companies often deducted the costs of food and accommodation from this. These are similar to wages paid at Chinese-owned companies in Africa, with casual workers at the Chambishi copper mine in Zambia paid as little as US$52 a month in 2007 (Muneku and Koyi 2007). However, wage rates in more developed African countries are higher than in China. For example average wages in Mauritius and South Africa were US$1.25 and US$1.38 per hour respectively in 2002, compared to just 66 cents an hour in China (Kaplinsky 2005).

While some African countries have lower wage rates than China, given extensive poverty, what is important in locating foreign investment, in addition to things like market access and infrastructure, is the 'real product wage': that is, how much labour costs as a proportion of the sale price of the final product. Given higher productivity of Chinese workers as a result of better technology and more developed skills and management techniques, and better infrastructure, most African countries still can't compete. Some estimates suggest that, even if African manufacturing workers laboured for free, African manufactures would still not be competitive with those from China (Carmody 2010).

There has, however, been some Asian investment in manufacturing in Africa, and Chinese companies can often outcompete domestic African companies in their home market, which has been a major problem in some countries. There are even reports of Chinese sex workers in Cameroon outcompeting locals by charging only 40 per cent of their price. They are able to do this because many of them also hold 'day jobs' working in Chinese-owned shops (Michel, Beuret and Woods 2009). This has led to protests by local sex workers against their Chinese counterparts (Perrot and Malaquais 2009). Competition between indigenous and Chinese for markets is consequently intense across a range of sectors.

Cheaper Chinese doughnuts are also outcompeting local ones in the capital city of Cameroon, Doula, and in Senegal and Togo local traders have waged campaigns against Chinese shopkeepers. However, according to one Chinese shopkeeper in Senegal, 'Senegalese merchants now have containers of goods sent to them from China. They pay less duty on their imports than we do, so it has become very difficult for us to keep our heads above water' (quoted in Michel, Beuret and Woods 2009, p. 122), so trade with China has also increased opportunities for some African traders. Many Chinese and African merchants source their imports from Yiwu, southwest of Shanghai in China, the largest wholesale market in the world at 2.5 million square metres. Spending just one minute in each of the 34,000 shops on the site would take seventy days. While the scale of increased Chinese economic engagement with Africa is now vast, it has a somewhat longer history than many people realize, and also a different structure.

In 1984 the People's Bank of China was designated as the Central Bank in China, and four different specialist banks were introduced to channel capital to different sectors of the economy (Breslin 2007). The Bank of China was made responsible for foreign exchange and established its first branch in Africa, in Zambia, in 1997.

Regional governments in China also have substantial autonomy in the formulation of economic development policy, which has had substantial implications for many African countries as many of the Chinese state-owned companies which have invested there are owned by regional governments in China. Many provincial governments in China have International Trust and Investment Corporations which borrow money on international markets to finance local investment projects. In China, provinces often subject products from other provinces to high taxes, and consequently the international market often offers greater potential for expansion (Gamora and Mathews 2010).

There is a debate in African Studies about the extent to which there is a coordinated Chinese government 'strategy' for Africa. The Chinese government issued its official Africa policy in 2006, but some scholars, such as Ian Taylor (2009), argue that there is no grand strategy for Africa as outcomes on the ground result from a negotiation process, and the central Chinese state often does not know what individual Chinese companies are doing. However, others argue that, while there may be no articulated grand strategy for Africa, structural imperatives, such as the necessity to secure access to increasing amounts of strategic minerals and fuels, shape Chinese engagement on the continent (Carmody and Owusu 2007). Also, while Chinese policymaking and implementation may be characterized as a system of 'fragmented authoritarianism' (Lieberthal 1992), the social relationships between private and public actors may achieve a surprising degree of coordination. According to some, it is impossible to distinguish between the public and the private in China: what is important is the *guanxi*, or trusting relationship, between the different actors involved – rather than the formal property rights, for example (Wank 1998).

The politico-economic reform process in China has also meant a restructuring of the class basis and support of the Chinese Communist Party. Interestingly, the class group with the highest number of party members in the Chinese Communist Party is 'New Private Entrepreneurs' (Breslin 2007). Thus Chinese engagement with Africa may be shaped by the structural, or indirect, power of domestic Chinese capital as it increasingly controls levels of investment and employment and also has direct influence within the Chinese Communist Party itself.

At the same time as China was undergoing economic reform, the Western-inspired policies of structural adjustment or free market opening in Africa presented both a political and economic opportunity for Chinese and other new economic power actors on the continent. The fact that trade barriers had been lowered, investment codes liberalized, labour costs reduced and currencies made convertible meant that these economies were now open to largely unregulated and unrestricted trade and investment from the new economic powers. However, the resentment over the often immiserizing impacts of these structural adjustment policies and the fact that African elites often detested the conditions attached to them, particularly the so-called 'governance conditions' – supporting transparency in resource allocation, for example – made China an attractive alternative 'partner' to the West. As has been argued, 'this new Chinese resource diplomacy, then, provides an alternative economic partner with no political strings attached for marginalized states (such as Zimbabwe) and those that reluctantly respond to US political initiatives because of economic dependence, providing a new challenge to the hegemon's attempts to construct a global liberal order that serves the US national interest' (Zweig 2002, cited in Breslin 2007, p. 139). Thus Africa is now an ideological battleground as China seeks to project its power 'asymmetrically': to outcompete the US economically, while avoiding military confrontation.

Sometimes Beijing uses economic liberalization strategically to grant duty-free 'early harvest' arrangements for African and Southeast Asian states in the Chinese market, as a means to offset the market's polarizing tendencies (Glosny 2007). For example, China now permits 440 products from countries with which it has trade agreements in Africa to be exported duty-free to the Chinese market. The Chinese government also has other innovative methods of cooperation with

African states – partly designed to secure resource access – such as the seven SEZs being built around the continent (Brautigam 2009).

According to Leonard (2008, p. 119):

> China will literally transplant its growth model into the African continent by building a series of industrial hubs with tax incentives that will be linked by rail, road and shipping lanes to the rest of the world. Zambia will be home to China's 'metal hub', providing the People's Republic with copper, cobalt, diamonds, tin and uranium. The second zone will be in Mauritius, providing China with a 'trading hub' that will give forty Chinese businesses preferential access to the twenty-member Common Market of East and South Africa that stretches from Libya to Zimbabwe as well as easy access to the Indian Ocean and South Asian markets. The third zone – a 'shipping hub' – will probably be in the Tanzanian capital, Dar es Salaam.

There are also geopolitical aspects to China's engagement in Africa. According to Marc Lanteigne, much of China's foreign policy is guided by the 'four nos': no hegemony, no power politics, no military alliances and no arms racing (Lanteigne 2009). In Africa, China is able to use its 'soft power' advantages of not having been an imperial power and its history of solidarity with liberation movements there to achieve the support of African states – in the United Nations General Assembly, for example.

While the Chinese also have military cooperation agreements with at least twenty-five African countries, they have for the most part eschewed direct military bases, despite having the largest army in the world, with around 2.5 million soldiers under arms. They do, however, have a military presence in Africa through their United Nations peacekeeping mission in the Congo, and are reportedly building a permanent military base in Kamina, in the mineral-rich Katanga Province of Congo (*La Lettre du Continent* 2008, cited in Michel, Beuret and Woods 2009), although this may be referring to the Congolese military reintegration centre there, which has had Chinese trainers for decades. It has also opened up its National Defence University to African, Latin American and Asian militaries.

Despite a high press profile, during the period 2003–6 China only supplied Africa with 15 per cent of its arms imports (Rupiya and Southall 2009). Even in Sudan, despite that country being a close Chinese ally, Russia supplies most of the country's arms by value, including helicopter gunships which are used by the government for population displacement (McFarland 2009). However, during 2004–6, China provided 90 per cent of the small arms entering Sudan (Eckert

2008, cited in Rupiya and Southall 2009) and has also sold the regime there 100 million dollars' worth of Shenyang and F7 fighter jets (Mbaye 2010). In 2000 China reportedly swapped a consignment of small arms for 8 tonnes of ivory from Zimbabwe (Mbaye 2010). What are the precise dimensions of China's resource diplomacy in Africa?

China's Resource Diplomacy in Africa

Recent influential books identify China's rise as of epochal and global significance (Arrighi 2007; Kurlantzick 2007). This contains both 'hard' and 'soft' power elements (Nye 2004). Hard power is more coercive and involves the use of economic or military power. Soft power is that acquired when other countries are acculturated to the power-seeking country's values and interests, so that they come to see those values as their own in some sense.

Joshua Kurlantzick argues that China is deploying its 'soft power' to gain access to resources and markets. However, this chapter argues that characterizations of China's global resource diplomacy as a form of 'soft power' are problematic for a variety of reasons. For instance, it is not at all clear that China's global resource diplomacy relies solely on 'soft power', as allies often receive military equipment, training and support – sometimes used to deadly effect, as in Sudan. While China sold arms to both Ethiopia and Eritrea during their war in the late 1990s, and consequently arms shipments could be seen as just another example of trade expansion, the actual construction of arms plants, as in Sudan, signals a strategic commitment, given the scale of investment in that country. This is indirect hard power then, whereby an ally uses military force to suppress dissenting social forces which might disrupt Chinese interests.

At a global scale, there appears to be a positive correlation between levels of Chinese investment and arms sales to recipient countries (Blank 2009). While China has received particularly negative attention for selling arms to the Sudanese state, it should be remembered that Indian, Malaysian, South African and European companies are still active in Sudan. European companies are involved in the construction of the Chinese-funded Merowe Dam, which has involved around 50,000 people being displaced, in addition to protestors being shot dead. Indeed, Sudan is a 'priority solidarity zone' for France, and the French oil giant Total has re-engaged the country (Clarke 2008). BP (formerly British Petroleum) also has a share in Petro China, which in turn has a share in the Greater Nile Petroleum Operating Company which has extensive operations in Sudan. In 2006 Sudan was the second-largest recipient of foreign investment in Africa; receiving US$5 billion, much of it from China, and pushing its growth rate to 13 per cent a year later (Michel, Beuret and Woods 2009). Despite British government condemnation of the regime there, interestingly, during 2005–6, it was also the largest recipient of British aid amongst its priority countries in SSA (Porteous 2008). This may indicate both humanitarian concern, around the crisis in Darfur, and strategic interest.

The Chinese state certainly does not shy away from engaging with autocratic states, when material interests dictate (Eisenman 2007). Some have suggested that, as an authoritarian state itself, China seems to find relations with other authoritarian states, which keep themselves closer to China through trade and diplomatic relations, generally less problematic than with more democratic states (Barma and Ratner 2006). Additionally, where African countries are under Western sanctions, this may be seen as providing a competitive advantage to Chinese companies.

In Zimbabwe, while Western companies are still permitted to invest, they are discouraged from doing so by their home governments. However, 'China emerged as a key minerals player. In 2006 a [US]$1.3 bn contract for coal mining and thermal generation construction was negotiated with China Machine Building International, and a chrome mining partnership was established between Zimbabwe's failing state owned Zimbabwe Mining Development Corporation and Beijing's Star Communications' (Saunders 2008, p. 74).

China's resource or geo-economic strategy in Africa is characterized by different strands of engagement and modes of governance. These include clientelism with African state elites, proxy force and other power elements, both soft and hard. There is an incipient new form of 'rule at a distance' (Abrahamsen 2000) in Africa – 'flexigemony' – whereby Chinese actors adapt their strategies to suit the particular histories and geographies of the African states with which they engage. This is in contradistinction to the United States' less flexible hegemonic vision of 'free market democracies' globally. Rather than being a neo-colonial, realist project based on raw hard power, Chinese actors must negotiate resource and market access through cooperation with African state elites. For example, the state-owned Industrial and Commercial Bank of China took a 20 per cent share of Standard Bank in 2008. Standard Bank has an extensive network of branches across eighteen countries in Africa (Shaw 2010). The precise contours of flexigemony will be described below.

This new configuration, of course, is unstable and has its own internal contradictions, which emerge in different geographic contexts. For example, in Sudan the Chinese government has recently appeared to be active in attempting to broker a peace deal in Darfur, whereas, as noted earlier, in previously 'peaceful'[2] Zambia, increased Chinese investment and migration have generated riots, strikes and shootings. The apparent contrast between war-torn Sudan and 'peaceful' Zambia is then examined to show how greater Chinese investment in resource extraction has led to outbreaks, or a renewal, of violence in both cases. Chinese strategies of engagement then are informed by the necessity to moderate the impacts of resource-based capital accumulation, which in other contexts have generated 'ungovernability' (Watts 2007).

'Soft Power' or Flexigemony? Strategy for an Emerging Presence in Africa

With the end of the Cold War, the USA appeared as the world's dominant power, militarily if not economically. In concert with its European and Japanese allies, it promoted through the international financial institutions and through its bilateral diplomacy and aid programmes a particular vision of what constituted 'good governance' in African states. The details of this have been described elsewhere (see Craig and Porter 2006). The model essentially comprised a free market economy and liberal democratic polity.

While the global free market or neoliberal system has shown itself to be very adaptive (Harvey 2003) and its 'persistent vulnerability to regulatory crises and market failures [was] associated with an ongoing dynamic of discursive adjustment, policy learning, and institutional reflexivity' (Peck and Tickell 2002, p. 392), the central tenets of 'free' trade, 'sound money' and broader economic liberalization remained unquestioned (Amsden 1994). In contrast, as discussed below, the Chinese mode of engagement in Africa is much less prescriptive about political and economic governance arrangements.

The Western hegemonic geopolitical and economic vision was informed by both material interests and ideals. A free market economy allowed for penetration by Western business and continued resource exploitation, while liberal democracy was seen to prevent 'excessive' government intervention in the economy (Joseph 1999). While the Western powers had supported autocrats, such as Mobutu in Zaire, during the Cold War as anti-communist bulwarks, during the 1990s their supposed 'natural preference for democracy' reasserted itself (Sandbrook 1993). While this Western reform programme encountered limited acceptance and also resistance in Africa (Van de Walle, 2001), its overall impact was to reinscribe Western dominance on the continent. This presented a challenge for Chinese actors in asserting their presence and influence (and securing resource access) as the 2000s progressed and as Africa was increasingly prioritized by Chinese policymakers.

In Western media accounts, China's 'march into Africa' is often presented as a threat to both Western interests and African populations (Mawdsley 2008). However, China's trade with Africa accounts for only 3 per cent of its total international trade and its expansion in Africa is part of its broader global expansion (Kurlantzick 2007). Nonetheless, Africa is perhaps more important than is suggested by the global trade statistics, with Angola, as noted earlier, being China's single largest supplier of oil in some years. While the US imports only 19 per cent of its oil from Africa, the figure for China, as noted earlier, is 31 per cent, making Africa of far greater strategic importance for the latter (Taylor 2009). For Africa's part, dramatically increased Chinese involvement is arguably the most momentous development on the continent since the end of the Cold War.

According to Tony Blair (2008), over the course of the last few years China has gone from a 'standing start' to being the most influential country on the continent. While Chinese foreign investment in Zambia, for example, accounted for only 10 per cent of the total stock in 2006 (van Dijk 2009), Kurlantzick (2007, p. xi) attributes this new power to the fact that 'in a short period of time, China appears to have created a systematic, coherent soft power strategy, and a set of power tools to implement that strategy'. Kurlantzick then goes on to assert, however, that 'soft power' for the Chinese is different from how it is for other actors such as the United States as 'it means anything outside of the military and security realm, including not only popular culture and public diplomacy but also more coercive economic and diplomatic levers like aid and investment and participation in multilateral organizations' (p. 6). The basis for this exceptionalism, or who is defining soft power in this way, is left unexplained though.

In fact, it would appear that the Chinese use, for the most part, hard economic power, albeit often cautiously, i.e. 'softly'. This more closely approximates Joseph Nye's (2008) more recent formulation of 'smart power'. However, China has also been willing to use its military technology and capabilities in Africa, through arming clients, such as Sudan. Hence the concept of flexigemony is better suited to understanding the way in which the Chinese have emerged from 'under the radar' to become, arguably, the most influential actors on the African continent.

China's strategy has been guided by the philosophy of *heping juequi* or 'peaceful rise'. This is perhaps the only option for China in seeking space in the international system, given the overwhelming preponderance of American military force, as the US now spends 45 per cent of the world's total military expenditure (SIPRI 2008). According to the Chinese Prime Minister Wen Jibao, the country's ascent in the international hierarchy would 'not come at the cost of any other country, will not stand in the way of any other country, nor pose a threat to any other country' (quoted in Kurlantzick 2007, p. 38). This pragmatic approach sought then not to transform other countries in the model of China (contra the neoconservative vision in the US which sought to bring democracy through violence to Iraq and Afghanistan) but rather to work through and with existing social relations and formations. Whereas neoliberal 'virtualism' (Carrier and Miller 1998) sought to make the real world of existing social relations conform to the ideal, Chinese interests dictate a more rhizome- or root-system-like approach, using existing, and creating new, networks of influence. As Mohan and Power (2008, p. 25) argue, 'the political outcomes of China's involvement in Africa will primarily be shaped by state–capital dynamics, particularly how Chinese capital and parts of the Chinese state intertwine with fractions of capital and political blocs within Africa', rather than any grand project of political and economic reform.

The Chinese government is, however, also conscious of the social licence to operate of its companies in Africa. In 2006, just in advance of the Forum on China–Africa Cooperation (FOCAC) meeting in Beijing, the Chinese government passed a law covering a code of ethics for companies operating overseas, which included adhering to local labour and other laws and protecting the environment (Michel, Beuret and Woods 2009). There is also now the doctrine of 'commercial prestige' whereby Chinese companies are meant to produce quality, rather than shoddy, products for sale overseas to protect and enhance the reputation of 'China Inc.'. Indeed, some analysts emphasize how relatively recent and consequently fragile China's engagement with Africa is. Additionally, competition from less threatening countries such as South Korea and Brazil is increasing (Michel, Beuret and Woods 2009).

One of the reasons why state elites have so eagerly received the Chinese in Africa is that their network or rhizome-like involvement supports prevailing distributions of power and patterns of corrupt – or what political scientists call neopatrimonial – governance (Clapham 2007) and also mirrors the rhizome structure of the African state itself (Bayart 1993). So, paradoxically while seeking to displace Western 'hegemonism', China is, in part, a status quo power in terms of domestic governance patterns and systems in Africa (Taylor 2007). Whereas former President of the World Bank James Wolfensohn ('The other crisis: address to the Board of Governors of the World Bank, Washington, D.C.', p. 11, quoted in Slater 2004, p. 106) argued that in today's global economy it was 'the *totality* of change in a country that matters' (original emphasis), the Chinese government is very much less prescriptive about domestic governance (and disorder) arrangements and has shown itself able and willing to work with and through both highly authoritarian states, such as Sudan and Zimbabwe, and more democratic polities and spaces such as South Africa and Zambia. While the US state tries to change the Sudanese or Zimbabwean polity, for example, the Chinese state does not, but rather works through them – a defining feature of flexigemony.

Rather than seeking a societal transformation, which is unlikely to be achieved in any event, the Chinese focus on two core aims: natural resource and market access, and the cultivation of key support constituencies. There are, of course, other motivations and dimensions to Chinese geo-economic and geopolitical strategy in Africa, which have been described elsewhere, particularly market access (Carmody and Owusu 2007).

The key elements of Chinese flexigemony in Africa might be summarized as follows.

- In line with the global regime of flexible, or free market, accumulation (Harvey 1989) and Beijing's 'go global' or 'go out' policy for its companies, it prioritizes the economic over political and security concerns.
- It uses a combination of economic, political and military levers in flexible strategic combinations to ensure continued raw material supplies.
- It does not use direct military force to secure interests, but rather proxy sub-contracting and the use of direct economic power.
- It is domestic and international sovereignty-strengthening for partner states: that is to say, it is not normalizing, or standardizing,

but works through extant institutions and diverse state–society formations.

• It is reinforced by frequent high-level state visits as a form of public diplomacy and to build inter-state trust in line with the Five Principles discussed later (political 'coming out', as a complement to economic 'going out').

If US hegemony is coercion tempered by consent to achieve neoliberal standardization or normalization, flexigemony is a more geographically differentiated strategy which varies the mix between these two elements more, without attracting the wrath of the hegemon. In fact, it more closely approximates the British colonial policy of indirect rule which worked through existing institutions, although without formal juridical control, than the hegemonic geopolitical model and vision born and projected during the Fordist era in the United States (see Ruppert 1995 and Agnew 2005). Another analogy is with the tributary state system which used diverse forms of power to encourage neighbouring kingdoms to emulate Chinese civilization (Alden 2008). How flexigemony in Africa plays out in practice is now demonstrated with reference to two case studies.

China and Sudan: Obstruction, But Also Evolution

Chinese companies are now Sudan's largest investors and, according to a study by PFC Strategic Studies, the Sudanese government could collect as much as US$30 billion or more in total oil revenue by 2012 (*Washington Post*, 23 December 2004). The bulk of this will come from Chinese-operated oil wells; China currently imports 60 per cent of Sudan's oil output. Given the extent of Chinese sunk costs in Sudan, it is arguably over an (oil) barrel in its dealings with Khartoum. Indeed, Beijing's relationship with Khartoum has become a major *cause célèbre*, and the campaign to link Chinese support for Khartoum and the conflict in Darfur with the 2008 Beijing Olympics was perhaps the most public manifestation of this. In turn, a full-scale foreign policy to play up China's contribution to conflict resolution in Africa took place in response.

Analysis of the conflict in Darfur has been covered in depth elsewhere: suffice it to say that the UN Security Council has been involved in trying to find a resolution to the crisis. For a long time, China sought to hamper or undermine such efforts. However, this has somewhat changed in recent years as Chinese flexigemony has developed. Indeed, Beijing's obstructionist policy began to shift *tentatively* from 2005 onwards. For instance, the Security Council passed three key Resolutions in March 2005, when 'the Chinese representative [began to strike] a more conciliatory tone and showed willingness to discuss the resolutions provided that the integrity of the country [Sudan] would be guaranteed' (*New Vision* [Kampala], 16 June 2007). Resolution 1593 (adopted on 31 March 2005) referred the situation in Darfur to the International Criminal Court (ICC). The Resolution was adopted under Chapter VII of the UN Charter authorizing coercive measures for non-compliance. China abstained, but noted that it 'believed that the perpetrators must be brought to justice'. Interestingly, this did not please Khartoum as the Sudanese Second Vice-President Ali Osman Mohamed Taha had told Sudan's cabinet that he had Chinese assurances the Resolution would not be passed (*Reuters* [Khartoum], 17 December 2005). China's 'abstention rather than a veto embarrassed Taha within the government', and 'the crowd following the ICC referral criticized China for not blocking the resolution' (*Sudan Tribune* [Paris], 15 January 2007). However, Beijing's overall position of either abstaining from UN Resolutions or seeking to water them down provoked a grassroots movement, primarily in the United States, that called for a campaign to highlight China's complicity in the conflict in Darfur. This was then directly linked to Beijing's hosting of the 2008 Olympics, with campaigners renaming the event the 'Genocide Olympics'. Editorials in the United States in late 2006 began declaring that 'The Chinese leadership must be forced to make a choice: work now to halt genocide in Darfur, or see the Olympic Games used, at every turn, as a means of highlighting the Chinese role in sustaining the ultimate human crime' (*Sunday Boston Globe*, 17 December 2006).

Frightened by the possibility that China's 'coming out' party might be tarnished, Beijing embarked on a major public relations exercise to convince the world of its positive role in Sudan. This was particularly spurred on when, in April 2007, the Chairman of the Senate Foreign Relations Committee, Joseph Biden, and ninety-six other Senators wrote a letter to Hu Jintao, who is sometimes called 'The African', calling on China to use its influence to help end the violence in Darfur. Soon after, on 10 May, 2007, the Chinese government appointed Ambassador Liu Guijin as the Special Representative of African Affairs, with a particular remit for Darfur. According to one Chinese informant, it was the Senate letter regarding Darfur and the Olympics that was the tipping point. China's foreign policy is still predicated on essentially state-to-state relations and while the 'Genocide Olympics' campaign remained non-governmental it was felt it could be ignored. However, once this drew in legislators and the American state apparatus, Beijing felt compelled to move on the issue (interview with He Wenping, Chinese Academy of Social Sciences (CASS), Beijing, China, 18 September 2007).

Meanwhile, the Chinese media began to publicize claims that Beijing had played a constructive role in Sudan, with the *Beijing Review* typically declaring that: 'Since the Darfur issue emerged, China has been in constant communication with the relevant people, playing mediator, promoting dialogue between top leaders, dispatching envoys, discussing the problem in the UN assembly' (*Beijing Review* [Beijing], 7 June 2007). Those involved in the Darfur issue at the diplomatic level largely saw these developments as positive. Certainly, Western diplomats began to assert that there had been a sea-change in China's position. Thus American Special Envoy to Sudan Andrew Natsios told a Senate panel that China 'have been largely supportive of our efforts to resolve the Darfur situation' (State Department 2007). The then British Foreign Secretary Margaret Beckett joined in, asserting that 'On Sudan, I know there has been some criticism of China, but actually China has played really quite a positive role, particularly in the negotiation of the Darfur peace agreement' (*Financial Times* [London], 18 May 2007).

A Change in China's Position?

It is absolutely true that China began to publicly advise Sudan to be more 'flexible' in accepting UN peace support personnel under the 'African Union (AU) / UN hybrid' proposal. And it began to give briefings on how much of a positive role China had been playing in Sudan. It is quite clear that, as 2007 developed, Beijing began to be ever more sensitive to accusations that it had colluded with a tyrannical regime. As a result, behind the scenes, Chinese diplomats sought to move Khartoum to a more accommodating stance on Darfur and outside involvement (interview with political scientist, Renmin University of China, Beijing, China, 19 October 2009). Yet China has at all times been hidebound by its intimate economic relationship with Khartoum and the billions of dollars' worth of investment in Sudan, as well as the position that 'China does not support bad governments.

What it does is engage with them but does not tell them what to do' (interview with Chinese diplomat, Addis Ababa, Ethiopia, 15 May 2007). This means that Beijing is limited in the pressure it is able and/or willing to place on the Sudanese government.

However, Chinese diplomacy vis-à-vis Darfur is not simply about oil, although it is a major part of the equation, particularly as China may now wish to build another pipeline from the oil fields in Chad to the Red Sea, which would require peace in Darfur (Massey and May 2009). As noted earlier, there is circumstantial evidence that China may indirectly have supported rebels in Chad, as the trucks which the rebels used to cross the desert and attack the capital in 2007 were bought by a Chinese oil company based in Sudan (*Journal du Dimanche*, 23 April 2006, cited in Massey and May 2009).

Critics of China might like to consider that, as far as the Chinese are concerned, there are important principles at stake in dealing with Khartoum. Chinese foreign policy remains wedded to the Five Principles of Peaceful Coexistence, formulated in 1954 and setting out the guidelines for Beijing's foreign policy and its relations with other countries (interview with Acting Head, Political Affairs Section, Chinese Embassy, Windhoek, Namibia, 13 August 2006). These Five Principles are namely: mutual respect for each other's territorial integrity; non-aggression; non-interference in each other's internal affairs; equality and mutual benefit; and peaceful coexistence (Taylor 1998). From the Chinese position, 'human rights are something covered by the sovereignty of a country. A country's sovereignty is the foremost collective human right...And sovereignty is the guarantor of human rights' (*Xinhua*, 12 December 2005). China is a state generally defensive of traditional beliefs about sovereignty when events deemed by policymakers to be threatening Chinese interests are occurring. Certainly a belief that non-intervention in the domestic affairs of states is vital for preserving international peace and stability has underpinned Beijing's international relations and is enshrined in the Five Principles of Peaceful Coexistence (interview with researcher, CASS, Beijing, China, 15 November 2009). More recently, these principles have been updated through the '28-character guidepost' stated by Deng in 1989 – the so-called 'New Security Concept' of China's peaceful rise. The twenty-eight characters were based on old Chinese sayings: 'watch and analyse developments calmly; secure our own positions; deal with change with confidence; conceal our capacities; be good at keeping a low profile; never become the leader and make some contributions' (Zhao 1996; Eisenman, Heginbotham and Mitchell 2007).

These characters fit well with the idea of flexigemony in which power and leadership in international relations are obscured through the idea of South–South cooperation and 'win-win' scenarios.

China has traditionally maintained that state sovereignty and the principle of non-interference must serve as the basis for international relations between states, though it needs emphasizing that this position is not static – as Beijing's movement on Darfur demonstrates. China has customarily emphasized the sovereignty of states in resolving issues amongst themselves also because of Beijing's sensitivity to possible outside involvement in affairs perceived by China as strictly domestic matters, such as Tibet and Taiwan (interview with Shu Zhan, Chinese ambassador, Asmara, Eritrea, 29 June 2006). The avoidance of establishing international precedents that may be later utilized in attempting to deal with China's 'domestic' issues is a policy thus scrupulously pursued by Beijing, even though it occasionally invites cynicism from non-Chinese observers. However, adherence to the Five Principles also serves instrumental functions as it is well received by African (resource) gatekeepers and also may serve to disguise the true extent of China's growing influence.

However, the rhetoric contained in official Chinese pronouncements 'has led many observers to reach the premature conclusion that Beijing opposes all forms of intervention and is wedded to an antiquated approach to sovereignty' (Carlson 2006, p. 218). In fact, it is possible to discern a subtle shift in China's position regarding state sovereignty (interview with He Wenping, CASS, Beijing, China, 18 September 2007), in keeping with the flexigemony concept outlined above. Four official guidelines on legitimate intervention now dictate Chinese positions: intervention must first proceed with respect for the concerned state's sovereignty; United Nations' authorization must be gained; the invitation of the concerned state must be secured; and force should only ever be used when all other possible options have been proven ineffective (Carlson 2006). This set of necessary conditions demonstrates that there *has* been movement in Beijing from a previous hard stand on state sovereignty and non-interference (Taylor 2008). Darfur is a case in point, although almost immediately after the Beijing Olympics ended the Sudanese government launched a major attack in Darfur, razing twenty villages in just ten days (Michel, Beuret and Woods 2009). It is arguably not in China's interest to find a complete solution to this conflict as that would enable American oil companies to return, thereby threatening the Chinese National Petroleum Companies' domination of the industry. Thus the poverty–conflict nexus can serve as a strategic resource for great powers. For example, while some Western countries reduced their aid, China has also stepped up its presence in Ethiopia since the disputed 2005 elections when there were shootings and mass detention of the opposition (Michel, Beuret and Woods 2009).

According to UN law, the notion of state sovereignty (which China has long promoted in its foreign policy) 'shall not prejudice the application of enforcement measures under Chapter VII' (Article 2 IV). This is a problem for Beijing, as Darfur exemplifies. In the post-Brahimi Report era,[3] Chinese foreign policy vis-à-vis peace operations has had to face a number of other thorny issues, particularly as the peace support aspect of peace operations is a quite novel type of peacekeeping (Bellamy and Williams 2004). For the Chinese, traditional peacekeeping 'is organized and deployed directly by the UN *with the consent of all parties*' (emphasis added) (Zhang Li 2003, p. 209). This has had implications for China's reactions to attempts to mediate in the Darfur issue, and the material aspect – i.e. oil – is not the only explanatory variable in accounting for China's policy stance regarding the ongoing crisis in Sudan (Fitzgerald 2008). Yet movement on the issue does reflect flexibility in Chinese foreign policy that many observers have previously overlooked. The fact that China is not guided by a standardizing or normalizing ideology in its relations with Africa – such as neoliberalism – and that it has many large state-owned corporations, whose decisions it can guide if not prescribe, gives it greater flexibility in its relations with African states – what we might term flexipower.

Chinese Flexipower and its Limits: The Zambian Case

While Chinese engagement and investment in Sudan have attracted international attention, the increased Chinese footprint in Zambia has also proven to be particularly controversial – especially in Zambia. Consequently Chinese foreign policy in Zambia has also seen evolution in recent years. The economic impacts of greater Asian investment in Africa will be described later.

Zambia's experience with World Bank / IMF structural adjustment during the 1990s was a painful and immiserating one, marked by deindustrialization which, according to a World Bank official, was the outcome of 'mark my words, the dogma of liberalization' (interview with World Bank official, Lusaka, Zambia, 10 January 2007). This provided an opening for an alternative economic philosophy and there are now discussions of a return to (some) development planning in Zambia, with the publication of the Fifth National Development Plan in 2006, rather than a new World Bank-inspired Poverty Reduction Strategy Paper (PRSP) (Larmer and Fraser 2007). In part this reorientation of development policy is a response to public pressure over China's role in the continent and the national division of rents from natural resources.

As noted earlier, Zambia is the third-largest recipient of Chinese foreign investment in Africa and the nineteenth-largest in the world (UNCTAD 2007b). China is now the world's largest consumer of copper, and consequently Zambia is of significant strategic importance. There are now an estimated 200 Chinese companies operating in Zambia (Bastholm and Kragelund 2007) and the Chinese government is building an US$800 million Multi-facility Economic Zone (MFEZ) in the Copperbelt. Establishing the SEZ in Zambia is partly to offset criticism about the effects of Chinese imports on local manufacturers, although it is to be anchored by a copper smelter, reducing transportation costs to China (interview with Zambian diplomat, Embassy of Zambia, Beijing, China, 20 October 2009). Furthermore, like some of the other smaller 'undeclared' zones in post-conflict countries such as Sierra Leone and Liberia, the zone in Zambia can process copper from, and take advantage of the market opportunities offered in, the DRC. More than 90 per cent of the DRC's resource-rich Katanga Province exports are reportedly sent to China (Raine 2009).

Certainly, the Chinese presence in conflict and post-conflict situations around the continent grants Chinese actors first-mover advantages in these 'frontier markets'. Consequently, the recently opened Chembe bridge between Zambia and the DRC was constructed by a Chinese company (Republic of Zambia (RoZ) 2006) and fifty Chinese companies have pledged investments worth up to, by some estimates, US$900m for the SEZ (Mwanawina 2008).

At the same time, Chinese investment in Zambia has been highly controversial. As noted earlier, forty-nine miners were killed in 2005 in an explosion at a plant which made explosives for the Chinese Chambishi copper mine, which operated a harsh labour regime, with workers reporting only being paid US$30 a month and forced to work seven-day weeks (Kurlantzick 2007). An official at the Ministry of Industry and Commerce in Zambia noted that 'back home in China they can give slave wages' (interview, Lusaka, August 2009). The Minister of Southern Province reportedly wept when she saw the working conditions in the Chinese coal mine in Kafue, where miners were not given any safety equipment (Mwanawina 2008).

The impacts of Chinese traders and the leasing of one of the main markets to Chinese management in the capital Lusaka have also been highly contentious, as local traders are displaced. According to some, many women traders selling imported second-hand clothes (*saluala*) find it difficult to compete with cheaper new Chinese imports (Fitzgerald 2008). In West Africa cheap Chinese clothes retail for as little as 10 per cent of the cost of second-hand Western imports (Lyons and Brown 2010), although, given the higher quality of *saluala*, there are still very active markets for it in Kamwala market and elsewhere in Lusaka (fieldnotes, August 2009).

These developments came together during the 2006 election, when the main opposition candidate Michael Sata ran on an explicitly populist anti-Chinese platform. According to Sata 'Chinese investment has not added any value to the people of Zambia' and 'we need investors, not infestors' (quoted in Fitzgerald 2008). In fact, similar sentiments had been expressed by incumbent government officials. The Minister for Commerce, Trade and Industry had previously argued that Chinese actors were 'displacing local people and causing a lot of friction. You have Chinese labourers here moving wheelbarrows. That's not the kind of investment we need. I understand they have 1.2 billion people, but they don't have to send them to Africa' (Dipak Patel, quoted in McGreal 2007, in Rupp 2008, p. 72).

Prior to the election, the Chinese ambassador threatened to cut diplomatic relations if Sata won – the first time since the era of Mao that China had attempted to influence the outcome of an African election. While Sata had threatened to recognize Taiwan, which would automatically have put an end to diplomatic relations with Beijing, the fact that China would have severed diplomatic relations if Sata was elected, rather than seeing what his actions would be when he was elected, constituted blatant interference in Zambian national politics. Ultimately, Sata took the majority of votes in the two regions with the greatest Chinese presence – the capital city Lusaka and the Copperbelt in the north of the country – and when he lost the election there were anti-Chinese riots in the capital. In the Copperbelt there have been riots, strikes and kidnapping of Chinese management, and the Chinese President had to cancel a planned visit to the Copperbelt in 2007 to lay the foundation stone for a new Chinese-built national stadium for fear of the public reaction (Taylor 2009). However, perhaps partly in an effort to defuse criticism of China's presence in Zambia, President

Hu cancelled some bilateral debt to China and announced the establishment of the SEZ (Jiang 2008).

Labour relations at the SEZ have been very contentious, particularly at the mine and the copper smelter where all workers are on temporary contracts (confidential interview, Zambia–China Cooperation Zone, Chambishi, Zambia, August 2009). Nonetheless, the influence of China is evidenced by the fact that the Zambian President reportedly holidayed with a Chinese deputy minister, and through the purchase of Chinese mobile hospitals, in contravention of the plans agreed with other aid donors (interview with diplomat, Lusaka, Zambia, August 2009). The disjuncture between elite and popular perceptions, and also the fact that the Zambian government must play to both domestic and foreign audiences, is evidenced by the Zambian Deputy Minister of Finance, who has argued: 'Why should we have a bad attitude towards the Chinese when they are doing all the right things? They are bringing investment, world class technology, jobs, value addition. What more could you ask for?' (quoted in Ndulo 2008, p. 146).

Paradoxically, it is Lusaka and the Copperbelt, the two regions of the country with the greatest Chinese presence, which have seen the most dramatic reductions in poverty in recent years (Carmody 2009), but there is a general feeling that, after years of immiseration, Zambians have not been benefiting proportionately from the recent economic recovery (Negi 2008) – a different type of resource conflict from more recent varieties (Le Billon 2004). This sentiment was reinforced by the closure in 2007 of the Zambia–China Mulungushi Textile Joint Venture with the Chinese state (McGreal 2007). The factory simply could not compete with Asian imports (interview with University of Zambia economist, Lusaka, Zambia, 1 September 2007) and with imports from neighbouring countries (Brautigam 2009). This had been the largest textile factory in Zambia, producing 17 million metres of fabric a year, in addition to 100,000 pieces of clothing, employing 1,000 people directly and around 5,000 cotton growers indirectly (Taylor 2006).

As the Zambian case shows, the Chinese government is not averse to using the threat of economic force (i.e. through cutting investment and trade relations) even in relatively more democratic states. However, this economic stick is also used as a carrot as China builds manufacturing zones, removes tariffs on African imports, etc. As noted earlier, Beijing uses economic liberalization strategically to grant duty-free 'early harvest' arrangements for African and Southeast Asian states in the Chinese market as a means to offset the market's polarizing tendencies (Glosny 2008).

Given that Zambia is sometimes cited as 'China's Perfect Storm' (Alden 2007), the government is in fact keen to repair its image there (interview with Zambian diplomat, Embassy of Zambia, Beijing, China, 20 October 2009). One Chinese journalist reports that China is developing ways to monitor its investment and nationals in Africa in order to repair its image (Negi 2008). However, this will prove increasingly difficult given the effects of economic liberalization in China (Taylor 2009). Nonetheless, some Chinese state-owned companies have earned goodwill by staying open and buying mines sold by Western investors as a result of the global economic crisis (interview with International Labour Organization official, Lusaka, Zambia, August 2009).

The Evolution of China's Africa Policy

James Tang has argued that 'as China has become more involved in regions where the Chinese presence formerly was limited, Beijing has encountered new challenges, such as the humanitarian problem in Sudan' (Tang 2006, p. 31). The strategies adopted by an incoming power, seeking to grab opportunities wherever it can, and those of a more established power, looking to protect its investments in an unstable environment, are intrinsically different and account for some of China's recent actions. Equally, and this needs emphasizing, Chinese corporations and the Chinese state are not the only actors involved with unsavoury regimes in Africa, as shown earlier. It has long been shown that Western companies, with the tacit approval of their home governments, have used all sorts of means to craft oil deals with African regimes and have overlooked notions of democracy and human rights (Shaxson 2007).

Paradoxically, keeping good relationships with major Western powers is a key foreign policy concern for Chinese policymakers, particularly given the control which the US navy has worldwide of vital shipping routes (Tang 2006) – a kind of 'choke space', instead of the 'choke points' the United States faces, in the Suez Canal for example. The events surrounding aspects of Chinese activities in Sudan arguably threatened this, or at least play into the hands of critics of China and those who like to speak of the 'China threat'. Chinese diplomats seem aware of this, asserting that 'China's policy of non-interference is appropriate for Beijing's diplomacy, but China has not been very successful in explaining this to the world. Consequently, we are concerned that people are "misinterpreting" our diplomacy' (interview with Chinese diplomat, Addis Ababa, Ethiopia, 15 May 2007).

Features of Chinese involvement in Sudan's oil industry unquestionably fit with ongoing external interactions with Africa. After all, French policy towards the oil-rich parts of the continent – such as Gabon – has never been guided by liberty, equality and fraternity. Washington's relations with oil-rich nations such as Equatorial Guinea, Nigeria and Angola are not guided by concerns over democracy, as discussed in more detail later. Business, as far as many actors are concerned, is business, and in this sense Western criticism of China's oil diplomacy in Africa is somewhat hypocritical (interview with Robin Sherborne, editor of *Insight*, Namibian political magazine, Windhoek, Namibia, August, 2006), although the scale of the genocide in Sudan does make it an exceptional case.

This is not the whole story, however. There is a growing consensus among the more effective governments in Africa on where they wish the continent to be heading. Yet, 'While in some countries China's involvement appears benign, in others its approach undercuts efforts by the AU and Western partners to make government and business more transparent and accountable' (*Africa Research Bulletin* 2006). Indeed, a key concern is that some of Beijing's activities in pursuit of resources threaten to reinforce patrimonial states and practices that NEPAD and the AU are ostensibly seeking to move away from (Taylor 2005).

Problems are compounded when one combines the nature of an African state such as Sudan with the way it is constituted through the so-called 'resource curse'. Here, Chinese interest in African oil mirrors the issues that other actors have to confront. The broader character of the oil industry and the way it has tended to undermine democracy and accountability in the developing world, particularly in Africa, is long-standing. China's experiences in Sudan are not particularly unique and Chinese corporations have had to deal with equally thorny issues in places such as Nigeria (Taylor 2007).

Leonard and Straus (2003, p. 13) argue that enclave economies in Africa (economies that export extractive products concentrated in relatively small geographic areas) are particularly problematic. Revenue generation is physically confined to small locales, with the prime markets for the products being external (the international market). This makes 'the general economic health of areas outside the enclave quite secondary, if not irrelevant. In enclave economies, then, elites gain little from any deep, growing, economic prosperity of the masses of the population.' Thus, while individuals who have gained access to rents from such enclaves may benefit handsomely, the system fundamentally fails to promote wider economic growth and development.

The fact that in Zambia some of the main perceived beneficiaries of 'enclave-led growth' are Chinese has fuelled conflict there. In Sudan the beneficiaries are drawn almost exclusively from Northern Sudanese ethnic cliques detailed in the 'Black Book' (El-Tom 2003). Thus, part of the problem is the way in which Chinese engagement with Africa is reinscribing this conflictual geography across different regime types.

Problematically, a distinct opaqueness in Chinese dealings in Africa compounds suspicions of Chinese motives, Sudan and Zambia being but two examples. As a Chinese scholar has noted, 'China shoulders much of the blame, as it has been poor at making its energy transactions with countries such as Iran and Sudan transparent. Lack of transparency fuels speculation that China has a well-coordinated project for countering US influence' (Zhao 2006).

Yet it is important to note that the 'China Inc.' model of a Beijing advancing centralized strategies around the world is simply incorrect. As Downs has noted with regard to Chinese National Oil Companies (NOCs) in Africa,

> when it comes to choosing where to invest, the companies are almost always in the driver's seat and the Chinese government, while occasionally offering general advice about the direction they should travel (for example, 'invest in Morocco'), is often just along for the ride with little idea of the final destination. Sudan's recent omission from the Chinese government's catalogue of countries that Chinese companies are encouraged to invest in is a case in point, but this absence has not prevented CNPC [China National Petroleum Company] from continuing to invest there. (Downs 2007, p. 48)

Indeed, as of 2003, Sudan was the country in which the CNPC had invested most (Mao 2008).

It is important not to exaggerate the capacity of the Chinese state to manage broad Chinese engagement with the African continent, but it would appear that Chinese foreign policy uses different instruments and shows different faces to different audiences: it is Janus-faced. For example, a Chinese company is building the new Presidential Palace in Sudan, leaving no doubt as to Beijing's commitment to the country, international (public) relations notwithstanding. However, the fact that Sudan is no longer a priority country for investment will reassure international investors, particularly after the flotation of one of China's NOCs on the New York stock exchange had to be withdrawn and reshaped after concerns over its investments in Sudan. The government may also feel there is already enough Chinese investment in that country. Yet China's stance of non-interference means that the values and interests of Sudan's elites exclusively decide domestic conduct. In short, until and unless the Khartoum elites themselves advance transparency, pro-development policies and equitable growth (and are prepared and competent enough to put them into force), no such course of action will be taken. Given the history of Sudan post-independence, the prospects for this are not encouraging.

Yet the international community, when looking at Chinese activity regarding energy in somewhere such as Sudan, is generally preoccupied with analysing how China can match its growing commercial influence with responsibility. In turn, Beijing is increasingly zealous in reassuring the world of its desire to be a responsible power. As one commentator noted, 'The challenge is for China and other leading energy-consuming countries to cooperate in defining and addressing the political and social challenges that arise in many of the oil states of the world' (Zhao 2006). Chinese policymakers do appear to be realizing this, although – as with Western policymakers – commercial considerations have a habit of trumping the best intentions.

Reflections on China's African Resource Diplomacy

Chinese policymakers use strategic levers and pressure points in their dealings with African states. There are ostensible soft power elements to this, such as the facts that China has reportedly sent 10,000 agricultural experts to Africa (Guijin 2004, cited in Eisenman 2007) and the China Export–Import Bank is now the largest supplier of loans to the continent.

China is emerging, as Robert Mugabe would have it, as an 'alternative global power point in Africa' (Eisenman 2007). This position of influence is being constructed through economic GPNs, bilateral state-to-state ties and multilateral institutions and fora such as FOCAC, which, when it met in Beijing in 2006, had leaders in attendance representing almost a third of humanity (Michel, Beuret and Woods 2009). In 2005 Beijing also launched a 'New Asian–African Strategic Partnership' which includes many other Asian countries in it, such as India and Japan (Okeke 2008). This then represents a claim by Beijing to global leadership in Afro-Asian relations.

In competing with the US and Europe for influence, Beijing's strategy can be compared to that of judo: to flexibly exploit opponents' strengths – such as the greater separation between Western corporations and governments – as weaknesses against them. Likewise, in the Chinese strategy game of Go, one way to win is to build relationships with smaller players until your rival is surrounded (Kurlantzick 2007).

As John Allen (2003) has noted, hegemony, or coercion tempered by consent, is only one form of power amongst others, including seduction and manipulation. However, he identifies two core forms of power: instrumental where 'power is something that is held over you and used to obtain leverage, or associational where power acts more like a collective medium enabling things to get done or facilitat[ing] some collective aim' (2000, p. 5). The success of Chinese power in Africa is based on its hybrid nature, where the prospect of economic sanction and benefit is combined with forms of collective power to achieve more secure incumbency for African state elites. African governments are also now able to triangulate or play off Western donors against Chinese investors, further increasing their relative power (Mohan and Power 2009). Thus, China in Africa is pursuing realist aims (increasing its own power), through empowering African states relative to Western donors.

China is pursuing a policy of what we can think of as platform growth and diplomacy. It uses its seat at the high table of international relations to protect and deeper embed client states, such as Sudan, and the diplomatic support it garners from African states can then be used as a platform to further protect and project its power. It is leveraging uneven development, using Africa and other global peripheries, as raw materials springboards, and the developed states as markets to fuel its economic rise. This ascent is cloaked in the rhetoric of 'win-win' and 'South–South' cooperation. However, the wins in Africa would appear to be primarily for elites and this rhetoric disguises the massive power inequalities between African states and China, despite the fact that China's GDP per capita is far below that of some African countries. Nonetheless, as this strategy will allow China to overtake the US as the world's largest economy, by most estimates, it can be seen through the prism of flexigemony.

Deng Xiaoping famously noted that the colour of the cat does not matter, as long as it catches the mouse. However, his was still a historical materialist project and perspective (Taylor 2009). Kurlantzick notes that whole regions of the world may become ensnared in a mercantilist cycle in which they sell raw materials in exchange for Chinese manufactures and, in this light, African publics must be wary of being the mouse caught by the new cat, whatever its colour (Kurlantzick 2007). Despite its stated policy of non-interference, selling arms to Sudan or Zimbabwe has dramatic implications for those countries' populations and could be viewed as perhaps the most dramatic form of interference in internal affairs as their peoples struggle for democracy and a fairer sharing of their countries' wealth. However, other emerging powers have also engaged with those regimes. We now move to consider other new economic power interests and strategies on the continent.

4 OTHER NEW ECONOMIC POWER INTERESTS AND RELATIONS WITH AFRICA

God forbid that India should ever take to industrialism after the manner of the West. The economic imperialism of a single tiny island kingdom [Britain] is today keeping the world in chains. If an entire nation of 300 million took to similar economic exploitation, it would strip the world bare like locusts. (Gandhi, quoted in Shiva 2008, p. 62)

The commerce between India and Africa will be of ideas and services, not of manufactured goods against raw materials after the fashion of the Western exploiters. (Gandhi, quoted in Bhattacharya 2010, p. 63)

Indian Interests and Strategies

These two opening quotes from Gandhi reflect on the process of globalization. As they show, he was not opposed to the idea of globalization, but was in favour of an alternative type to that promoted during the colonial era; an alter globalization based on ideas and services rather than the unequal trade of raw materials for manufactured goods. On the other hand, his political comrade and competitor Nehru had a high modernist vision of an industrialized India. His vision would seem now to be in the ascendant there, although he might not have approved of the distributional consequences of India's current growth model.

While Chinese interests and engagement in Africa have dominated the media and academic literature recently, India is also becoming an important economic and political player in Africa. The Indian economy is only about a sixth of the size of the Chinese one, but it is still growing fast and consequently exerts considerable demand for natural resources. While it was once commonly felt that China was a global manufacturing hub and India a service one, the picture is more complicated.

India is 'home' to major manufacturing companies such as Tata and ArcelorMittal,[1] the world's largest steel company – which require natural resources for their growth, in addition to major global service suppliers such as the well-known information technology company InfoSys. Like in China, provincial governments are also involved in other Asian-driver economies. For example the Southern Indian state of Andhra Predesh signed an agreement with Kenya and Uganda to send 500 farmers to farm 20,000 and 8,000 hectares in each of those countries respectively (Perrot and Malaquais 2009), although this has not yet come to fruition. Mohandas Gandhi was only partly correct. While services are an increasingly important part of India's relations with Africa, raw materials, agriculture and manufacturing are also key sectors.

As many of the largest Chinese companies operative in Africa are state-owned, it is easier to examine and theorize the links between the government's geo-economic strategy and state-owned corporate ones, although it is very important to pay attention to context and detail in examining these relationships (Brautigam 2009). The Indian case is more difficult as there is generally a clearer separation between state and corporate interests, although there are also Indian state-owned corporations engaged in Africa. Consequently, Indian engagements with Africa appear somewhat more 'messy' or uncoordinated than Chinese ones, although there is substantial variation within and between cases. While much of the incipient literature on India's engagements with Africa details different resource and infrastructure deals, in this chapter, while making reference to some of these, the broader goal is to examine the drivers and some of the impacts of increased Indian state and corporate involvement and investment in Africa.

Like China, although starting the process of economic reform later – the Indian political economy has undergone a fundamental restructuring in the last twenty years. This began in earnest with the economic liberalization programme of 1991, whose architect, Manmohan Singh, was then Minister of Finance and is now Prime Minister. India adopted economic liberalization, or free market policies, because it faced a balance of payments crisis, with very little foreign exchange left to pay for imports (Corbridge and Harriss 2000). If you do not have enough foreign exchange to buy fuel and other essential economic inputs, the economy grinds to a halt.

Prior to this programme of liberalization India had been characterized by its famous, but very slow, 'Hindu rate of growth', although some dispute this interpretation (Sen 2007). Once the economy was liberalized it began to grow quickly, particularly as foreign investors were attracted by the highly educated scientific workforce which had been developed under the Indian Institutes of Technology system and elite universities during the previous more state-led era.

Outsourcing of basic back-office functions led to the setting-up of call centres in India, with operators sometimes being given English or American names and briefed on the plots of soap operas so that callers from the West would not know they were Indians – a kind of veiled globalization, with echoes of India's current relations with Africa. Liberalization also enabled previously domestic-focused Indian conglomerates to grow and expand overseas and access technology more easily. However, the fruits of growth have been highly unevenly distributed, with some social classes and areas continuing to be mired in deepening poverty (Shiva 2008; Patnaik 2008). For example, suicides among farmers driven to despair by declining productivity and profitability of agriculture have caused outrage for many in India. This private-sector-driven, unplanned, polarizing and chaotic model of 'economic development' is in evidence in Indian economic relations with Africa. However, there are signs that the Indian government is beginning to wake slowly in Africa from its previous 'sleepwalking' and is now devoting serious diplomatic and economic resources to the continent (Naidu 2010).

Indian Trade and Investment in Africa

Indian trade with Africa amounted to US$35 billion in 2008, around a third of the figure for China. In 2006 India imported 12 per cent of its gold imports, 79 per cent of its phosphates, 91 per cent of its nuts and 16 per cent of its copper from the continent (Naidu 2009). Nine out of every ten rough diamonds around the world are cut and polished in India and they are the country's single largest export, at around US$14 billion a year (*AsiaPulse News* 2008). Of the US$10 billion in rough diamonds imported each year into India, around 80 per cent are thought to come from Africa, and the Indian government is keen to source these directly, rather than through traders in Europe. The Indian government is reportedly keen to disrupt De Beers' near-monopoly of the global diamond trade and to source them directly from Botswana, for example (Benza 2010). In Angola it has reportedly been promised that the Indian government will sponsor a diamond cutting and polishing centre in order to retain locally more of the value added (Bhattacharya 2010). As part of the first India–Africa Forum Summit in 2008 it was announced that India, like China, would allow duty-free imports for selected products from the thirty-four African countries with which it has trade agreements. These products include mineral ores and gem diamonds which can be further processed in India and the added value consequently captured there.

Indian trade with Africa almost doubled to 7.7 per cent of its total trade from 1990/1 to 2006/7 (Naidu 2010), in contrast to China's current 3 per cent. Thus Africa is proportionately a much more important trading partner for India than it is for China, a fact often neglected in the current literature.

Trade promotion is supported through the Indian Export–Import (EXIM) Bank Focus Africa Programme. The EXIM Bank has around half a billion dollars in lines of credit operative in Africa under this programme, which is very small compared to the Chinese EXIM Bank's operations. However, when all its lines of credit are included, those active in SSA amounted to over US$2 billion in 2009, 60 per cent of the bank's total (Bhatacharya 2010), again showing the strategic priority which is attached to the region. These loans are at concessional interest rates which mean that, for low-income countries, the grant, or aid, element amounts to 41 per cent of the loan. Some of these lines of credit are to develop information and communication technology infrastructure, which may be relatively inexpensive to develop when compared to massive Chinese loans for road and rail infrastructure for example.

Despite the relatively small scale of India's EXIM Bank operations in Africa, it was Indian firms which topped the list of greenfield FDI sites in Africa at forty-eight – compared to thirty-two from China – between 2002 and 2005 (UNCTAD 2007), although this is now likely to have changed. India is the second-largest investor in Uganda and the largest in Ghana by a number of projects (Bhattacharya 2010) – two countries with very liberal foreign investment regimes.

In contrast to China, India does not have a stated 'go global' policy for its corporations to encourage them to enter international markets. The absence of such a formal stated policy may mean Indian investment attracts less attention and actually conforms more closely to the Chinese foreign policy: 'be good at keeping a low profile; never become the leader and make some contributions'. China's leadership position in Africa means India attracts less attention around its oil investments, in Sudan for example. As China has a permanent seat on the United Nations Security Council, which has been used at times to shelter the Sudanese government, and as it has also sold substantial amounts of arms there, its involvement in Sudan has been much more controversial. India then is arguably engaged in a kind of 'globalization slipstreaming' behind China in Africa.

Resource Access

Oil imports are arguably of even greater strategic importance for India than for China as the country has only 0.4 per cent of the world's proven reserves (Naidu 2008). Consequently it imports 75 per cent of its oil needs, compared to only a third for China (McCormick 2008). To maintain an 8 per cent average economic growth rate, India needs to increase its primary energy supply by three to four times its 2003/4 levels (Naidu 2010), and it is also estimated that India will run out of coal in the next forty years. Consequently it currently needs – and will increasingly need – to import the majority of its energy needs, and it is projected that by 2030 India may be the world's third-largest consumer of energy after the United States and China (Naidu 2009). India now imports 11 per cent of its oil from Africa, partly to fuel its rapidly growing car fleet (Arnold 2009). In the capital of India, Delhi, by itself, an extra 200,000 cars are added to the streets every year (Shiva 2008).

In 2005 India offered US$1 billion in lines of credit to West African petro states in exchange for oil exploration rights (Frynas and Paulo 2007), and new lines have been negotiated since then. Energy – and resource security more broadly – is then an important driver of Indian engagement with Africa, and this can be acquired through state-owned corporations, in addition to private ones (Singh 2007).

Indian companies have been very active in resource deals in Africa. For example, in 2003 OVL, the overseas arc of India's state-owned energy company, Oil and Natural Gas Corporation (ONGC), bought a 25 per cent stake in the Greater Nile Petroleum Operating Corporation in Sudan for US$250 million from the Canadian Talisman company, which had been forced to relinquish its stake by US sanctions applied against the regime there (Arnold 2009). ONGC also has major investments in Nigeria and Côte d'Ivoire and other countries, and the private conglomerate ArcelorMittal had expressed an interest in buying the Port Harcourt Refinery in Nigeria. However, in 2008 the new Nigerian government revoked its contracts to run a number of steel plants in the country, because it was felt they were overly favourable to

ArcelorMittal. While Indian oil and gas companies have sometimes been outbid by their cash-rich Chinese rivals for oil and mineral concessions in Africa, in 2006 the governments of these two Asian powers reached an agreement not to bid against each other for energy resources in an effort to contain spiralling energy prices (Obi 2010).

In Zambia the country's most important copper mine, Konkola, accounting for 65 per cent of mineral production in the country, was sold to Vedanta Resources, which is an Indian company in origin. In order to attract investment, on the advice/insistence of the World Bank the mineral royalty rate was set at 0.6 per cent giving the Zambian government US$12 million in 2006 from the US$2 billion in copper extracted that year (Arnold 2009). When tax write-offs for new investment were included, the World Bank estimated that the effective rate of taxation on copper in Zambia was zero – a shocking statistic given that it is by far the country's dominant export (Fraser and Lungu 2007). While there has been new investment and some associated job creation as a result of this investment, there have also been environmental costs. The Konkola Copper Mine (KCM) polluted one of the rivers in Copperbelt Province. An environmental assessment noted: 'The contamination from this latter plant area is, at least periodically, very severe, with Ph [*sic*] sometimes as low as 2.2 being experienced in the South Uchi stream' (Zambia Consolidated Copper Mines 2005), which flows into the Kafue River.[2]

ArcelorMittal has also signed a major iron ore deal with Liberia, although the government of Ellen Sirleaf Johnson renegotiated the unfavourable terms (Alden 2007). Global Witness had previously criticized ArcelorMittal for the extractive nature of the deal in post-conflict Liberia and for setting up a 'state within a state'. ArcelorMittal had previously abrogated sovereign power unto itself in Liberia, controlling 'company and capital structure, taxation, royalties, transfer pricing, rights to minerals and confidentiality' (Global Witness, quoted in Arnold 2009, p. 86). This quasi-sovereignty is something which is arguably replicated in Chinese-built SEZs in Africa, and in American oil compounds (Maass 2009). However, the resource boom which lasted through 2008 gave greater bargaining power to African states, which they have asserted in the two cases detailed above with ArcelorMittal. Perhaps because it is a private company, it is felt that renegotiating deals *ex post* is less likely to damage relations with the 'home country' government (India), than if the same were to be attempted with Chinese state-owned corporations. Also the fact that Indian aid and loans are on a much smaller scale than Chinese ones makes the trade-off easier to make. Nonetheless, Indian conglomerates do have continuing structural power, depending on context. ArcelorMittal is South Africa's largest steel producer, for example (Cheru and Obi 2010).

Sanusha Naidu (2010) also argues that the bureaucratic nature of the Indian state makes it difficult to sign off quickly on investment agreements. For example, when the Indian Parliament blocked the purchase of the Akpo oil field in Nigeria, deciding it would be unprofitable for the Indian ONGC, the Chinese National Offshore Oil Corporation bought it for US$2.3 billion in 2006 (Michel, Beuret and Woods 2009). As in the example above, India's democracy may put it at a disadvantage in competition against China in Africa.

Other Economic Sectors and Legacy of Migration

From 1961 to 2007, 56 per cent of Indian FDI in Africa was in the manufacturing sector, and 26 per cent in the service and 18 per cent in the primary sectors (Pradhan 2008). However, this seemingly high level of manufacturing investment is undoubtedly boosted by mineral processing activities. There has also been investment in 'pure' manufacturing and other sectors, however.

'Zambia ha[s] been declared a major investment destination under the Tata Group expansion program in Africa' (RoZ 2006), with investments in the agricultural sector and in hydro-power. However, a manager at the Indo-Zambian Bank, which was set up after an agreement between Indira Gandhi and Kenneth Kaunda, noted (interview, Lusaka, December 2007) that 'I don't see assembly lines', although there has been some foreign investment in the production of juices, which compete with those produced by local companies such as Manzi (Nordic/SADC 2005, cited in Fick 2006). Tata has also opened a new bus and truck assembly plant in Ndola in Zambia (*India News* 2006), although according to a World Bank economist interviewed (Lusaka, December 2007), this project would not have taken place without government incentives, and government will be the major buyer of the few hundred buses and trucks assembled each year.

Some Indian companies have also been active in the tourism sector. For example, Tata invested US$8 million in the renovation of the Taj Pamodji Hotel in Lusaka, Zambia (Naidu 2009). Investment flows are not all one way, however. For example, Mauritius, whose population is largely of Asian extraction, was the largest single foreign investor in

India during the June quarter of 2007, with investments of US$1.9 billion (Reuters 2007). In fact, from 2000 to November 2009 Mauritian companies invested over US$40 billion in India, making it the single largest foreign investor there during that time period (India Brand Equity Foundation 2010a). In contrast to what is often assumed, African investment is sometimes being used to develop India's infrastructure. For example, in March 2010 the India Infrastructure Development Fund (Mauritius) received Indian cabinet approval for a fund which it was thought would bring US$163.8 million dollars for infrastructure investment into the country (India Brand Equity Foundation 2010b). There has also been substantial South African investment in the tourism and manufacturing sectors in India in the last number of years.

India is now digitally linked to East Africa through the East African Submarine Cable (EASSY) and to Mauritius, South Africa and West African countries through the new South Atlantic 3 / West Africa Submarine Fibre Optic Cable (SAT-3/WASC). This latter project undoubtedly facilitates joint ventures between Indian and Mauritian companies. An example of this is the joint venture that Nextcell, an Indian mobile phone company, and AquaSan, which is a Mauritian company specializing in water and sanitation set up as Nextcell Mauritius (India Brand Equity Foundation 2010c), demonstrating the recursive nature of globalization. They hope to capture substantial mobile phone market share in Africa.

India is thus seeking not only the extraction of natural resources from Africa but also capital resources or investment. While the Indian state may be paying increased attention to resource-rich African states, the fact that there is an extensive Indian diaspora in Mauritius and that there is a potential strategic coupling of their economies based on information technology makes it something of an exception. This deepening South–South economic globalization also has security implications, discussed in more detail below.

There were earlier forms of South–South globalization, although they were often previously Northern-directed. There is a substantial Indian-originating diaspora in Africa. Many Indians came to Africa during the colonial period to work as indentured labourers and as 'free' traders, and some of their descendants maintain close connections with their areas of origin. In some colonies they served as an ethnicized intermediate class, with Europeans controlling the 'commanding heights' of large-scale commercial agriculture, banking, manufacturing and mining, and indigenous Africans supplying manual labour for the most part. After their periods of indentured labour were up, many stayed on and became involved in trading. A commonly held assumption is that this diaspora provides India with an automatic entrée into Africa. However, there is not necessarily the coincidence of interests that intuition might suggest (McCann 2010a).

According to a senior official in the Indian Ministry of Commerce, East African countries – where, along with South Africa, the diaspora is concentrated – are in the process of being eclipsed in India's strategy of engagement with the continent in favour of West African oil producers (Mawdsley and McCann 2010). Even Central Africa will arguably be of greater economic interest, they argued, because of its rich mineral resources. The first India – Central Africa Trade Forum was held in Congo-Brazzaville in 2009, for instance.

In countries such as Kenya, where there is a substantial 'Indian' diaspora, Indian engagement is largely private-sector-driven and market-seeking (McCann 2010b). Indian investment in non-resource-rich countries has concentrated in areas such as mobile telecommunications, such as the investment by the Mumbai-based Essar group.

Essar also acquired a 50 per cent stake in Kenya Petroleum Refineries in 2009, which is the sole petrol refiner in East Africa. Indian trade with Kenya reached almost half a billion dollars in 2004–5, which was more than a 55 per cent increase over two years and meant that Indian trade with Kenya was only slightly below that of China. India's main exports to Kenya are engineering products, cotton and pharmaceuticals, while the principal imports are gemstones and inorganic chemicals (Vines and Oruitemeka 2008).

Indian Overseas Assistance to Africa

Somewhat questionably, given the acute need at home and the fact that there are proportionally more malnourished children in India than in Africa, India also gives aid to Africa. Indeed average incomes in Africa, across the continent, are about US$200 a head per year higher than in India (Melber and Southall 2009). The motivation for this is thus surely primarily political/economic, rather than humanitarian.

India donated food to Namibia, Chad and Lesotho in 2003/4 and several hundred thousand mosquito nets to the Republic of Congo (Naidu 2009), in addition to being involved in UN peacekeeping missions on the continent (Singh 2007). According to Naidu (2009, p. 130), 'this use of soft power for humanitarian purposes is possibly intended to downplay India's image of scrambling in Africa and instead project New Delhi as a development partner'. According to the Minister of State for Commerce 'the first principle of India's involvement in Africa [is] unlike that of China. China says go out and exploit the natural resources, our strategy is to go out there and add value' (Dawes 2008, quoted in Naidu 2009, p. 134). However, she argues that ultimately it will be how African governments engage with India which will determine whether it is a 'scrambler' or a development partner. As Chris Alden (2007) has pointed out in relation to China, however, the two are not incommensurable and international relations contain elements of both self- and mutual interest.

India's aid relations are also tied up with its own self-image. For example, despite the fact that it ranks seven places below South Africa on the United Nations Human Development Index (no. 127, as compared to no. 120), in 2003 the Indian government announced it would suspend taking bilateral development assistance from twenty-two donor countries (McCormick 2008). This was a symbolic statement that the country was independent and could begin to assert itself as a 'great power'. As Alex Wendt (1999) has noted, ideas are what drive the creation of social structures, so states do not necessarily only follow their material interests, but may also undertake seemingly irrational actions, such as wars, for this reason. In the 2007/8 budget speech, the government of India asserted its intention to establish its own overseas aid agency – the India International Development Cooperation Agency.

As a poor country itself, India does not see its role as giving substantial grants-in-aid, but instead concentrates its aid in Africa on technical training and assistance (McCormick 2008; Mawdsley 2010). Much of India's aid is delivered through the Indian Technical and Economic Cooperation (ITEC), which was set up in 1964 to examine ways of improving cooperation with Africa (Naidu 2010). For example India has an African e-Network project which will connect African countries through satellite and fibre optics and facilitate telemedicine and tele-education programmes. African universities and hospitals will have links with each other and with institutions in India. This network may also facilitate communication between African heads of state and, perhaps, Indian politicians.

According to a professor of African Studies in Delhi, India needs African votes to get a permanent seat on the United Nations Security Council but does not have the money of the Chinese or America's military might. Consequently, India has to rely on cooperation in information technology, agriculture and engineering, where India has experience (quoted in Arnold 2009), although this opportunity has now arguably passed for a variety of geopolitical reasons, including lack of Chinese support for a permanent Indian seat. For Sanusha Naidu (2010, p. 47), 'the launch of the Pan-African e-Network reflects the first step towards strengthening the ICT partnership before losing out to the Chinese, designed perhaps to enable India's telecom giants to become industry-shapers in the continent', although empirical support for this statement is currently lacking.

There are also some high-level initiatives which are worth examining. For example the 'Techno-Economic Approach to Africa–India Movement' (TEAM-9) was initiated in 2004. The '9' is because it is a partnership between India and eight resource-rich West African states. The goal of the programme is to improve healthcare, food security, transport and telecommunications in the African countries through a focus on technology (Mawdsley and McCann 2010). It has, however, also cancelled the bilateral debt of some less resource-rich African countries, such as Mozambique and Tanzania (Vines and Oruitemeka 2008; Mawdsley 2010).

The Indian government does not have the same economic weight behind it as the Chinese government, in terms of access to foreign exchange reserves or indeed granting access to its domestic market. Consequently the Indian government has gone for the direct approach in its dealings with African governments. The Pan-African e-Network, noted earlier, was launched in 2007 in Addis Ababa, Ethiopia, the site of the Headquarters of the AU. The e-Network provides facilities for telemedicine and education, but, perhaps more importantly from a political point of view, it allows videoconferencing for all fifty-three heads of state in the AU. According to the e-Network website, this is the VVIP's (very, very important people's) network. Undoubtedly African heads of state will be flattered if they didn't already know this. This overt support for sitting heads of state is more 'top down' than China's approach, as India does not have the same economic resources to bring to bear in its African relations. Consequently, it must rely more on the goodwill of African elites, as it can exercise less 'hard' or coercive power over them.

The Geopolitics of Indian Economic Engagement

According to Cheru and Obi (2010), while Indian Foreign Ministry attempts to support private sector engagement in Africa are minor compared to the resources Chinese state-owned corporations can draw on, over the longer term India will have a comparative advantage over China in Africa as a result of its diaspora, its strong educational system, its proximity to the continent and its democratic tradition. Whether this is the case remains to be seen, but India is using a variety of strategies to cooperate and compete with China. One of these is 'balancing' through alliances with other 'middle powers'.

In part to offset the influence of China, India has been involved in the IBSA (India, Brazil, South Africa) group which was launched in 2003. South–South globalization thus has a variable geometry to it. A host of agreements have been signed between the participating parties on issues such as health and wind resources, but despite proclamations of a desire to move towards a free trade area amongst the participants, little progress has been made on tariff reductions. China, with the support of South Africa, requested to be included in the IBSA dialogue forum on commercial issues. However, fearing a loss of influence, India blocked this on the basis that China is not a democracy (Vines and Oruitemeka 2008).

The Indian navy has patrolled Mauritius' Exclusive Economic Zone (EEZ) since 2003 and has a similar agreement with the Seychelles (Vines and Oruitemeka 2008). India has also signed defence agreements with other countries on Africa's East – Mozambique, Madagascar and Kenya – and has had joint training exercises with other African navies (Vines 2010). These defence agreements are also reportedly driven by fears of Chinese expansionism.

India is keen to protect its shipping routes and its enhanced military capabilities also signal its emergence as a 'great power' (Vines and Oruitemeka 2008). This preoccupation may be a reflection of the fact that 90 per cent of India's trade by volume, and almost three-quarters by value, is done by sea (Bhattacharya 2010). This regional geo-economy finds institutional expression through the Indian Ocean Rim Association for Regional Cooperation, which meets every two years. This organization has assumed greater salience recently as a result of heightened economic engagements.

According to the Indian Minister of State for Defence, 'if India and Africa are able to synergize energies and initiatives and adapt to a changing world, the 21st century could surely belong to them' (Rao Inderjit Singh, quoted in Naidu 2008, p. 116). The rhetoric of Indo-African relations follows closely that of the Chinese, with an emphasis on 'win-win' relationships. The first Indo-African conclave was held in 2005 and the 'India–Africa partnership' launched. Many potential economic development projects were discussed at this. As noted earlier, at a subsequent meeting in 2008 the Indian Prime Minister Manmohan Singh announced a 'Duty Free Tariff Preference Scheme' to allow preferential market access to India for exports from fifty of the world's 'least developed countries', of which thirty-four are in Africa. At this meeting he also announced half a billion dollars of new aid for Africa and an increase in lines of credit to the continent to US$5.4 billion by 2013 (Mawdsley and McCann 2010).

While China's influence in Africa is much more prominent and powerful than that of India, India is nonetheless an important emerging actor on the continent, where relations between the two are characterized by competition and collaboration. In contrast to the Western promotion of 'good governance' on the continent, India, like China, also subscribes to the principle of 'non-interference' in the sovereign affairs of other nation states. This 'non-interference' serves to placate African political elites and thereby to aid or ensure continued resource access. India also cooperates with South Africa through the India, Brazil, South Africa (IBSA) forum. We now turn to examine Brazil's relations with and interests in Africa.

Brazil's Relations with and Interest in Africa

I want to sell a lot more to those who never bought from us in a continent that will have 700 million inhabitants within 25 years. (Brazilian President Lula da Silva 2009, quoted in Ogier 2009)

Brazil is an emerging economic power, with a long history of engagement with Africa, particularly with Lusophone Africa through the slave trade. As noted earlier, Brazil was also only recently replaced as the largest source of SSA's imports. This is in part because much Brazilian technology is appropriate to African conditions and because the Brazilian government made a deliberate effort to cultivate economic and other relations with African states in the post-independence period.

Brazil is now the world's tenth-largest economy in dollar terms (United States Central Intelligence Agency 2009) and the government of Lula da Silva pursued an active Africa policy for reasons of national interest and also solidarity. Lula's government introduced many progressive initiatives domestically in Brazil, such as the zero hunger policy, and, despite criticism from some quarters over the orthodox nature of economic management in Brazil, there would appear to have been genuine concern to foster South–South cooperation for pragmatic economic, solidaristic and humanitarian reasons. Africa is also of immense strategic importance to Brazil as it now accounts for over 73 per cent of its imports of crude oil (UNCTAD 2010). Quite simply, and in contrast to other large powers, the Brazilian economy would not function without Africa.

In the first four years of his government, President da Silva opened or reopened thirteen Brazilian embassies in Africa. This was reciprocated by African governments, as the number of African embassies in Brazil rose from sixteen to twenty-five (Ribeiro 2009a). Lula also established a dedicated Department for Africa in the Foreign Relations Ministry in Brazil and has toured Africa ten times, visiting twenty countries (Ogier 2009). The website for the Africa–Brazil Cooperation Programme on Social Development notes that it seeks to 'promote international technical cooperation between developing countries to foster social protection policies' (United Nations Development Programme 2009). President Lula also initiated the Africa – South America Summit in 2006, and in 2009 was a special guest at the AU Summit in Sirte, Libya (Freemantle and Stevens 2009).

The pattern of relations has followed that established by the other BRICs in Africa. Deepening commercial engagement and investment, such as the acquisition of a contract to mine the Moatize coalfields in Mozambique by Companhia Vale do Rio Doce (CVRD) of Brazil, was preceded by 95 per cent bilateral debt relief amounting to US$315 million – a very substantial sum for the Mozambican economy. According to Yager (2005, section 30.2), CVRD planned to complete a feasibility study on the development of the Moatize coalfield in June 2006. If the feasibility study yielded favourable results, CVRD planned to build a mine that would produce 14 Mt/yr (million tonnes per year) of coal. Production is expected to begin in 2011. The company also planned to build a coal-fired power station with a capacity of 1,500 megawatts (MW). Most of the production from the new mine would be coking coal for consumption by steel plants in Brazil; the remainder was expected to be thermal coal for domestic consumption and export to African markets. Development of the Moatize Mine would also require rehabilitation of the railway from Beira to Tete, and the construction of a maritime export terminal at Beira. Total costs of the project were expected to be US$1 billion.

In this project then, Mozambique would get investment, while Brazil would receive business for one of its major companies and a raw material for its steel industry. This follows the logic of bargains cut with other African governments. For example, in Angola the Brazilian government provided a credit line of US$580 million for 2005–7 to enable the construction of the Capanda hydroelectric power plant and to purchase cars – for the police, for example – from Brazil, in addition to signing other agreements on infrastructure, sanitation and agriculture (Ribeiro 2009). Thus, while Western countries have recently been attempting to untie their aid, so that recipients are not required to purchase products or services produced by the donor in exchange for the aid, in Brazil – as with China – the vectors of aid (or concessional loans) are linked with trade and investment, in a pattern reminiscent of the colonial period (Kaplinsky 2008). The fact that new economic powers are not the former colonial powers means that they bring 'soft power' advantages to their negotiations with African governments, and even exploitative trade and investment deals with them do not readily raise the spectre of 'recolonization'. This can work to African governing elites' advantage.

Brazilian exports to Africa increased 315 per cent from 2002 to 2006, while imports from Africa grew by a similar proportion (Ribeiro 2009). From 2002 to 2009, total trade grew fivefold between Africa and Brazil. Together Angola, Nigeria and South Africa account for 48 per cent of Brazil's exports to Africa and 53 per cent of African imports to Brazil. Unsurprisingly most of Brazil's exports are manufactures and food, while Africa's exports to Brazil are raw materials, particularly oil (from Nigeria and Angola) and also coal (from South Africa), again replicating a colonial pattern. Approximately 87 per cent of Brazilian imports from Africa are minerals (including oil and base metals) (Trade Law Centre for Southern Africa 2009).

Just as the US and China are keen to diversify their energy supplies away from the volatile Middle East, Brazil is concerned with energy import diversification, particularly as a result of the nationalization of Bolivian gas fields. Increased oil imports largely account for the fact that Brazil experienced a rising trade deficit with Africa, from US$312 million in 2002 to US$5.6 billion in 2008. Petrobras, which is the 34th-largest company in the world, has plans to invest US$3 billion in Africa to 2013, largely in Angola and Nigeria (Ogier 2009).

Brazil has a major sugarcane-based ethanol industry which produces 160,000 barrels of oil-equivalent per day (Amigun, Sigamoney and von Blottnitz 2006) and there is growing cooperation with African countries in this area. For example, the Ghanaian Parliament has approved the building of an ethanol plant by the São Paulo-based company Ethanol Trading (Ogier 2009).

While China is often castigated in the Western media for supporting so-called 'rogue regimes', such as Zimbabwe and Sudan, diplomatically and economically, Brazilian companies are also investing heavily in mining operations in Zimbabwe (Horne 2009). New trade webs are being created as China is now Brazil's biggest trading partner as well, with soy exports from the Brazilian Amazon having increased 10,000 per cent in recent years. Is this then a new model of globalization where, in Africa and elsewhere in the post-colonial world, China and other Asian countries have emerged as 'nodal points for commodity flows, often completely independent of colonial structures' (Dobler 2008, p. 410)?

At a more local level, there is now an agreement between the Gauteng Economic Development Agency (GEDA) and the Brazilian Machinery Manufacturers' Association to encourage trade and investment in the sector. According to GEDA's General Manager, 'today we buy machinery from manufacturers the world over. What we're now beginning to realise is that most of what we buy in foreign markets is available in Brazil at comparable, if not better, quality and price. Instead of importing such machinery, we believe we should be cooperatively manufacturing locally, at the same time creating new industry using South African resources' (quoted in Nevin 2004).

In 2008 the Brazilian Agricultural Research Company opened an office in Accra, Ghana, to facilitate transfer of agricultural technology to Africa (UNCTAD 2010). The UK/Irish company Tullow Oil announced a major oil find off the Ghanaian coast in 2007, and Petrobras has indicated its interest in developing one of the oil blocks (emii.com 2008).

Other Emerging Power Interests

There are also many other emerging middle – and some potentially great – powers involved in Africa. For example Vladimir Putin, the Russian Prime Minister, recently toured the continent, and the state-owned gas company Gazprom is active in Nigeria, Algeria and Libya (Clarke 2008). However, as the world's largest exporter of energy, Russia is not driven by the same imperatives as some of the other great powers in terms of securing access to supplies. Consequently its involvement in Africa is likely to be much more limited than that of other BRICs. Other Asian players such as Malaysia do have extensive and growing interests, however. For example, the Malaysian state-owned oil company, PETRONAS (Petroliam Nasional Berhad), has operations in at least fourteen African countries (Clarke 2008).

Turkey is also rapidly expanding its economic engagement with Africa, although according to some this is primarily in order to access new markets rather than resources or diplomatic support (Kaplinsky and Farooki 2009). Turkish exports to Africa rose from US$1.5 billion to over US$10 billion from 2001 to 2009 (*The Economist*, 27 March 2010, p. 40, cited in Scott, vom Hau et al. 2010, p. 4). In some ways Turkey was ahead of the game as it adopted an 'Opening up to Africa' policy in 2008, in addition to designating 2005 the 'Year of Africa' (UNCTAD 2010). It also hosted a summit in Istanbul in 2008 which attracted twenty-nine African Presidents or Prime Ministers. Trade with Africa was already worth over US$15 billion in 2009, and exports to Africa were heavily concentrated in textiles. According to Abdou Diallo, a Senegalese businessman based in Istanbul, 'we have begun to distinguish Turkish goods from Chinese products due to their quality. Turkish goods mean European quality at a cheaper price' (quoted in Africathegoodnews 2010). Interestingly, Turkey is Africa's only major developing country export market where manufactures have increased as a proportion of total exports in recent years (UNCTAD 2010) as some manufacturers offshore labour-intensive assembly operations to the continent. This is partly because Turkey is the EU's second-largest external supplier of clothing, after China.

As the Turkish economy grew in the 2000s, it also imported more oil. Nigeria is Turkey's eighth-largest oil supplier, and exports of Nigerian oil to Turkey grew two and a half times from 2005 to 2009 (calculated from International Trade Centre 2010). Oil is central to the functioning of the global economy and it is to an examination of competition over that resource in Africa that we now turn.

5 DRIVING THE GLOBAL ECONOMY: WEST AFRICAN AND SAHELIAN OIL

Más Petróleo = Más Pobreza (More Oil = More Poverty). (Graffiti on an Amazonian oil pipeline, quoted in Maass 2009, p. 6)

The intensified struggle for oil in Africa is not a replay of the partition of the nineteenth century, yet the continent is haunted by a ghost from the past. Its natural resources are being increasingly exploited by competing transnational actors that marginalize and impoverish people in Africa's oil producing countries. (Obi 2009, p. 198)

The former Minister of Oil in Venezuela once referred to it as the 'devil's excrement'. Others have likened it to a drug. If you are healthy (a country with good institutions such as Norway or the UK), some argue it is like taking speed: it will raise your rate of economic growth without immediately adverse consequences. However, if you are unhealthy it has been likened to heroin: it can kill – or nearly kill – you. This is the 'oil curse'.

As the global economy has continued to grow, generally, there has been increasing demand for oil and conflict over access to it. It is estimated that demand for oil will rise by around 60 per cent from 2002 levels by 2020 (Institute for the Analysis of Global Security 2004, cited in Southall 2009), with increased demand being largely driven by rising Asian economies. China by itself now accounts for 40 per cent of total global growth in oil demand (The US Energy Information Administration, cited in Pan 2006). China's demand for oil increases by 1 per cent for every percentage increase in its GDP, versus 0.4 per cent for the OECD countries, whose economies are heavily biased towards services (Dumas 2006). This means that 'with demand rising a few percentage points every year at times of economic expansion, and with the output of older and larger [oil] fields declining by a few percentage points annually, the industry needed to find vast amounts of new oil to maintain an equilibrium of supply and demand. "That's like [finding] a whole new Saudi Arabia every couple of years"' (Sadad al-Husseini, quoted in Maass 2009, p. 23). By 2020 the Chinese government expects the country to consume between 10 and 15 million barrels of oil per day, which is double Saudi Arabia's total production, or roughly equal to Africa's entire production (Michel, Beuret and Woods 2009). Already, by 2005, the United States imported more oil from Africa than from the Middle East (Shaxson 2007).

Two-thirds of global oil reserves are found in the Middle East, much of which is potentially hostile to the United States, in particular as a result of its support for Israel, amongst other reasons, and consequently the US is very keen to diversify its oil supplies away from that region towards Africa, where proven reserves have risen by 45 per cent since the turn of the century (French and Chambers 2010). Gas reserves are also of substantial interest to the US, as natural gas can now be compressed and exported by tanker, with Nigeria holding 78 per cent of proven reserves in Africa. However, oil and gas production has often been associated with corruption in Africa.

Halliburton, the energy company with which former US Vice-President Dick Cheney was associated, agreed to pay US$382 million in criminal fines over payments to Nigerian government officials in relation to the Bonny Island natural gas liquefaction plant (Anonymous 2009). It is not coincidental that the countries in Africa with the highest rates of foreign investment are not those that score the highest on indices of democracy or transparency, but those that are mineral- and oil-rich (Southall and Melber 2009). Partly because of problems associated with oil wealth, Sudan and Chad come out in forty-fifth and forty-sixth places respectively, out of forty-eight, on the Mo Ibrahim Governance Index of Africa, for example (*The Economist* 2007), and disaffection with poverty and corruption has fuelled internal opposition in both Chad and Nigeria (Marchal 2006).

Nigeria in West Africa has pumped more than 400 billion dollars' worth of oil since it was discovered there in the 1950s – enough to cancel all of SSA's debt. However, more than 80 per cent of oil revenue has accrued to just 1 per cent of the population (World Bank, cited in Watts 2006), while the majority of the population have got poorer, leading to a rebellion in the oil-rich Niger Delta.

The Niger Delta is perhaps the ultimate example of the 'paradox of plenty'. The Delta by itself has 35 billion barrels of proven oil and gas reserves, which is more than the entire United States. It supplies almost 10 per cent of that country's oil imports by itself (BP 2005, cited in Shaxson 2007).

While the Niger Delta produces all of the country's oil and gas, there is no electricity or public water infrastructure for most of the population. It is the poorest region of the country and there is only 1 secondary school per 14,000 people (Ghazvinian 2007). Meanwhile, the former head of ExxonMobil, the world's largest private oil company, earned US$145,000 a day during his tenure, as oil production brought environmental destruction to local communities from spills and the 'flaring' of gas from oil fields.

Agriculture in the Niger Delta has been devastated by oil spills and the practice of gas flaring – the practice of burning off unwanted or uneconomic gas from the oil fields. According to the Worldwide Fund for Nature, an estimated 1.5 million tons of oil have been spilt in the Delta over the last fifty years (Ghazvinian 2007). This is the equivalent of an *Exxon Valdez* disaster – in which an oil tanker ran aground in Alaska in 1989 – every year.

Acid rain is so bad in parts of Nigeria that it eats through corrugated iron roofs every few years. Gas flaring from oil fields also releases carcinogens including benzene, benzopyrene and toluene; however, local people sometimes cook bread and other foods beside gas flares. Despite, or perhaps because of, its oil wealth, Nigeria has a lower per capita income than Senegal, also in West Africa, whose main exports are fish and nuts.

Nigeria has also become a by-word internationally for corruption, with even the national police chief convicted of embezzling US$98 million, although he only served six months for the offence (Maass 2009). Indeed, where the state ends and private-sector interests in Nigeria begin is open to debate. In a recent topical example, one large-scale Chinese entrepreneur was granted permission to register his fleet of sport utility vehicles as police cars (Michel, Beuret and Woods 2009). An old Chinese proverb has it that when a tree moves it dies, but when a man moves he can make a fortune.

Oil has promoted not only corruption but also, given the scale of inequality associated with its extraction, conflict. Rebel movements, such as the Movement for the Emancipation of the Niger Delta, funded their campaign through kidnappings and through the practice of 'bunkering', in which oil is stolen from pipelines and then resold to oil companies. Sometimes it has been alleged that the Nigerian military itself is involved in this practice, which can have tragic consequences when the oil pipelines explode.

In 2003 200,000 barrels of oil were thought to be stolen this way each week, costing the Nigerian Treasury around US$5.2 billion a year (Ghazvinian 2007). An internal report for the oil company Shell concluded that, 'after over 50 years in Nigeria, it is therefore reasonable to say that [Shell] has become an integral part of the Niger Delta conflict system' (quoted in Maass 2009, p. 78).

While the practice of gas flaring is meant now to be illegal in Nigeria, it still continues and is a major source of greenhouse gas emissions worldwide, amazingly producing more of these than the rest of SSA combined (Shaxson 2007). More than a quarter of all gas flaring worldwide happens in SSA and around 20 billion cubic metres of gas is flared each year from the Niger Delta (Intergovernmental Panel on Climate Change 2007).

The number of people killed in the Delta each year as a result of the conflict is roughly 1,000, making it a borderline 'high intensity' conflict. While there has been a recent amnesty for militants the peace agreement had stalled as of 2010. Perhaps this is a result of what Joseph Hurst-Croft refers to as the 'hydra approach', whereby temporary concessions are made by the government only for renewed trouble to sprout up elsewhere as the overall structure of the political economy remains intact. This approach has even extended to granting oil exploration licences to companies controlled by militants in the Niger Delta (Shaxson 2007).

The Scale of Oil Company Investment in Africa and Impacts

ExxonMobil is the world's largest oil company and now produces more oil in Africa than in any other region of the world, with 25 per cent of its oil production coming from the continent. It holds 8.5 billion barrels of oil equivalent in reserves in Africa in an area extending 65 million acres (if Somalia is included) (Clarke 2008) and West Africa is expected to generate 45 per cent of its new global production growth.

Other huge oil companies such as Shell, Total and Chevron are also heavily invested and are spending 15, 30 and 35 per cent of their global production and exploration budgets in Africa, respectively (Ghazvinian 2007). The French company Total has the largest operations in Africa and holds 30 per cent of its total reserves there (Michel, Beuret and Woods 2009) and this is reflected in the fact that Air France has a nonstop 'Dedicate' service to an increasing number of African oil cities. Regular passengers are encouraged to join its 'Petroleum Club' which offers 'exclusive services for the oil and gas industry' (Ghazvinian 2007, p. 7).

Total is heavily invested in Gabon which is almost the same size as Nigeria, but with less than a hundredth of the population, giving it one of the highest per capita incomes in Africa (US$6,700 a year). It is the world's largest consumer of champagne per head but inequality there is stark with two-thirds of the population living on less than a dollar a day. Previously the former President Bongo had spent several billion dollars building a Transgabonais railway project for which there was insufficient traffic. As part of a privatization programme, a twenty-year licence to operate it was sold to French timber companies that paid less than a hundredth of what it had cost to build it (Economist Intelligence Unit, cited in Shaxson 2007).

French and European aid also went to mining and timber interests in Gabon, sometimes in the name of 'rural development', and French companies also have uranium mining contracts in the country. There is a garrison of 650 French troops stationed beside the Presidential Palace in Gabon, and it is the Western African station for France's air force fighter squadron (Oliveira 2007; Clarke 2008). While we often think of globalization as an economic and cultural phenomenon it is also a military one (Barkawi 2006). The extraction of point resources, in this case oil, is implicated in this military deployment. Oil generates wealth for some, poverty for many, and military spending to repress consequent dissent and conflict.

Western companies, such as those mentioned above, have much more sophisticated offshore technology than Asian competitors, which enables them to exploit oil fields effectively, and most of the big discoveries in recent years have been made offshore (Ghazvinian 2007). Offshore production also offers the advantage of being removed from conflict dynamics onshore, although there have been cases where militants have boarded offshore oil production platforms and demanded ransoms – in Nigerian territorial waters, for example.

According to the well-known World Bank economist Harry Broadman, the bulk of Chinese investment is in the oil sector in Africa, although he does note that there are many other investments and, as oil is a classic enclave industry, these are more likely to create jobs and technology transfer. In Africa the Chinese state operates through three national oil companies: the CNPC, the Chinese National Overseas Oil

Corporation and Sinopec (Obi 2009). Around 60 per cent of Africa's exports to China are made up of oil (Breslin 2007) but according to some analysts China is still only a bit player in the African oil industry. While Chinese national oil companies reportedly have good onshore drilling technology, in response to their relatively poor offshore technology some Chinese companies have gone into partnership with Western companies and established joint ventures. For example, in 2006 the Chinese National Overseas Oil Company invested US$2.3 billion in an oil concession in Nigeria owned by Total. This followed a visit by the Chinese President a few months earlier in which he had given Nigeria loans of US$4 billion for infrastructure projects, to be paid off in oil. In order to promote deals such as this and diversify sources of investment, for a time Asian companies were given 'right of first refusal' on new oil blocks in Nigeria (Vines et al. 2009).

It was the former US Assistant Secretary of State for Africa under the second Bush Administration, Jendayi Frazer, who referred to South Africa, Kenya, Ethiopia and Nigeria as 'keys' to the different regions of Africa for the United States (Hills 2006). The Chinese also have their key or anchor states in Africa, some of which overlap with the American ones, such as Nigeria given the extent of its oil reserves. Consequently the Chinese state has been particularly facilitative; signing an US$8.3 billion contract in November 2006 to build a railway in Nigeria and launching a satellite for the Nigerian government in 2007, which subsequently malfunctioned.[1]

According to the noted analyst Erica Downs, Chinese oil interests in Africa are still minuscule when compared to those of Western companies, and the country still has to purchase most of its oil on the open market (Downs 2007). However, its oil contracts are not insignificant and are growing rapidly. Chinese oil consumption doubled from 1996 to 2006 and PetroChina is reducing output by 7 per cent a year in its biggest domestic oil field in China to try to extend its life, giving added impetus to sourcing oil overseas (French and Chambers 2010).

By early 2008 Chinese companies had seventy-five oil contracts in sixteen countries, covering over 872,000 square kilometres (Clarke 2008). While there is competition amongst the main Chinese state-owned oil corporations (Taylor 2009), oil analyst Duncan Clarke (2008) notes that Chinese overseas oil strategy is coordinated through the China Petroleum Commerce and Industry Association and that 'China prefers to take 100 per cent concession, build and own pipelines, and ship its crude using its own tankers under the Chinese flag' (p. 401).

While Erica Downs has noted that concerns about China 'locking up barrels at source' are misplaced – because the country would otherwise have to purchase more of its oil on the open market, thereby reducing available supply for other countries – this is only true in the short to medium term. Once global resource scarcity begins truly to bite, these state-controlled supply chains will be crucially important in maintaining exclusive resource access. However, Cambridge business Professor Peter Nolan notes that, with an oil price about US$70 a barrel, oil production from shale and tar sands, of which Canada has huge deposits, is economically viable and would supply global demand for several hundred years (Nolan 2009). This economic logic changes calculations about the world already having passed 'peak oil', when half of the world's oil supply is gone. There are also, however, worrying implications for climate change.[2]

The fact that there are now new, and consequently more, competitors for Africa's oil resources has given greater bargaining power to the governing elites of oil-rich states. Cyril Obi (2009, p. 206) argues that 'there is no doubt that the leverage given to the Nigerian state by the new scramble for its oil has partly fed into a new kind of economic nationalism, driven by the quest for more profit and political patronage calculations of the national ruling elite'. The Nigerian government receives 90 per cent of production revenues from oil and this easy money has fed grand corruption, with the result that much of Nigeria's infrastructure – including its oil refineries – does not function satisfactorily. Nigeria has to import refined petroleum.

As noted, oil is a classic enclave industry. It is capital-intensive and consequently does not create many jobs, particularly for locals, although Shell notes that, in its case, 70 per cent of its staff in Nigeria are from the Niger Delta (Ghazvinian 2007). Even the multi-million-dollar floating production, storage and offloading vessels (FPSOs) that now dot the West African coastline are manufactured in industrial countries. Consequently, only about 5 per cent of the billions of dollars invested in African oil production each year is actually spent in Africa (Ghazvinian 2007).

While Nigeria is Africa's largest oil producer, it looks likely that it will soon be eclipsed by Angola, which by 2009 was producing almost 2 million barrels a day, or over 80 per cent of Nigeria's output (United States Central Intelligence Agency 2010). Along with Algeria, Sudan is now also a major oil producer (see Carmody 2010 for a discussion), but less has been written about Angola and Africa's third-largest oil producer, Equatorial Guinea. Consequently the discussion below focuses on these.

Oiling the Wheels of Repression: Equatorial Guinea

In Equatorial Guinea, oil production by itself accounts for 86 per cent of the economy or GDP (Oliveira 2007). It is a particularly attractive supplier of oil to the United States as it is not Muslim and not a member of OPEC, although Chinese oil companies are also active there.

Oil and gas companies in Equatorial Guinea operate as enclaves removed from the broader economy and society. When Marathon Oil built its US$1.5 billion gas facility there, it flew in manual workers from India, Sri Lanka and the Philippines who had previous experience of working on similar projects, and required less oversight than local workers who would have to be trained (Maass 2009). If you pick up a phone in the complex you are in the Texas area dialling code and consequently placing a call to a number in the rest of Equatorial Guinea is calling 'internationally'. These oil compounds then operate as almost separate sovereignties for MNCs, similar in ways to the Chinese SEZs discussed later. One area, again, where there is local job creation, however, is in the sex industry, which has sprung up around oil compounds. This contributes to the spread of sexually transmitted diseases and puts strain on the rudimentary and under-funded health infrastructure in the country.

Equatorial Guinea, by virtue of its oil wealth, is one of the richest countries in the world in per-head terms. From when oil was discovered in the mid-1990s, the country's economy has grown an incredible forty times bigger. During that time it has sometimes had the fastest-growing economy in the world, although this is merely a reflection of a rising oil price and production, rather than economic diversification and development. It performs poorly in terms of educational attainment and life expectancy, showing that the standard of living is very low for most people.

In 2009 there was a difference of ninety places in its position in the Human Development Index of the United Nations – which is a composite of literacy, life expectancy and income – versus its GDP. While Equatorial Guinea has a higher income per head than Italy at number 28 in the world, in terms of what can be bought locally it comes in at 118th position on the Index. Meanwhile the size of oil revenues is a state secret and President Obiang has purchased himself a US$55 million Boeing 737 airliner with gold-plated bathroom fixtures.

According to a Marathon Oil executive, however, Equatorial Guinea's oil reserves may be gone in a decade (Oliveira 2007), leaving open the question of what will replace them.

Relations between the oil companies and the Obiang autocracy are close, with many companies renting properties from Obiang's relatives, for example. Not only that but, as one of the President's sons explained, 'Cabinet ministers and public servants in Equatorial Guinea are by law allowed to own companies that, in consortium with a foreign company, can bid for foreign contracts' (quoted in Maass 2009, p. 43). Perhaps unsurprisingly, the oil companies received very good deals, with the government getting only 15 to 40 per cent of the revenues from its oil and gas, and only 12 per cent of oil revenues in the first year of its contract with ExxonMobil (Klein 2005), which was still sufficient to provide untold riches to the Obiang family.

In 2006 more than two-fifths of the country's cabinet were relatives of President Obiang, and his bodyguard is Moroccan as locals – or, in the President's terminology, 'strangers' from outside his family – cannot be trusted (Ghazvinian 2007; Shaxson 2007). The Minister for Agriculture and Forestry is the President's son Teodoro, who owns the country's only private radio station, has a mansion in Malibu and dated the American pop star Eve. He is widely tipped to succeed his father.

Relations with the United States are now also close, in spite of the former Equato-Guinean Foreign Minister claiming the American ambassador there in the 1990s was involved in witchcraft, and the regime harassing and killing journalists, missionaries and aid workers (Oliveira 2007). Perhaps this is because Equatorial Guinea is ostensibly a 'democratic country', with President Obiang getting 97 per cent of the votes in the last election. Perhaps having his name pre-printed on ballots and soldiers overseeing voting helped (Shaxson 2007).

Although the US State Department noted these elections were 'flawed', relations continue to deepen. This mirrors relations with Nigeria where the deeply unpopular President Obasanjo purportedly won over 90 per cent of the votes in the Niger Delta region in the 2003 election (Oliveira 2007). As Joseph Stalin once remarked, 'It's not who votes that counts but who counts the votes' (quoted in Clarke 2008, p. 369). As one of President Obiang's sons noted, 'The United States, like China, is careful not to get into internal issues' (quoted in Maass 2009, p. 48). Although, strictly speaking, this is not true, as the regime is effectively now buttressed by both the US and China. The US embassy in the capital Malebo is rented from President Obiang's uncle.

Such support is sometimes justified on the basis that, if American interests did not deal with unsavoury regimes, the Chinese would with even fewer conditions. So in this way the 'China threat' is actually useful to the US in Africa (Maass 2009). In reality, neither side sets any conditions on Obiang's government, which is close to Robert Mugabe in Zimbabwe, for example.[3] The social theorist Bauman (1998) has noted that globalization 'unites as it divides'. This is certainly true in an African context where state leaders are very supportive of each other and their struggles to remain in power, as the gulf between them and the masses grows wider. The Venezuelan state oil company PDVSA (Petróleos de Venezuela, SA) also cooperates with Equatorial Guinea. Thus it would appear when it comes to oil, human rights are a secondary concern for both 'socialist' and capitalist powers alike.

Corruption, Inequality, Wealth and Poverty: The Impacts of Oil in Angola

Angola has also had one of the world's fastest-growing economy in several of the last few years. While Angola is now China's largest supplier of oil (Alden 2007), the US is its main export market. China imported 9 billion dollars' worth of oil from Angola in 2006 (Michel, Beuret and Woods 2009).

The country is a paradox in that it is characterized by both huge wealth and poverty. You can now buy a $7,000 candelabra in Angola's new $35 m shopping mall, while 70 per cent of the country live below the poverty line (Perry 2007). Luanda is now the most expensive city on the planet and hotel rooms are booked months in advance (Ritzer 2010). Reportedly there are seven politicians or former politicians in Angola who are worth over US$100 million each. Meanwhile half of all children in Angola are malnourished and a child under five years of age dies of illness or hunger every three minutes (Michel, Beuret and Woods 2009).

President Dos Santos of Angola, who has been in power for thirty years, because of his overseas assets is thought to be the sixth-richest person in Brazil. He is protected by paramilitary 'ninjas', dressed in black. Thoughtfully, he sent 2,500 of these to Zimbabwe to protect the regime of fellow former 'socialist' leader Robert Mugabe in 2007.

Noted academic Ricardo Soares de Oliveira refers to West Africa's petro nations as 'successful failed states' (Oliveira 2007). For him, 'failed states provide nothing in the way of public goods to their citizenry, cannot cover their nominal territory and are frequently assaulted by insurgent groups which may prioritize plunder over the more classic goal of regime change' (p. 29).

The Angolan state has failed in terms of providing services and jobs for its population, but is successful in maintaining itself and enriching its office holders. According to one European diplomat, 'the trains may not run on time but the army and Sonangol [Angola's national oil company] work and that's all that's necessary' (quoted in Oliveira 2007, p. 63). The Angolan military is thought to be the second most capable in Africa, after South Africa's, and is 'battle-hardened' after years of civil war.

As the oil price soared until mid-2008, Angola had the world's fastest-growing economy that year and with the oil price rising again in 2009–10 Angola's government once again has a substantial revenue stream. However, the ordinary people see few of the benefits of this windfall, particularly as new loans are taken out and much of the oil revenue disappears. The anthropologist James Ferguson notes that the government in recent years has had very little net revenue because receipts from oil have been mortgaged through debt, and that the Angolan government has only been able to continue to run its day-to-day operations through additional borrowing (Ferguson 2006). Angolan politicians, generals and power brokers – 'Special Angolans' – specialize in 'evaporating' oil revenues. The IMF estimates that, at a *minimum*, US$1 billion 'evaporates' every year from Angolan government accounts.

Given the scale of inequality, oil production is associated with militarization and conflict in the country. Much of Angola's oil production takes place in Cabinda, an enclave in the north which is physically separated from the rest of the country by the Congo but, like the Niger Delta, racked by poverty. Separatists have been fighting for independence and 30,000 Angolan soldiers are deployed there (Oliveira 2007). Thus, while there is internal competition over the division of oil rents, this is mirrored in external competition for influence over the Angolan state.

There was substantial controversy in the early 2000s around the fact that the Angolan government rejected a loan from the IMF in favour of one from China's EXIM Bank, which is now the largest lender of funds to African governments. The IMF, at least in the post-Cold War era, has insisted on government transparency as part of its loan packages, whereas Chinese government lending famously comes with 'no [political] strings attached'. From 2002 to the time of writing, China's

EXIM Bank had lent the Angolan government US$4.5 billion, with the 'private' China International Fund (CIF) lending at least another 3 billion (*The Economist* 2010).[4]

The CIF is registered in Hong Kong and is the parent firm for all of the Chinese companies in Angola receiving funding under the loan agreements. It also receives all of the oil Angola supplies in return for loans (Michel, Beuret and Woods 2009). According to its website its mission is:

> To aim at South–South cooperation;
> To consider win-win situation as the key criterion while pursuing profits;
> To sincerely share experiences and achievements of China's economic
>   reforms with developing countries;
> To explore a new framework for Chinese enterprises to expand overseas;
> To introduce laudable concepts and worth-learning ideas from other
>   developing countries into China.

It is also active in Guinea but most of its website focuses on Angola, where it is building airports, railways, industrial zones, and hundreds of thousands of units of public housing, and an 'automotive industrial park' which will produce 30,000 sport utility vehicles a year (1 every 3 to 6 minutes), presumably for sale in Angola and the region.

While there are no political strings attached to Chinese loans, they do often come with economic conditions. In the case of the EXIM Bank loans to Angola, 70 per cent of the public tenders for the civil engineering and construction projects that the money finances have to be given to Chinese companies approved by Beijing. The Chinese government is fond of emphasizing the 'win-win' nature of Sino-African interactions; however, deals such as this could be considered a multifold 'win' on both economic and political grounds for China. In the first instance, they enable China to recycle its massive foreign exchange reserves, generated by export growth in China, and to access critical natural resources. They also enable China to build up its MNCs. For the infrastructure projects, the loans return to China twice, as they are repaid and Chinese companies are being contracted to implement them (Isaac 2010).

Chinese state-owned companies are less concerned about profit-ability, and somewhat more about strategic objectives, as they have access to China's massive foreign exchange reserves. The fact that Chinese companies often have access to state-subsidized finance means that they can outcompete rivals from other countries. As loans are often given to build infrastructure, this facilitates Chinese resource extraction and imports of manufactured goods, in a colonial-style pattern. The China Road and Bridge Corporation has around 500 active projects in Africa, for example (Ghazvinian 2007).

In line with China's 'go global' policy, overseas loans facilitate the development of Chinese MNCs, while at the same time building political capital and (inter)dependency with African political elites. Associated labour migration flows to Africa also deepen and lock in longer-term economic engagement.

In 2004 the Angolan government prevented BP from selling half of its oil Block 18 to the Indian Oil and Natural Gas Corporation, favouring the Chinese state-owned Sinopec company instead. Later, when the French oil giant Total's licence for its block was not renewed, Sinopec also got that. However, increased Chinese engagement is also subject to setbacks. In 2007 a deal to have Sinopec build a US$3 billion oil refinery in Lobito broke down as the Angolan state-owned oil company Sonangol announced it would build it itself. Money was now not an object for the Angolan government in the way that it had been a few years previously, as the country earned US$45 billion from oil sales in 2007 (Michel, Beuret and Woods 2009).

With the slump in the oil price in 2008–9, the power of Western-dominated financial institutions in Africa increased again. Angola, which was desperate for funds, consequently accepted a 27-month US$1.4 billion loan from the IMF. Thus the Angolan political economy is a cauldron in which the power of the West, China and local elites comes into competition and collaboration, with little benefit to local people. However, since the end of the civil war in 2002, the government has engaged in more 'legitimation' expenditures, as health and education are being improved and the government has a plan to build a million homes for shack dwellers by 2012, some of them delivered by the CIF as noted (*The Economist* 2010). Whether this ambitious target will be met remains to be seen.

Oil has been a mixed blessing for Angola. It has strengthened the corrupt and authoritarian government, while also opening up the possibility of limited redistribution. This has often been the case with other resources as well. While the oil sector has attracted much recent foreign investment in Africa, there has also been substantial interest in other energy resources, particularly uranium and biofuels as global oil reserves dwindle. The next chapter will focus on the nature and impacts of uranium exploration, and those of another increasingly important strategic metal, coltan.

6 POWERING AND CONNECTING THE GLOBAL ECONOMY THROUGH CONFLICT: URANIUM AND COLTAN

In their quest to obtain a highly priced mineral, colombo tantalite, which is used in cell phones and computers, rebel miners are killing thousands of highly endangered eastern lowland gorillas and elephants. (US Congressman Gilchrest, in Congressional Record 2001, p. 10330)

Uranium and (In)Security in the Sahel

Most people in Africa continue to rely on biomass for energy to cook – timber and sometimes dung, for example. However, as concerns about global climate disruption and the depletion of fossil fuels have increased, nuclear energy has received increasing interest as a potential alternative source of energy, at least in the rich countries. Given the dangers of climate change, even the well-known environmentalist James Lovelock is in favour of the further development of nuclear energy (Lovelock 2009).

China is now the world's largest greenhouse gas emitter and opens approximately one new coal-fired power plant weekly. However, the French builder of nuclear reactors Areva forecasts that between 150 and 300 new nuclear reactors will be built worldwide by 2030, and that a minimum of 50 of these will be in China and India (Shiva 2008). The newspaper the *International Herald Tribune* refers to this as a 'nuclear renaissance'.

France is heavily dependent on nuclear power, which accounts for over 70 per cent of all of the electricity generated in the country. Consequently it, and its companies, are keen to maintain good relations with uranium suppliers, and where these are former colonial possessions existing networks of influence may create a competitive advantage and/or resistance, depending on the context.

The scale of mining and processing of uranium is vast. As most deposits are low-grade, roughly 100,000 tons of rock have to be mined to get a ton of uranium and each standard reactor requires around 100 tons of uranium to function (Shiva 2008). Through a chemical process the uranium is treated so that it becomes enriched, while the remaining 85 per cent becomes depleted uranium which must be disposed of (or other uses found for it, such as in munitions). Depleted uranium shells are sometime used by the American military to pierce enemy armour, for example.

As noted earlier, Africa holds 18 per cent of the world's known recoverable uranium resources. There is already substantial competition around access to this resource on the continent, with Russia an important emerging player. Uranium mining has been associated with pollution and violent conflict in Niger, one of the world's biggest producers.

While worldwide demand for uranium was 80,000 tons in 2006 only 46,000 tons were mined (Michel, Beuret and Woods 2009). Consequently the price of the uranium used in nuclear reactors (U308) rose more than tenfold, from US$7.10 a pound in December 2001 to US$85 a pound in March 2007, before falling to US$45 by late 2009. This price spike generated a rush of new exploration interest in Africa, with active prospecting being undertaken in thirty-one countries.

Africa has two of the world's top ten uranium producers: Niger (8 per cent of world production), which is the world's third-biggest producer, and Namibia (7 per cent) (Southall 2009). Such was the scale of interest in new uranium exploration that the Ministry of Mines and Energy in Namibia had to suspend issuing new prospecting licences in 2007. As Namibia is a middle-income country with a strong regulatory environment, this led to a shift of interest to Niger, which is a very low-income country which has experienced significant conflict, detailed below.

More recently there are reports that an Indian company has signed a uranium exploration agreement in Namibia, and Chinese and Russian companies have also been active there. This fits with the broader Chinese strategy of diversification of energy suppliers. According to the Vice-President of China National Nuclear, 'China won't rely on any single supplier of uranium because of energy security considerations' (quoted in Finch 2007a). The Chinese President had visited Namibia in 2007 and given out a grant and low-interest loans in order to boost Chinese tourism there – using China's economic power to build trust and gratitude and pave the way for resource deals.

While there is competition between different national companies for access to resources, there is also cooperation between them, as noted earlier in relation to the oil sector. In 2007 the French nuclear giant Areva bought out the South African company Uramin, which had operations in both Namibia and Niger. However, it later agreed to sell a 49 per cent stake in the company to China Guangdong Nuclear Power Company and China's sovereign wealth funds.[1] In this case this partnership would enable Areva to access more easily the growing Chinese market, including that for construction of power plants (*Shanghai Daily* 2008). Competition in Niger has been intense, partly around uranium, but also partly and indirectly around oil.

Oil, (In)Security and Uranium in Niger: A Volatile Mix

Niger has the lowest Human Development Index rating in the world and recently, again, has suffered from 'internal' conflict. This is, in part, the outcome of US security strategy in the Sahel.

In 2003 32 European tourists were kidnapped in Algeria and transported out of the country, purportedly by an Islamic fundamentalist group led by a former army officer known popularly by his *nomme de guerre* – 'El Para'. This led to the United States sending 400 Army Rangers special forces to the Chad–Niger border regions in the following weeks to pursue him.

According to the noted Africa expert Jeremy Kennan, this was part of an elaborate deception to achieve a US military presence in the region for strategic reasons (Kennan 2009). As he puts it, 'prior to March 2003, there had almost certainly been no act of terror, in the conventional meaning of the term, anywhere in this vast region of Africa. And yet, by the end of 2004, senior US military personnel were describing the Sahara as a "swamp of terror"' (p. 40). Insurance rates on major projects in Africa, which are a good measure of terrorist risk, were amongst the lowest in the world at that time. However, this region is between oil-rich North and West Africa, and particularly strategically important for that reason. This rhetoric of terror laid the groundwork for the setting up of AFRICOM, and between 2002 and 2008 the United States gave half a billion dollars to Mali, Chad,

Niger and Mauritania for border security (Michel, Beuret and Woods 2009).

The insertion of US special forces in this region led to militarization and conflict and was partly responsible for sparking a rebellion amongst the Tuareg people in Niger (Kennan 2009). In 2007 the Niger Movement for Justice targeted national security forces for attack, in addition to foreign mining interests. In common with rebels in Darfur, Sudan and the Niger Delta, they were aggrieved by the lack of perceived benefit from the region's mineral resources, and also pollution from uranium mining. This exclusion of local African populations from the benefits of mineral resources, while they are often forced to bear the environmental costs, was a pattern established under colonialism. For example in Namibia, the Germans established the *Sperrgebiet* ('forbidden zone') along parts of its coastline to prevent locals looking for diamonds (Philips 2007).

A Tuareg spokesman in Niger, Boutali Tchiwerin, argued that:

The exploitation of uranium by Areva and its subsidiaries has contributed to the impoverishment of the area by accelerating the phenomenon of turning the area into more of a desert by plundering of the natural resources and the draining of the fossil deposits. It is undoubtedly an ecological catastrophe and a continuing human tragedy which threatens the existence of one of the oldest civilizations of this Sahara. (quoted in Finch 2007b)

As with many other natural resource exploitation projects in Africa, foreign workers have been brought in, exacerbating local grievances. Nonetheless, Areva is Niger's largest private-sector employer, with 2,000 workers at its Akouta and Arlit mines, in addition to other jobs around the country, and the income from these jobs supports an estimated 200,000 people (Michel, Beuret and Woods 2009).

While Areva does give money for health and educational programmes in Niger, as do many other multinational companies in other resource-rich regions in Africa, the company website notes: 'But it's true that the local conflict facing the country complicates the exercise of social and corporate responsibility. The expectations of the population and the communities are, frankly, huge' (Areva 2009). It depends of course what 'huge' means in this context – a clean environment and a reasonable standard of living?

The government of Niger has been looking to reduce its traditional dependence on France and as competition over resource access increases, its bargaining power over royalties from uranium is strengthened. In 2007 the government established a joint venture with the China National Uranium Corporation to develop the uranium deposits at Azelik, Agadez and Madaouela (the latter beside Areva's operation in Arlit).

According to the Niger Minister of Foreign Affairs in 2007, 'Areva's monopoly has been smashed' (quoted in Michel, Beuret and Woods 2009, p. 59). The timing of the signing of the uranium mining agreement with the Chinese may have been calculated as a provocation to France as it was signed on 14 July – Bastille Day. The Niger President's son was commercial attaché in Hong Kong at the time and was involved in the negotiations, and Canadian and British companies and the Indian firm Taurian Resources Pvt. Ltd have also been granted permits to prospect for uranium in the southern part of the country (Naidu 2008).

Some Chinese companies had previously established a presence in Niger, with textile company Enitex being bought by a Chinese company in 1997 (Michel, Beuret and Woods 2009). Paradoxically, Western-dominated institutions which give loans to Niger – such as the World Bank – facilitated Chinese involvement there. As part of its free market policies of economic liberalization, the World Bank had insisted that all infrastructure contracts be opened up to international bidding in order to reduce prices and potential corruption. Chinese companies won all of the contracts.

After the signing of the uranium agreement, however, the Chinese Deputy Manager was kidnapped and the Tuareg rebels declared the Chinese contracts invalid. All of the Chinese workers at the Teguiddan-Tessoum site were evacuated, and the Niger government accused Areva of sponsoring the rebels, despite the fact that they had also attacked Areva facilities in April of that year (Michel, Beuret and Woods 2009). This may have been partly a way of exerting pressure on Areva to improve the terms of its deals with the Niger government. Work on the Azelik deposit was suspended, although there are now attempts to revive it.

There were more dramatic events to follow in July of 2007 when the commander in Niger's army tasked with protecting Areva's interests defected to the Tuareg rebels, along with two dozen of his men (Michel, Beuret and Woods 2009). After this defection the rebels seemed to lose interest in, and indeed tolerated, Areva, instead directing their attention to the Chinese investments.

Areva also refused to hand over the geographical surveys it had completed of the Madaouela site to the new Chinese incumbent. The

Chinese subsequently backed out and the contract for this site went to a company called Ivanhoe, which is affiliated with the giant mining conglomerate Rio Tinto, whose founder and co-director is known as 'Toxic Bob' Friedland as a result of his involvement in a number of ecological scandals (Michel, Beuret and Woods 2009). One company he chaired was responsible for the worst cyanide release in the history of the United States.

In 2008 Areva had re-established better relations with the government and signed a deal to develop a uranium mine in Imouraren, which may become the second-biggest in the world. 'Of course, things have changed since the competition rode into town. Areva will have to pay twice as much to mine the yellow cake as it did previously and will have to surrender a significant amount of it to the government, that is, President Tandja and his inner circle' (Michel, Beuret and Woods 2009, p. 110). While the uranium sector attracts increased investment as a result of the conflict the tourism industry collapsed, and when the Niger military banned stockpiling of fuel to try to disrupt rebel movements, local farmers had trouble bringing their produce to market. The makings of a 'conflict complex' were being put in place.

The Central African Republic (CAR) also holds substantial uranium reserves and has been historically afflicted by conflict. According to one commentator,

> the overarching goal is to take African resources and funnel them towards French corporations. The CAR itself is a base from which the French can access resources all over Africa. That is why it is so important. They use it to keep the oil flowing to French companies in Chad, the resources flowing from Congo, and so on...CAR has a lot of uranium, which the French badly need because they are so dependent on nuclear power. At the moment they get their uranium from Niger, but CAR is their back-up plan. (John Hari, *The Independent*, 19 February 2007, quoted in Arnold 2009, p. 119)

In 2006 French jets fired on rebel positions in CAR to enable government troops to advance (Reuters 2006).

The globalization of the economy is implicated in the globalization of militarization but there are many other chains or webs brought about and facilitated by this phenomenon, which is ultimately dependent on resources. Uranium is used to provide power which can be stored in another metal vital to the functioning of the global economy, which is also associated with conflict in Africa: coltan.

Conflict and Coltan in the Congo: War in the Great Lakes

> Foreign powers, with the collaboration of some of our Congolese brothers, organise wars with the resources of our country. These resources, which should be used for our development, for the education of our children, to cure our illnesses, in short so that we can have a more decent human life, serve only to kill us. (Bishop Emmanuel Kataliko, quoted in Renton, Seddon et al. 2007, p. 172)

> Seriously, someone help me. I want to go to Congo so that I can also get something to show my grand children in future. (Letter to the Editor, *The Monitor*, Kampala, quoted in Turner 2007, p. 49)

The Great Lakes region of Africa gets its physical geography and name from the fact that the region's underlying tectonic plates are separating. Here is one of the places where the continent is slowly being broken apart (Jenkins 2007). This physical process is mirrored in the tearing of the socio-political fabric of many countries of the region as a result of conflict centred on resources.

Coltan is an abbreviation for colombite-tantalite from which the precious metals Colombium and Tantalum are extracted (Tantalum-Niobium International Study Centre, cited in Tegera, Mikolo et al. 2002). This is a rare metal which looks like black mud, but serves a vital role in the global informational economy. Tantalum is twice as dense as steel and can capture and release an electrical charge, which makes it vital for capacitors in portable miniaturized electronic equipment such as mobile phones and computers (Hayes and Burge n.d.).

Much of the world's reserves of coltan – around 9% by some estimates – is found in the DRC, although Australia is the world's largest producer given greater economic and institutional stability in that country. As the use of mobile phones and other personal electronic devices around the world exploded in the 1990s, demand for coltan skyrocketed. From 1990 to 1999 the sales of tantalum capacitors increased by 300 per cent (Montague 2002).

Since the colonial era, what is now the DRC has been plagued by conflict. The initial post-independence leader, Patrice Lumumba, was deposed, and subsequently executed, in a coup reportedly carried out by elements of the military with the support and encouragement of the Belgian and American governments. Mobutu Seso Seko, who was Chief of Staff in the army, then came to power until 1997. His given name was previously Joseph Mobutu, but on assuming the presidency he adopted his new name, which had at least two translations: 'The Ngbandi translation reads, "the warrior who knows no defeat because of his endurance and inflexible will and is all powerful, leaving fire in his wake as he goes from conquest to conquest". In Tshiluba, the name translates to "invincible warrior, Cock who leaves no chick intact"' (Callaghy 1979, p. 341, quoted in Dunn 2001, p. 239). Mobutu ran down the country over thirty years, until he was eventually deposed by a rebellion.

While copper had been Zaire's (now DRC's) main export, the disastrously corrupt reign of Mobutu meant it declined in importance during his rule. Whereas the United States supported Mobutu during the Cold War as an anti-communist bulwark, it subsequently withdrew its support, and while the World Bank and the IMF had previously been willing to overlook gross abuses, perhaps in deference to the wishes of their most important shareholder (the US), they also withdrew their support from Zaire. Some argue that this was what sparked the collapse of the copper industry, and indeed the economy at large in Zaire, creating fertile conditions for conflict (Clark 2002a).

Copper mining requires substantial capital investment and institutionalization to be successful. It was replaced in Zaire as an export by diamonds, which, if they are arable or found in the soil, can be harvested with picks and shovels. By 1995 diamonds accounted for roughly 47 per cent of Zaire's export earnings, and an estimated three-quarters of them were being smuggled out of the country (MacGaffey, Bazenguissa-Ganga et al. 2000, cited in Renton, Seddon et al. 2007).

When Laurent Kabila launched his rebellion against Mobutu in 1996 he was supported by the governments of Uganda and Rwanda. The Rwandan military invasion of Congo was spurred by the desire to attack the remnants of the *Interahamwe* ('we hunt together') militias responsible for the genocide in Rwanda in 1994 and who continued to attack the country from bases in Congo. Some have also suggested that 'over-populated' Rwanda was seeking 'Lebensraum' ('living room') over the border in Congo. Others argue that it wished to create a buffer zone in Congo as an obstacle to rebels staging attacks from there (Turner 2002). However, these governments were certainly not unaware of Congo's immense mineral wealth. Beginning in 1998, aircraft began to fly to Congo from military airports in Uganda and Rwanda carrying military equipment, arms and soldiers. On the return trips, they brought back gold, coffee and apparently diamond traders and soldiers (Turner 2007).

There was also global geopolitics involved in the Rwandan and Ugandan armies' invasion of the DRC. According to Renton, Seddon et al. (2007), the White House backed the invasion and planned to use the Rwandan army as an instrument of American influence in the region. The RPF troops were trained under the American Enhanced International Military and Education and Training Programme (E-IMET). There was already intense geo-economic and political competition between France and the United States in the Great Lakes region at that time (Schraeder 2000). The shift of Rwanda into the Anglo sphere of influence was evidenced subsequently by the dropping of French as an official language and its replacement by English, and the country joining the Commonwealth in 2009. American interest centred on 'containing' Sudan regionally, although there may also have been economic interests at play as the US Department of Defense classifies coltan as a strategic mineral (Lalji 2007). Despite being a small impoverished country, with Western support Rwanda fielded 10,000 troops in the Congo (Arnold 2009).

Before Mobutu was overthrown, Western and South African mining houses were signing huge deals with Laurent Kabila. De Beers and American Mineral Fields reportedly signed contracts with him worth an estimated US$3 billion a year, for example (Renton, Seddon et al. 2007). In some cases companies such as Barrick Gold and Banro American Resources were accused of 'funding military operations in exchange for lucrative contracts in the east of the DRC' (Braeckman 1999, quoted in Montague 2002, p. 106). The co-founder of American Mineral Fields even allowed rebels to use his private Lear Jet (Block 1997, cited in Montague 2002). Numerous other companies either expressed interest or signed contracts to exploit mineral resources. Sometimes these small 'junior' mining companies may have bought the concessions on a speculative basis.

In July 1998 when Laurent Kabila made the decision, for domestic political reasons, to expel the Rwandan army, this led to a second war. This coincided with another nationalist or nationalizing decision. It was two days after his government moved to nationalize the main coltan mining company in 1998 that the rebellion to overthrow him began, reportedly with the support of the directors of the company which was being expropriated.

This war in Congo brought in seven other African armies at its height (those of Rwanda, Uganda, Burundi, Namibia, Chad, Angola and Zimbabwe), and this regional scramble was partly fuelled by coltan (Nest 2006). According to Dena Montague (2002, p. 102), 'the Uganda People's Defence Forces and the Rwandan Patriotic Army, as well as the Congolese rebels they each support – the Rally for Congolese Democracy (RCD) and Congolese Liberation Front – have each ruthlessly exploited the mineral wealth from the territories under their respective control'. In areas controlled by the Rwandan army, the Walikale people were 'driven into regroupment camps' where they were then forced to mine coltan (Longman 2002). Brutal techniques were used to gain control of these areas, with the United Nations arguing that the various rebel groups, with which the Rwandans and Ugandans colluded, used rape and cannibalism in order to intimidate people into submission. It was, in part, a 'war against women' (Colette Braeckman, quoted in Turner 2007). The freedom offered by mobile phones is not free for some people, who have to pay for the 'bloody externalities of electronics' (Patel 2009). In 2000, prices for coltan spiked tenfold – largely as a result of the launch of the Sony PlayStation 2 games console and new mobile phone handsets – rising to US$365 a pound in the Eastern DRC (Lalji 2007).

Much of the coltan in Eastern Congo is mined in two world heritage sites: Kahuzi-Biega National Park and Okapi Wildlife Reserve (World Conservation Union 2001). In the Kahuzi-Biega park, which was at one point controlled by Congolese rebels and the Rwandan army, only 2 elephant families out of 350 remained in 2000 (Koyome and Clark 2002).[2] Outside of the parks in Rwanda, unregulated coltan mining destabilized hillsides, leading to landslides and damaging future agricultural potential. Half of the land that was seized for unplanned artisanal coltan mining cannot now be used for agriculture (Tegera, Mikolo et al. 2002; Nest and Grignon 2006). The 'resource pull effect' has also been in evidence (Basedau 2005). According to a coltan miner in the DRC: 'We think that agricultural activities are a good thing, but we cannot see ourselves taking them up again in the short term because we earn much more money from coltan. However we are thinking of investing coltan money in agriculture and cattle once peace returns' (quoted in Tegera, Mikolo et al. 2002).

Other wildlife has also been affected by coltan mining. ' "I'm not in favor of killing gorillas," says Dick Rosen, CEO of AVX, a tantalum capacitor maker in Myrtle Beach, S.C. [South Carolina] but "we don't have an idea where [the metal] comes from. There's no way to tell. I don't know how to control it," he says' (quoted in Essick 2001). As the British MP Oona King noted, 'Kids in Congo are being sent down into mines to die so that kids in Europe and America can kill imaginary aliens in their living rooms' – or text each other (quoted in Bush and Seeds 2008, p. 1). Up to 30,000 child soldiers were also conscripted into the Mai Mai militia to fight for control of the coltan-producing regions. They are known for their use of cannibalism as a weapon of war.

'The Congo's mineral affluence is balanced by a global greed for gadgets in which death becomes a currency (or in more crudely economic terms, an "externality") for the efficient flow of capital to digital distributors and investors' (Mantz 2008, p. 37). Apple Corporation, which produces iPods and iPhones that use coltan, says that it requires its suppliers to certify that the materials they use have been produced in a 'socially and environmentally responsible process', but argues that the supply chain is long and complex (Fung 2010).

Other precious metals were also looted in Congo. The IMF has praised Uganda for its export-led growth, driven by commodities such as gold, despite the fact that the country has almost no domestic deposits (Renton, Seddon et al. 2007). Indeed, in 1997 gold and gold compounds became Uganda's second-largest export earner (Clark 2002). This 'strong economic performance' ensured continuing inflows of aid from the West, with aid accounting for 55 per cent of Uganda's budget between 2000 and 2001. However, the United States showed its displeasure at the second Ugandan invasion of Congo by suspending all military aid (Clark 2002). In Uganda, taxpayers paid for the cost of the war while President Museveni and close associates reaped its economic benefits (Koyome and Clark 2002).

As implied above, the Rwandan and Ugandan invasion of DRC sparked other African governments to send in their militaries to protect the Kabila government. For example, Robert Mugabe's government had loaned Kabila several million dollars to fund his overthrow of Mobutu. Consequently Zimbabwe's army intervened on Kabila's side, at great expense, estimated at up to US$1 million a day (Carmody 2007). Zimbabwe's ruling party was rewarded for its support by a company run by some of its 'leading lights' receiving a contract to log or exploit 33 million hectares of forest in Congo, an area roughly ten times the size of Switzerland or the same size as the UK (Zeilig 2002). Timber and diamonds were also used as conflict resources.

After the second Ugandan invasion of 1998, the Ugandan-Thai forest company DARA-Forest set up operations in the Ituri region of Orientale Province. Satellite imagery subsequently showed that a huge area of forest had been logged by the company (Koyome and Clark 2002). In 2007 the son of the Chief Executive Officer of Zimbabwe Defence Industries was arrested in Zimbabwe with consignments of diamonds and gold, presumably from Congo. At the same time a Major in the air force was arrested holding US$49 million in diamonds and US$98 million in gold (Southall and Comninos 2009).

By 2000 Zimbabweans had secured rights to exploit two of the DRC's main diamond areas, and Namibians and Angolans, who also fought on Kabila's side, received similar concessions (Renton, Seddon et al. 2007). Nonetheless, the Angolans may have ordered Kabila's subsequent assassination, as he was thought to be ineffective at winning the war through force or negotiating a conclusion (Turner 2002).

When the price of coltan fell dramatically in 2001, rebels in Eastern Congo were forced to look for other sources of revenue and the war appeared to end in 2003 (*Gorilla Journal* 2001). However, problems with the Australian coltan supply chain, which accounts for 41 per cent of global production, again led to rapidly rising prices. The spot price for tantalum ore rose approximately 30 per cent from 2007 to 2008 (Vetter 2008) and was implicated in the return to large-scale conflict in the Eastern DRC (John Prendergast, interviewed on CNN's *Daily Show, Global Edition*). However, the Rwandan government 'arrested' the warlord responsible for the renewed violence, Laurent Nkunda, whom it had previously supported in 2009, perhaps in an attempt to curry favour with the incoming Obama administration in the US (Erlinder 2009).

Laurent Nkunda, who likes to be referred to as 'the chairman', one of the main rebel leaders in Congo, was apparently being bankrolled by Rwandan businessmen eager to maintain access to coltan in North Kivu (François Grignon, cited in Arnold 2009). Within a month of Barack Obama coming to power, his former Rwandan government backers had mounted a joint military operation against him with the Congolese. According to Peter Erlinder, Nkunda simply knew too much about the Rwandan government's crimes in Congo to be left on the loose. A draft United Nations report accuses the Rwandans of genocide in Congo.

Another possible explanation for the change of heart by the Rwandan government was that Nkunda had challenged the Chinese presence in Congo. Reportedly, when the former Nigerian President, Obasanjo, visited him on behalf of the UN, one of Nkunda's demands was that DRC revisit its contracts with Chinese companies so that its natural resources would not be 'sold off on the cheap' (quoted in Michel, Beuret and Woods 2009, p. 256). The new President, Joseph Kabila, who came to power after his father had been assassinated, had trained at a military academy in Beijing and declared that he wanted to make Congo 'the China of Africa' (Marriage 2010).

The exploitation of cassiterite, which is used in electronic circuitry, in Congo has also been highly controversial. In 2008, 'some of the world's best known consumer electronics companies', such as Microsoft and Hitachi, were forced to examine their global supply chains after it was suspected that some of the cassiterite used in their products was being mined illegally at a site controlled by a renegade brigade of the Congolese army, using slave labour (*Financial Times*, 6 March 2008). When the Congolese government suspended all mining activities in the district, the price of cassiterite shot up to US$18,000 a tonne. The army was also reportedly confiscating cassiterite from artisanal miners, some of whom were as young as twelve.[3]

While a Conflict Coltan and Cassiterite Act was introduced in the US Congress to prohibit the importation of these minerals from Congo if any rebel groups would benefit from their sale, this may simply have led to geographical substitution effects as coltan mined in Congo was rerouted to other markets. In any event, according to a British journalist, 80 per cent of Congo's coltan is sent to Australia for processing (cited in Bush and Seeds 2008).

There are, however, efforts underway to institutionalize resource extraction in Congo as, in 2008, China agreed a US$9 billion loan to rebuild thousands of miles of roads and railways and build hospitals and health centres in exchange for the rights to five copper and cobalt mines in the south of the country. This was subsequently reduced to US$6 billion under pressure from the World Bank and IMF (Kabemba 2010). This deal will allow the extraction of an incredible 10 million tonnes of copper over thirty years.

In contrast to deals sponsored by some Western institutions, this one was by some accounts only seven pages long, and did not include any environmental or social impact assessment statements. When investing, China is often able to cut through bureaucratic red tape which hampers other investors, because Chinese investment is 'tied to grants and takes place at executive levels at the stage of negotiation' (Dubosse 2010, p. 80).

The Congolese were not in a strong bargaining position as the minerals they were giving access to are worth between US$39.7 billion and US$83.6 billion, but 'if you are drowning, you don't look at the hand that is reached towards you, you just grab it' (Kabwe 2007, quoted in Marysse and Geenen 2009, p. 373). The Congolese government did, however, manage to secure agreement that only 20 per cent of the workforce would be Chinese; that half of 1 per cent of the investment would be allocated to training; and that 1 and 3 per cent would be spent on social and environmental projects respectively in the surrounding areas (Kaplinsky and Farooki 2009). The government was also able to use the leverage afforded by the Chinese to renegotiate sixty 35-year mining agreements with Western companies.

According to one major Belgian-Congolese investor, 'the West talks about good governance and attaches some impossible conditions to its development aid. The Chinese niggle less and they are taking the best parts' (Georges Forrest, quoted in Marysse and Geenen 2009, p. 375). In 2007 the heads of more than a dozen Western mining companies meeting in Switzerland complained that they were being undercut by Chinese companies who were able to link infrastructure deals with resource provision (Southall 2009).

In Congo the government has previously looked at potential Western investors to develop the mines granted to the Chinese in Katanga, but it was not felt they could raise sufficient resources. On the other hand, as noted earlier, the fact that Chinese state-owned companies are able to access China's several trillion dollars in foreign exchange reserves (the largest in the world), indirectly through China's EXIM Bank, puts them at a substantial competitive advantage. The long-term developmental impacts of the Chinese investment in Congo remain open or unclear. The country is also a major source of timber for China, to which the next chapter now turns.

7 FURNISHING AND FEEDING THE WORLD? TIMBER, BIOFUELS, PLANTS, FOOD AND FISHERIES

Timber traders have effectively bought the right to pillage the country's [Madagascar's] parks with impunity. They are extracting up to $800,000 a day worth of timber. (Reiner Tegtmeyer, quoted in Lough 2009)

It is not just Africa's minerals which are of increasing interest to outside powers and companies, but also land: not necessarily to grow old staple cash crops, such as cotton, the vital raw material for the first industrial revolution, but now to gain access to timber, food and bio-fuels. Land is what the famous historian Karl Polanyi called a fictitious commodity (Polanyi 1944). It is something bought and sold on the market, but not produced through market mechanisms. It is consequently a limited resource over which there will be increasing competition, despite the fact that there are now some substitutes – such as hydroponics, which allow vegetables to be grown in a chemical solution for example.

Fuelling Dispossession? Biofuels

Biofuels, as the name implies, are fuels (solid, liquid and gas) derived from biomass, a renewable resource that can potentially be harvested sustainably. Biofuels are made from biomass through biochemical (fermentation of sugar to alcohol, and anaerobic digestion or fermentation) or thermochemical processes (gasification, pyrolysis, liquefaction). (Amigun, Sigamoney and von Blottnitz 2006, p. 695)

The development of biofuels has been highly controversial both in Africa and globally for a number of reasons. So-called 'first generation' biofuels are derived from sugar, vegetable oil, starch or animal fats and the feedstocks for these are often grains, such as wheat, or maize. Without getting into the technical details, these feedstocks are being diverted from the human and animal food chain and consequently the price of these grains is pushed up. According to Vandana Shiva, 'industrial biofuels are not the fuels of the poor; they are the foods of the poor transformed into heat, electricity, and fuel for the rich' (Shiva 2008, p. 78). One UN official recently claimed that turning food crops into biofuel was a 'crime against humanity' because of the way in which it contributed to food price increases and left millions of people hungry (Ferrett 2007). He called for a five-year moratorium on the production of biofuels. Thus, while the deals currently being negotiated in Africa may enhance other places' food and energy security, they may compromise them in Africa. Filling up a 25-gallon tank of a sport utility vehicle uses the equivalent of over 450 pounds of corn, containing enough calories to feed a person for a full year (Runge and Senauer 2007).

According to John Mathews (2007, p. 3550), 'if the United States and Europe are serious about biofuels they must turn to the South for their supplies', while Amigun, Sigamoney and von Blottnitz (2006, p. 694) simply state: 'Africa is an unexploited resource for biofuels development.' The EU has set targets for 20 per cent renewable energy and 10 per cent biofuels in vehicle fuel by 2020 (Boddinger 2007). While the diversion of feedstock to biofuels could not account for the entire food price inflation of recent years, it certainly contributed substantially. Wheat prices rose 86 per cent in 2007 globally, and the World Bank estimated that an additional 130–55 million people around the world would be pushed into poverty by increases in food and fuel prices in 2008 (cited in Honahan 2009). Even after price falls in the latter part of 2008, global food prices remained above their long-term levels and, at retail level, prices continued to increase in many African countries as a result of local supply issues. For example, prices of white maize (the staple food) increased by 107 per cent in Malawi in the first eleven months of 2008. According to an internal World Bank report, biofuels were responsible for forcing up food prices by 75 per cent. Thus industrial biofuel crops may contribute to hunger and landlessness.

Cassava is the cheapest source of calories for most tropical countries. Cassava is a tuber like a potato and a staple food across much of Africa. However, it can also be used to make ethanol (a biofuel).

In Africa 200 million people depend on cassava as their staple food; however, largely as a result of its diversion to make the alcohol ethanol, prices for it are projected to increase by 135 per cent, according to one study (Boddinger 2007).

So-called 'second generation' biofuels, which are not derived from food crops – such as those derived from switch grass – do not compete with food production and therefore do not create food price inflation, except in as much as they may reduce available land area. Advocates also argue that, as they fix carbon from the atmosphere while growing, they are a carbon-neutral source of energy. However, there may still be issues with population displacement and deforestation, and a number of studies in the journal *Science* have shown that biofuels release more carbon dioxide than conventional fuels if the costs of forest clearing and processing are taken into account (Shiva 2008). Furthermore, a recent study of biofuels by the Smithsonian Tropical Research Institute found that while twenty-one of them did have reduced greenhouse gas emissions of 30 per cent or more when compared to petrol, twelve actually had a worse environmental impact than fossil fuels (Cochrane 2008). According to Runge and Senauer (2007, p. 7), the 'full cycle of the production and use of corn-based ethanol releases less greenhouse gases than does that of gasoline, but only by 12 to 26 per cent'.

Some studies have estimated that there are up to 700 million hectares of 'surplus land' in SSA which could be used to grow energy crops (Smeets, Faaij and Lewandowsky 2004). This is almost the same amount of land as the total for the contiguous land area of the United States (the forty-eight states). This idea, that there are surplus land and labour in Africa, which can be used for the benefit of other places and to raise incomes in Africa, has a long history. It is known as 'vent-for-surplus'. However, some have cast doubt on this idea that African societies have extensive underutilized resources. In fact, in many African societies at harvest time there are labour shortages, so which crops get harvested becomes an important consideration. Will labour diverted to biofuel crops detract from food production?

Mozambique is one of the countries which have been identified as having high biofuel production potential. However, 64 per cent of Mozambicans suffer from poor nutrition, with a calorie intake below 2,100 per day (Batidzirai, Faaij et al. 2006). Plantations for biofuels require a minimum of 100 acres for large-scale production, and consequently the vast majority of them are corporate-owned. While the government of Mozambique has stated that only 9 per cent of the arable land in that country is currently under cultivation, local people rely on this land for grazing animals and wild food gathering (Toulmin 2009). Furthermore, if biofuel production increases land prices, this will put additional pressure on the poor.

Jatropha curcas is a biofuel tree indigenous to Central America and was brought to Asia and Africa by Dutch and Portuguese mariners (Shiva 2008). The advantage of this plant is that it can grow in poor soil not suitable for other crops. According to some proponents, it doesn't need water, fertilizers or pesticides, and a recent study by Goldman Sachs found that it only cost US$43 to produce a barrel of fuel from *Jatropha*, so it is highly cost-effective (Cochrane 2008). However, other studies have cast doubt on its benefits, arguing that it does require substantial quantities of water for it to grow and that it also needs to be weeded, thereby contributing to soil erosion. Two states in Australia have banned the plant, particularly as it also has an invasive character – a tendency to spread uncontrollably. There are also concerns that it may have negative health consequences and contribute to elevated cancer risk for those who harvest it.

The production of biofuels has other class impacts. Who will benefit and who will lose from biofuels development is partly dependent on land tenure structures, which in Africa and many other parts of the developing world tend to be highly uneven. According to the Food and Agriculture Organization of the United Nations, 'unless the "complex agricultural structures that divert most profits to a small group become more equitable", the biofuel boom is not likely to benefit most of the world's poor' (Boddinger 2007, p. 924).[1]

Some of the deals being done are also reminiscent of the colonial era, as local leaders are sometimes duped into giving up their rights, as King Lobengula of the Ndebeles was in what is now Zimbabwe in 1889, when he signed the Rudd Concession which supposedly guaranteed that his kingdom would not be colonized (Pakenham 1991). In Ghana a Norwegian company called Biofuel Africa got the rights to clear and cultivate land after a village leader who could neither read nor write gave his consent with a thumbprint. The Ghanaian government eventually put a stop to the clear-cutting of forested land there, but reportedly only after 6,422 acres had been cut down (Knaup 2008), although the company involved disputes this figure (Kolnes 2008). In Tanzania thousands of residents have been displaced by the Swedish company Sekab so it can grow sugarcane to make ethanol.

In some cases African governments are actually – somewhat unbelievably – giving land away for free to promote biofuel production. In Tanzania the government has granted the British firm Sun Biofuels a 99-year lease on an area equivalent in size to 12,000 soccer pitches to grow *Jatropha*, for free. In return the company will be expected to spend US$20 million to build roads and schools (Knaup 2008). Prokon, a German company, has plans to cultivate with *Jatropha* an area the size of Luxembourg in Tanzania. As noted earlier there is also increased demand for African land to grow food for export.

Water is Life? Food, Flowers and Fuel for Whom?

Aside from biofuels, another aspect of the agricultural extroversion of Africa is that, as Bruce Lankford of the University of East Anglia has argued, 'we are exporting drought'. The UK's consumption of virtual water is much bigger than its actual consumption of water. Virtual water is a concept which takes into account the water used in the production of agricultural products. For example a mixed salad requires around 300 litres of water to grow it (Shiva 2008).

Recently there was a controversy in the British media when it was found that large-scale flower farms in Kenya growing for Tesco were diverting water from rivers, to the detriment of small-scale farmers. There are concerns that flower farming will dry out the Rift Valley Lakes as the Lake Naivasha region in Kenya is now Africa's biggest exporter of cut flowers to Europe. This trade was severely disrupted by the Icelandic ash cloud of 2009 as these flowers are air-freighted in chilled containers.

According to Tandon (2007, p. 8):

> Britain imported 18,000 tonnes of flowers from Kenya in 2005, nearly twice the amount it imported in 2001. There are no publicly available figures for how much water the companies extract from the lake but they are conservatively estimated to take at least 20,000 cubic metres of water a day on average. A combination of climate change, which is increasing the severity and frequency of droughts, and the over-extraction of water is now stretching the lake to its limits. 'Last year, we could walk right into the heart of the lake through the mud. We are literally watching over the lake as it makes its last kicks', said a security guard at one of the biggest flower farms (O Ogodo and J Vidal, 'The African paradise ravaged by roses', *The Guardian*, 14 February 2007).

Food exports are also an increasingly contentious issue. Whereas Africa was food self-sufficient in the 1960s, it now imports a quarter of all its food (Bello 2009). According to the United Nations, food price increases in the latter part of the 2000s may have completely reversed any poverty reduction in the previous decade and a half (United Nations Dept. of Economic and Social Affairs and UNCTAD 2008).

According to the noted economic historian Kevin O'Rourke (2009, p. 11):

> One of the most worrying news stories of last year was that involving Korea's Daewoo Logistics leasing almost half of Madagascar's arable land on a 99 year basis. According to initial reports, the land was to be leased for around US$12 an acre, but an article in the *Financial Times* subsequently reported that in fact Daewoo was planning to lease the land at zero cost, with increased employment opportunities for the locals being the sole payoff which would accrue to the African island.
>
> The alarming aspect of this story was not the fact that Daewoo's behaviour was pretty obviously exploitative. Rather, it was the Korean motivation for the deal: 'We want to plant corn there to ensure our food security. Food can be a weapon in this world,' said Hong Jong-wan, a manager at Daewoo. 'We can either export the harvests to other countries or ship them back to Korea in case of a food crisis.' In turn, this rationale can be explained by the fact that '[Food-importing countries] have lost trust in trade because of the price crisis this year' (in the words of Joachim von Braun, director of the International Policy Food Research Institute in Washington).

This deal provides a lens on a variety of issues. Daewoo planned to put three-quarters of the land area under corn, while the rest would be used to produce palm oil for biofuels (Walt 2008). South Korea is the third-largest corn importer in the world and had planned to replace half of its imported corn with supply from Madagascar. As noted in the quote above, in part this move was prompted by rapidly rising food prices in 2008, which sparked riots in poor countries around the world. More land cannot be produced to grow food and, as rising population and consumption put it at a premium, countries and companies will become increasingly keen to establish direct supply chains, rather than relying on the market. Thus, because of the growth which it has unleashed, market-led globalization may actually undercut itself over the longer term.

The South Koreans are also keen to diversify their energy supplies through biofuels and sourcing fossil fuels from non-traditional sources. In 2006 the South Korean President undertook an African tour to resource-rich countries, and a South Korean minister commented on the visit that 'closer cooperation with Africa's oil producers will help South Korea diversify its petroleum import sources' (Sohn Se-joo, quoted in Frynas and Paulo 2007, p. 232). According to a Professor at Hankuk University of Foreign Service, South Korea is also interested in receiving diplomatic support from African countries in the United Nations, as it contests with North Korea (Durban, South Africa, 27 July 2010), and Africa is becoming much more important as a market for the country. By 2009 there were forty-seven South Korean companies invested in Angola for example (Vines et al. 2009), and Africa's share of South Korean overseas development assistance rose from 8 to 19 per cent from 2005 to 2008 (UNCTAD 2010).

In Madagascar, the fact that land was being given on long-term lease to a foreign company while many people go hungry was partly responsible for the coup which brought Andry Rajoelina to power in 2009, and one of his first acts was to scrap the land deal. As he noted, 'in the constitution, it is stipulated that Madagascar's land is neither for sale nor for rent, so the agreement with Daewoo is cancelled' (quoted in BBC 2009). There were subsequent reports that, despite the coup and bloodshed, Daewoo continued to hold the land it had been granted, surreptitiously – although, given the political instability in the country, it was not clear whether or not the deal would go ahead. In addition to South Korea, the oil-rich countries of the Persian Gulf which run huge trade surpluses are also concerned about their food security, and their sovereign wealth funds also have potentially vast amounts of money to invest in the purchase of African land. In 2007 the Gulf States alone were earning from oil US$5 billion a week that they had to reinvest, much of it overseas. This is also potentially the case for China, which is increasingly concerned about sourcing sufficient food.

'In the first half of 2004, China had a trade deficit of foodstuffs of US$3.7 billion, including imports of 4.1 million tonnes of food grains. It is predicted that this deficit will soar in the future – in the case of food grains, to around 40 million tonnes in 2007' (Cutler, pers. comm., cited in Kaplinsky 2006, p. 990). However, according to UNCTAD, China exported more food than it imported in 2005, whereas – using different definitions – the Food and Agriculture Organization of the United Nations showed China having a food trade deficit of US$11.8 billion in 2005, although US$8.7 billion dollars of this was in soya beans, which are not a staple food in China and are mostly used for animal feed (Lines 2008).[2]

Given the strategic priority which China places on food security, it is not then a major importer of food, although with changing consumption patterns it is importing more animal feed. Of the US$138 billion increase in China's annual primary commodity imports since 1995, over US$85 billion was in ores, metals and fuels (UNCTAD 2007, cited in Lines 2008). This situation may change in the future though as water scarcity reduces grain yields in China as it is diverted to industrial and commercial uses. Grain production in Northern China fell by 50 million tons between 1998 and 2004 (Bergsten, Peterson Institute for International Economics et al. 2008). Chinese demand for another African land-based resource has, however, been voracious: timber.

The Timber Trade

Another issue which has generated worldwide concern in relation to the new scramble for Africa is its environmental impacts, with the Western media particularly focused on the impacts of Chinese investment and trade. In China, 30 per cent of the country has acid rain, three-quarters of its lakes are polluted, and two-thirds of a billion people drink water which is contaminated with human and animal waste (Leonard 2008). Consequently, environmental quality is not a top priority for most Chinese companies operating in Africa, although it is important not to overgeneralize and to analyse these problems dispassionately.[3] Some apocalyptic projections estimated that the last tree in Tanzania would already have been cut down by now (Chambers 2005).

Deforestation in Africa is, however, a serious problem, with an estimated 4 million hectares of forest lost each year: twice the world average rate of deforestation (Arnold 2009). According to some estimates, exports of forest products from SSA actually declined in the late 1990s – a reflection of forest depletion; however, wood removals are thought to have increased from 500 to 661 million cubic metres from 1990 to 2005, largely as a result of increased production of fuel wood (Holmberg 2005, cited in Southall 2009). The true figures are disputed but wide-scale legal and illegal logging continues.

Wood products, especially furniture and furniture components, flooring, and construction materials (e.g., doors, window frames), are significant value-adding industries for developing countries, and in 2005 nine out of twenty of the world's leading exporters of wood manufactures were developing or emerging economies (International Trade Centre 2008). Wood products are especially significant for developing economies because they are traditionally resource- and labour-intensive activities undertaken by a diverse group of enterprises, from craft-based micro-enterprises to larger-scale and high-volume producers (Kaplinsky and Readman 2000). China is the world's largest exporter of furniture as of 2006, when it overtook Italy.

Depending on the type, a single tropical tree can take more than 100 years to mature, and be worth tens of thousands of US dollars. The moabi tree, which grows in the Congo Basin, reaches up to 90 feet tall and can live for several hundred years, is particularly favoured by logging companies because its wood is hard and dark and consequently can fetch a high price. It is used for garden decking, for example, in Europe and the United States, although much of it is machined in China.

In Congo-Brazzaville the Chinese company Sicofor hires people to walk through the forests marking trees to be cut down. This particular forest concession includes a quota for cutting down 189 trees a day (Michel, Beuret and Woods 2009), and Congo-Brazzaville's Minister for Forestry and Environment is a major shareholder in the company. According to him:

> opening up the undergrowth to the logging of usable trees has allowed us to restore and rejuvenate the forest, creating better conditions for wildlife. Nowadays, you find more wildlife in the parts of the forest that have been opened up to logging companies than in the National Parks. In fact there's so much wild game in the logging areas that we're hoping to start holding big game hunts there. (Quoted in Michel, Beuret and Woods 2009, p. 57)

The Chinese have also built a large house for Jean-Jacques Bouya, the Managing Director of the state company which manages the country's large infrastructure projects, in Congo-Brazzaville. Many of these contracts have been awarded to Chinese firms.[4]

Globalization, or the increased connectedness of places around the world, means that consumers do not often see the ecological costs associated with their consumption. While European and American consumers benefit in the short term from deforestation in Africa, the local forest-dwelling communities are severely affected. For example, the Baka people in Cameroon depend on the moabi tree for nuts, which are sometimes pressed in order to make oil – 'people rely on it for their survival' (Nelson 2008) and Ngola Baka is now a 'poorer, hungrier place as a result of European tastes for luxury', an example of what David Harvey (2003) calls 'accumulation by dispossession'. Moabi trees cut down in Congo-Brazzaville go to make British parquet flooring, or furniture for the Swedish furniture giant IKEA, which gets about 30 per cent of its wood through China (Michel, Beuret and Woods 2009). IKEA says it 'aims' for wood sold in its stores to be Forest Stewardship Council-certified.

China buys 60 per cent of Congo-Brazzaville's wood, and Europe, particularly Finland, is also a major importer of illegal wood products according to the Worldwide Fund for Nature. In 2006 Congo-Brazzaville had wood exports of almost 1 million cubic metres (Michel, Beuret and Woods 2009) and, while there is a local law in place which stipulates that 85 per cent of felled trees should be processed on site, this does not appear to be observed. One Chinese-linked firm in Central Africa was fined over US$1 million for cutting undersized trees and logging in unallocated concessions (Lyman and Dorff 2007).

The UK government has given substantial amounts of money to protecting the rainforests of the Congo Basin, but it is largely Euro-American consumption which is driving the demand for tropical timber, and often European and American companies which are involved in the deforestation. In the United States a law was recently passed making the exporters of furniture and other wood products being imported into the country liable if they use illegally harvested wood. This may be partly motivated by economics, however, as, in the absence of this regulation, if American companies observe stricter environmental standards, they may be put at a competitive disadvantage relative to their Chinese and other Asian counterpart – although, of course, many American companies produce in China for export.

The Worldwide Fund for Nature estimates that at current rates of deforestation Congo-Brazzaville's forests will be two-thirds gone by 2050. Access roads, which make up 60 per cent of all roads in the country, also contribute substantially to deforestation, directly, and by opening up remote regions to colonization and mineral extraction projects. In Gabon, the China National Machinery and Equipment Import–Export Corporation was given a concession in one of the heretofore national parks (Belinga) to extract 500 million tonnes of iron ore. This project will also need huge amounts of energy and the construction of two massive hydroelectric dams with resultant population displacement and habitat loss (Michel, Beuret and Woods 2009). Around 70 per cent of Gabon's timber exports are sent illegally to China, while the figure for Equatorial Guinea is thought to be 90 per cent (Lee 2006).

There has also been substantial concern about the deforestation process in Mozambique, which is known locally as the 'Chinese takeaway' (Carmody 2010). It is estimated that clandestine timber production accounts for between half and 70 per cent of the total for Mozambique. And in 2007 1,000 illegal logs were seized in one raid, and 700 containers of hardwood were seized at Nacala port (Ribeiro 2010). They were cut down by the Mozambican–Chinese joint venture MOFID. Another binational Mozambican–Chinese joint venture was operating illegally in the buffer zone of the Gile National Reserve Park. In one weekend, ten times as much of the black wood *Dalbergia melanoxylon* was exported as was meant to have been cut down in a whole year. This tree takes an estimated 200 years to reach a 20-centimetre diameter.[5] The Chinese government is, however, aware of problems arising from deforestation overseas and the Global Environmental Institute in Beijing played an important role in the drafting of overseas forestry management guidelines (Zhi and Bai 2010), although the extent to which this will be enforced or represents a form of 'green-washing' remains to be seen.

According to the International Tropical Timber Organization, the Chinese State Forestry Administration will 'soon begin the process of selecting companies to implement the guidelines, which include bans on illegal logging and clearing of natural forests for plantations, on a "trial basis"' (IllegalLoggingInfo 2010). Trying to enforce compliance with local laws on a trial basis is unusual and may bespeak: (1) the need to continue to access timber and that this should not be compromised, irrespective of the legality; or (2) the limited ability of the Chinese state to enforce compliance on its companies with operations overseas; or both.

The chopping down of trees in the Congo Basin and elsewhere in Africa sets off a complex series of flows in which wood is exported to China and other destinations for processing into furniture and other wood products for the US and Europe, and then the Chinese government builds up its foreign exchange reserves which it then uses to finance projects in Africa and elsewhere and to buy US government debt. Globalization then is a cumulative and expanding process, although it does suffer periodic setbacks as evidenced by the recent global financial crisis and drop in world trade. Some resources are themselves, however, naturally mobile.

The African Fish Rush: Protein and Piracy

Global trade in fish and fish products has grown very strongly during the last twenty-five years, with export values increasing by 600 per cent during this time, in nominal (not inflation-adjusted) terms (Ponte

2008). Around 50 per cent of the world's fish exports come from developing countries and surprisingly they are one of their most valuable exports, surpassing the combined revenues from agricultural products such as tea, coffee, rice, bananas and meat (Ahmed 2005, cited in Ponte 2008). Under globalization, fish have even been financialized through trading in fish futures, or options to buy future fish catches (Boyes 2010), and Angola is reportedly repaying some of its debts to the Chinese government through not only oil, but also fish (Isaac 2010).

Fisheries in Africa produce around 7.3 million tonnes of fish a year, with about 90 per cent of this caught by small-scale fisherpeople. However, there is competition between internal and external demand for fish in Africa and the continent exports around 2.7 billion dollars' worth of fish annually. 'Western Africa (from Morocco to South Africa) is increasingly becoming a fish basket for Western Europe, Russia and China' (Alder and Sumaila 2004, p. 156). These waters are some of the most productive in the world and the EU now imports 60 per cent of its fish requirements, primarily from Africa (Standing 2009). Of all animal proteins consumed in Africa, fish provides around 19 per cent. Worryingly, this is the lowest proportion amongst world regions and is in decline (Southall 2009). Sometimes the planes taking fish from Africa bring arms in return (Sauper 2006).

The EU pays annual lump sums to African countries for fishing agreements, so that its boats can fish in their waters. For example, in the Tanzanian case the EU pays around €600,000 a year for seventy-nine fishing boats to be able to catch 8,000 tonnes of tuna (Standing 2009). According to the then Director of Marine Fisheries in Senegal in relation to the fishing agreement, 'the EU actively resisted numerous conservation measures and drove a hard bargain on price' (Ilnyckyj 2007, quoted in Standing, 2009, p. 349).

There appears to be even less transparency in relation to Chinese fish access agreements than European ones, however. According to the head of the Artisanal Fisheries Council of Senegal, 'here and there we see infrastructures being built with the support of China and we say these may be part of the access agreements, but we know nothing about the contents of these agreements...a partnership must be based on transparency and participation from the artisanal sector (Bartels 2007, p. 81, quoted in Standing 2009, p. 352). A representative of the Wildlife Conservation Society in Congo-Brazzaville recounted how 'one of the Chinese boats ran out of diesel the other day so we took the opportunity to board her and conduct an inspection. We thought we had them, but they produced special licenses from the fishing minister' (quoted in Michel, Beuret and Woods 2009, p. 46).

South Africa is also a major fish exporter and some scholars go as far as to claim that 'the most visible sign of South Africa's reintegration into the global economy has been the boom in exports to the EU and other developed regions' (Crosoer, van Sittert and Ponte 2006, p. 21). Off the coast of Namibia and South Africa the waters are particularly rich as a result of the Benguela upwelling system. This is an ocean current which brings nutrient-rich waters up from around 200–300 metres' depth, which fuels phytoplankton growth on which fish can feed. The annual sardine run around the coast of South Africa brings millions of fish together in a shoal up to 7 kilometres long, in addition to thousands of dolphins and sharks which feed on them. Hake accounts for about 40 per cent of the value of fish and fish products exported from South Africa, with the EU taking about 80 per cent of this (Ponte 2008). As a result of overfishing, the average landings in the Benguela section decreased by 41 per cent from the 1960s to the 1990s (Alder and Sumaila 2004).

While only 600,000 tonnes of fish were landed from Western Africa in 1950, by 2000 this had reached 4.5 million tonnes. The fact that much of this catch is by foreign fishing fleets has depleted stocks and provided intense competition for domestic artisanal or small-scale fishing fleets. According to some estimates, 68 per cent of the most productive areas, or main capture fisheries, in the eastern central Atlantic are in decline and the trophic level of fish landings is declining.

The trophic level refers to the number of positions away on the food chain organisms are from plants, which are trophic level one, so there is massive 'fishing down the chain' taking place in this part of the world, as fishing fleets focus on smaller and more abundant fish to maintain their catch levels. As noted earlier, some estimates are that 90 per cent of abalone shellfish are now fished out in Southern Africa, casting doubt on the renewability of this resource (Alden 2007). Southern African abalone were 'looted by high seas and home grown pirates trading on international markets' (Crosoer, van Sittert and Ponte 2006, p. 25).

Fishing down the chain has caused genetic distortions in most oceans (Morato 2006, cited in Standing 2009) as trawlers have become more efficient. Trawlers increasingly use fish aggregation devices which notify ships of the presence and location of fish. Foreign fishing fleets often use larger and more efficient vessels than local artisanal fishers. Whereas in 1990 there were twenty Spanish purse-seine fishing boats, which use huge nets in the shape of a purse, which caught 96,666 tonnes of tuna in the Indian Ocean, by 2006, twenty-two boats caught

200,543 tonnes (Standing 2009). Off the coast of Congo-Brazzaville, Chinese trawlers use nets several kilometres long, which disrupt those used by local fisherpeople. Sometimes these practices are illegal, but as a result of corruption few prosecutions take place.

As is common with most African resources, very few of their benefits 'trickle down' to local communities, as foreign interests predominate. Foreign fleets have often manipulated access agreements in order to overfish. Because of weak enforcement many foreign fishing vessels also fish inside countries' EEZs. One survey off Guinea's coast found that 60 per cent of the 2,313 vessels spotted were committing offences, with Guinea losing an estimated US$100 million a year as a result of this pirate fishing (Environmental Justice Foundation 2009; Greenpeace 2009).

Local fishers also often object to the large amounts of fish that are thrown away (the 'by-catch') because they are not of commercial value to industrial fishing fleets. For example, sometimes trawlers are only looking for prawns, but catch other species which they then discard. Industrial trawlers may discard up to 90 per cent of their catch (Patel 2009). This decreases fish reproduction rates and also disrupts the food chain resulting in further reductions in fish stocks. As local fishers are put out of business some use their boats to bring illegal migrants to Europe (Ritzer 2010).

One study found that usually less than 10 per cent of the observed increase in landed catch actually remained in the region (Kaczynski and Fluharty 2002) and many fishers in Ghana actually became poorer, even as the landed values of their fisheries increased, as the bulk of profits went to foreign interests. Additionally, in many countries employment in the fishing sector is in decline, as are some coastal communities. In part whether this happens or not depends on how strong the onshore country's economy is and its sources of revenue. In Mauritania, incredibly, 27 per cent of the entire state budget is funded by fishing access fees, mostly paid by the EU. Africa's EEZs, the largest in the world, are not so exclusive (Clarke 2008) as African governments are often in a very weak bargaining position.

Namibia, on the other hand, has a much more diversified economy than Mauritania, and consequently the government has been able to adopt a more nationalist approach to try to capture locally more of the benefits of fisheries. For example, there are tax reductions depending on how much Namibian involvement there is in fishing ventures. This resulted in a 1 per cent increase in employment and a 1.5 per cent increase in Namibian ownership for every percentage point lost in foreign fishing fees between 1993 and 1998 (Armstrong, Sumaila et al.

2004). Likewise, South Africa's hake fishing industry is currently certified by the Maritime Stewardship Council as sustainable – one of only ten in the world (Crosoer, van Sittert and Ponte 2006).

In some cases fish taken from African countries' EEZs by European fishing vessels is sold back to regional governments, reportedly to be processed in local canning factories (Standing 2009). According to some academics, European vessels even charge governments in Africa a premium for this fish as they know that fish caught by European boats face lower tariffs into the EU (Ponte, Raakjaer and Campling 2007, cited in Standing 2009).

While this local processing creates added value for African economies, the jobs created are very low-paid, with around half of all workers in the Seychelles canning industry coming from outside the country, as many locals consider the work too demeaning. Generally though, the level of local processing is low, with one report for the United Nations Environment Programme estimating that only 12 per cent of the fish caught in Mauritania's waters are locally processed (United Nations Environment Programme 2007, cited in Standing 2009). Part of the reason for this is the very strict hygiene and sanitary standards that food entering the EU has to pass, which many African producers find difficult to meet.

Even though EU boats, under the terms of fishing agreements, are meant to employ local staff where possible, this does not always happen. Also trawlers are much more capital-intensive than small fishing boats, with each job on a trawler 'costing' about US$300,000 in capital to create, versus a maximum of about US$3,000 on a small boat (Pauly 2006, cited in Standing 2009). One estimate suggests that for every 100 tonnes of shrimp caught in Madagascar a trawler will generate 42 jobs, whereas the equivalent figure for small-scale fisheries is 230 (Gorez 2000, cited in Standing 2009).

In addition to registered vessels committing offences, there are unregistered pirate vessels operating off the coast of Africa. In Guinea in the first six months of 2005, the authorities reportedly arrested eight boats of Asian origin for fishing without permission (Standing 2009). This pattern of looting of African resources by outsiders fits into a broader pattern of resource extraction from the continent, which has generated resistance (Bond 2006).

According to Carol Thompson (2009, p. 300), 'piracy refers to refusal to compensate or even acknowledge the original cultivators of the bioresource'. Up to US$300 million a year in tuna, shrimp and lobster are being stolen by foreign trawlers in Somali waters each year (French and Chambers 2010). Another report from the Marine

Resources Assessment Group in 2005 estimated that the Somali economy lost an estimated £73 million a year to illegal fishing, with other estimates going as high as £230 million (Phillips 2009). The plundering of Somali territorial waters by foreign fishing fleets gave rise to an armed response by local fisherpeople. This 'piracy of the rich' was what sparked the 'piracy of the poor' in response.[6]

According to one pirate in Somalia, Mohamed Hayesi:

> The first day joining the pirates came into my mind was in 2006...A group of our villagers, mainly fishermen I knew, were arming themselves. Years ago we used to fish a lot, enough for us to eat and sell in the markets. Then illegal fishing and dumping of toxic wastes by foreign fishing vessels affected our livelihood, depleting the fish stocks...The first hijack I attended was in February 2007 when we seized a World Food Programme-chartered ship with twelve crew...I only want one more chance in piracy to increase my cash assets, then I will get married and give up. (Quoted in McLister 2009)

According to one of the pirates who kidnapped Captain Richard Phillips of the *Maersk Alabama* in 2009, everyone has to die at some point and piracy at least offered an opportunity for a living (Phillips and Talty 2010). The US military did shoot dead these people who captured Captain Phillips.

One of the features of globalization is that things and knowledge become more 'liquid' and can move more easily between places (Ritzer 2010). However, in some cases liquids are literally moved and can generate resistance. The dumping of toxic waste was also implicated in the rise of piracy off Somalia.

According to the United Nations Environment Programme, which is headquartered in neighbouring Kenya, the tsunami of 2005 broke up tonnes of rusting barrels of toxic waste which had been dumped in Somali waters. Reportedly, 300 people died from coming into contact with this waste at the time, while many others developed respiratory and skin infections, mouth ulcers and abdominal bleeding (Phillips 2009). It only cost European companies roughly US$2.50 to dump a tonne of toxic waste there, versus US$250 to have it processed in Europe.[7]

According to some analysts, pirate raiding groups in Somalia are now composed of ex-fishermen with the necessary sea-faring skill, technical experts who operate tracking equipment and automatic identification systems, and militia members who board the ships, and they split the profits between them (French and Chambers 2010). In some cases there have been reports that the proceeds of piracy are used to fund militant Islamic groups in Somalia, whereas in other cases such groups are reported to be suppressing piracy as an affront to Islam.

The globalization of fishing is generating resistance and disrupting further globalization. In November 2008 the American-flagged *Sirius Star*, carrying 100 million dollars' worth of oil, was captured. This single event drove up the price of oil globally by 1 per cent (Howden 2008). In the first nine months of 2009, the International Maritime Bureau found that there were 306 pirate attacks off the coast of Somalia, which was more than the entire number for 2008 (McLister 2009). This was lucrative business for those who were successful, with average ransoms for commercial ships and tankers reportedly rising from US$1 to 2 to 3 million, driving up the cost of land and other prices in parts of Somalia (Hassan 2009). In 2008, up to November, an estimated US$150 million in ransom was paid to Somali pirates (Arnold 2009), with ransoms often dropped onto ships by helicopter.

In response to piracy, Western powers and also China have sent their navies to patrol off the coast of Somalia, showing their common interest in keeping trade routes open and also ensuring continued access to African resources. In this case military globalization again follows economic globalization. The EU has also set up a 'Maritime Security Centre – Horn of Africa', based in the UK, which coordinates naval protection closely with the private sector off the Somali coast (EUNAVFOR: Somalia 2010).

It is well understood that piracy off the coast of Somalia is just one manifestation of the complex crisis which has engulfed that country since the collapse of its government in 1991 when the United States withdrew its support of the dictator Siad Barre. Furthermore, piracy, and disorder generally, increased in Somalia after the American-backed Ethiopian invasion of the country in 2006 to support the Transitional Federal Government and depose the Islamic Courts Union, which was gaining territory in much of the south of the country. The Americans had been concerned that this group, which contained both 'radical' and 'moderate' elements, would give sanctuary to Islamic terrorist groups. This put the Americans in the unusual position of supporting some of the warlords they had fought against in the early 1990s. While the 'justice' of the Islamic Courts Union was sometimes brutal – against women wearing jeans or people playing rock music, for example – it had succeeded for the first time in decades in bringing order to Southern Somalia.

In contrast the Ethiopian invasion spurred resistance as the invading forces reportedly engaged in practices such as shackling their prisoners and driving vehicles over them, according to Human Rights Watch (cited in Michel, Beuret and Woods 2009). Subsequently they were forced to withdraw and the Americans, realizing their mistake, attempted to reinstate Sheikh Sharif Sheikh Ahmed as President of Somalia. He had formerly been Commander in Chief of the Islamic Courts Union. Now EU troops, including those of officially 'neutral' Ireland, will train Somali soldiers to combat Islamic militants (Downey 2010). As Somali scholar and authority Abdi Samatar writes, 'America's gifts to the Somali people in the last few years have been warlords, and Ethiopian invasion, and an authoritarian, sectarian and incompetent regime' which cannot police its territory or waters (quoted in Campbell 2008, p. 20). Piracy has flourished in this environment. Interestingly however, most of the pirates are based in the autonomous and functioning region of Puntland (French and Chambers 2010). Insecurity is too high in the rest of Somalia for pirates to protect their assets and function effectively.

Illegal fishing in Somalia by European and other fleets has led to a reverse scramble to get access to wealth by pirates – a form of violent wealth redistribution. This in turn has led to world powers sending their navies to patrol the waters off Somalia, which is an attempt to contain coercively the contradictions of globalization (Gill 2003), but this is likely to lead to further conflict and deeper engagement.

Biopiracy

Another example of the piracy of the rich is so-called 'biopiracy', which is also a major issue in Africa. For example in 2003, Aventis, which is a major biotechnology corporation, took out patents which claim legal ownership of compounds from a vine (*Uvaria klaineri*) which is found in Gabon. The World Intellectual Property Organization notes that Aventis was planning to apply for patents on these compounds in 105 countries, including Gabon (McGown 2003).

In West Africa there has also been controversy about the brazzein berry, which is several hundred times sweeter than sugar. Extracts from this were patented by researchers at the University of Wisconsin so that it could be produced synthetically in labs and used as a sweetener. When this synthetic substitute was introduced onto the market it resulted in the price of brazzein collapsing and many women who had previously picked it becoming unemployed.[8]

Ironically, conservation efforts have sometimes facilitated biopiracy. For example, scientists have identified various biodiversity 'hotspots' around the world, such as Madagascar – 'the hottest of the hot'. Many of the plant species in these hotspots are known to have medicinal properties. For example the bark of the *Prunus africana* tree is used to treat inflammation of the prostate gland in men (Neimark and Schroeder 2009). However, once the medical benefits of this plant were identified, harvesting of it increased to such an extent that it had to be added into the Convention on International Trade in Endangered Species.

According to Neimark and Schroeder (2009, p. 46), this case 'illustrates that commercial drug development can potentially result in levels of material extraction that are comparable to mining'. While pharmaceutical companies may get rich from extracting these biological resources from designated conservation areas, local people may be excluded and have their livelihoods undermined and criminalized. This has echoes of previous colonial practices whereby Europeans excluded Africans from conservation areas, whereas in reality it was often European overhunting which had created the problem in the first instance. These practices of dispossession and enclosure are increasing again, with large tracts of land in Tanzania being leased to an investor from the United Arab Emirates 'to use as a private unregulated hunting reserve for the very rich who wanted to kill leopards' (Theroux 2003, p. 256). In addition to the land market, there is now also intense competition for other African markets, to which we now turn.

8 THE ASIAN SCRAMBLE FOR INVESTMENT AND MARKETS: EVIDENCE AND IMPACTS IN ZAMBIA [WITH GODFREY HAMPWAYE]

While resources are central to the new scramble, markets, as noted earlier, are increasingly important. Chinese and Indian trade with Africa is only a small fraction of their trade with Asia. However, Africa is becoming a much more significant market, for Asian products in particular. For example, some have noted that Africa experienced an Asian 'textile tsunami' in the last decade, although clothing accounts for only 4 per cent of China's exports to Africa, in contrast to the biggest category, machinery, at 10 per cent (Trade Law Centre for Southern Africa 2010). Nonetheless some trade unionists estimated that over 100,000 jobs were lost in the Nigerian textile industry as a result of Chinese import competition (Carmody 2010). This was one of the factors which led the Nigerian government to impose an outright import ban on a wide range of products, including textiles, in 2004–5, in contravention of its World Trade Organization obligations (Ikhuoria 2010). The government may feel that it has the latitude to impose repeated import bans because of global demand for its oil, perhaps showing how globalization tends to undercut itself. The South African government has also negotiated a voluntary export restraint agreement with China, although there are concerns that this will simply mean substitutions will take place from other Asian garment producers such as Vietnam.

Africa is also becoming a more important site for Asian manufacturing and service investment. Whereas in 2003 over half of Chinese FDI went into mining, by 2005 this had fallen to 15 per cent (Zhi and

Bai 2010), and while trade relations with China are geographically extensive throughout the continent, investment is heavily concentrated in oil- and mineral-rich states. What are the nature and impacts of Asian investment in manufacturing, mining and services?

With some notable exceptions (see Strauss and Saavedra 2009, for example), much of the literature on this topic to date has been based on secondary sources or has not adopted a systematic methodological approach. In contrast, this chapter, co-authored with Godfrey Hampwaye, undertakes an empirical investigation based on a survey of twenty-seven Chinese and Indian (hereafter 'Asian') firms and fourteen interviews with stakeholders and Asian businesses on the nature and developmental impacts of their investment in Zambia. In particular it seeks to interrogate whether the nature and scale of current Asian investment is potentially economically transformative or merely represents a reworking of a colonial-style economy.

Recently there have been major theoretical advances in our understanding of the process of globalization, particularly through the development of the concept of GPNs (Coe et al. 2004). The GPN concept seeks to go beyond the linear structures of global commodity or value chain analysis to incorporate different types of network configuration involving the totality of relevant groups of actors and relationships (Coe, Dicken et al. 2008). However, to date there has been little empirical analysis of Asian companies and their investments in Africa using this concept. This is an important lacuna because the GPNs some of these companies create are often quite different from those of other TNCs as a result of heavy state involvement, ownership and engagement, in many large-scale Chinese companies in particular. All twenty-one Chinese firms in the Global Fortune 500 are majority state-owned (Nolan 2009). While India has a distinctive history of engagement with Zambia (see Kapferer 1972), as approved Indian investment from 2000 to 2007 was only 12 per cent of Chinese investment the focus of this chapter is more heavily on Chinese companies (Zambia Development Agency (ZDA) various years).

Zambia in Southern Africa is the third-largest recipient of Chinese foreign investment in Africa, and the nineteenth-largest in the world (UNCTAD 2007). China is now the primary source of new direct investment in Zambia, and has over 140 officially recorded projects covering various sectors (*Times of Zambia*, 20 October 2008). It was projected that, by mid-2009, Chinese investment in Zambia would have exceeded US$1.5 billion (*Times of Zambia*, 20 October 2008), and China is already the third-largest investor in terms of stock of FDI, after South Africa and the UK (Ndulo 2008). Indian investment in

Zambia has also been growing rapidly, although, mirroring patterns in the rest of Africa and as noted above, it is dwarfed by Chinese investment (Indian High Commission 2009; Broadman and Isik 2007). Does this new investment represent a break with previous patterns of extractive globalization, or reinforce existing trends of exclusionary inclusion in the global economy?

As noted earlier, previous rounds of globalization in Africa have incorporated most of the continent on unfavourable terms, resulting in deepening impoverishment and marginalization (Bond 2006), in contrast to South-East Asia, for example, where foreign investment, in manufacturing in particular, has facilitated job creation and poverty reduction: a more inclusive type of globalization. In large part the answer to the question above depends on the scale and type of investment. In order to answer this question, it is necessary to provide more context on Asian–Zambian, and particularly Sino-Zambian, relations, which the next section of the chapter does, paying particular attention to the new Chinese-owned MFEZ in that country. The rest of the chapter then reports on the results of a survey of Asian-owned firms and assesses their developmental impacts. These results are complemented by qualitative interview data with stakeholders and firms. The chapter then assesses how the current global economic crisis of the late 2000s affected Sino-Zambian relations.

Chinese and Indian Investment in Zambia: History and Context

China has a long history of engagement in Africa and, between 1973 and 1979, China spent almost 7 per cent of its GDP on aid to Africa (Liu 2010). There are arguably three phases of the Sino-Zambian relationship, driven by solidarity, geopolitics and geo-economics. Zambia's relationship with China can be traced back to the 1970s when the latter constructed a railway line from Dar-es-Salaam in Tanzania to Kapiri-Mposhi in Central Zambia (McGreal 2007). This was necessary to facilitate Zambian copper exports following the closure of the traditional southern route as a result of sanctions on apartheid South Africa and Southern Rhodesia (Hampwaye 2008). Geopolitically it was spurred by the fact that during the 1960s and 1970s the Chinese state was in competition with the Soviet Union for support in Africa. More recently, China has forgiven some of the debts associated with the construction of this railway, arguably for geo-economic rather than geopolitical reasons: as China is now the world's largest consumer of copper, it is anxious to secure access to this major Zambian resource.

The next major investment by China in Zambia was the Zambia–China Mulungushi Textile Factory in Kabwe in the 1980s (McGreal 2007; Carmody 2009b). The Chinese initially built this factory as a turn-key facility for the Zambian government, but when it ran into operational difficulties the Chinese Premier suggested it should be run as a joint Chinese–Zambian venture from 1997. This factory created thousands of jobs and contributed to poverty reduction (McGreal 2007), although 'perpetual reorganizations at the textiles plant...brought about job losses and the suffering of workers' (Muneku and Koyi 2007, p. 22). Ultimately, this project ceased to operate in the mid-2000s as it couldn't compete with imports from Asia and the surrounding region (Brautigam 2009; Carmody 2009b). Thousands of jobs were lost directly, but it also affected thousands of local cotton growers (see Taylor 2006 for a fuller description).

Since the early 2000s, the scale of Chinese investment and associated in-migration in Zambia has increased dramatically. There are now an estimated 200 Chinese companies operating in the country, ranging from state-owned to entrepreneurial companies, and these investments are spread across sectors (Bastholm and Kragelund 2007). Mining in Copperbelt Province has received the most investment. The Chinese own the Chambishi Copper Mine through the China Non-Ferrous Mining (Group) Co. Ltd, and Chambishi Copper Smelter (Bastholm and Kragelund 2007; Carmody 2009b). Other Chinese investments in the mining industry are scattered across several towns – for example Sunfeng Minerals in Ndola, and Jiaxing Mining in Kitwe. Examples of Indian investment include the KCM which is owned by Vedanta Resources,[1] and Kagem Mining (Bastholm and Kragelund 2007; Hampwaye 2008).

With the global economic downturn of 2008–9, Chinese companies are buying up other foreign investments in the country at bargain-basement prices – such as the Luanshya Copper Mine (Rundell 2009). A global economic upturn will mean Chinese companies are well positioned to supply the increased amounts of raw materials required. As noted earlier, China already imports 52 per cent of the world's iron ore, and Chinese stockpiling of copper led to a near-doubling of the copper price during 2009, as Chinese mining companies sought to spend their reserves of devaluing US dollars. A new Chinese mining investment of US$3.5 billion in Zambia was announced in 2009 (*Lusaka Times*, 2009).

The construction sector is also among those which have attracted Chinese investment in Zambia. This sector is perceived as strategic in terms of gaining access to resources through the construction of infrastructure (Centre for Chinese Studies (CCS) 2006). There are at least fifteen Asian-owned construction companies in Zambia (National Council for Construction 2009), which have won contracts ranging from maintenance to building of infrastructure such as roads, railways and airports. Among the major Chinese construction companies which are active is the state-owned Overseas Engineering Corp., which has signed contracts to construct several schools and hospitals in Zambia.[2] A poster for the Anhui Foreign Economic Construction Group, which is building the new Sino-Zambian Friendship stadium in Ndola, notes that the company has 'abided by the national "going out" strategy since 1992' (fieldnotes, August 2009).

The Chinese have also invested in agriculture, although this is difficult to quantify given numerous unrecorded 'small' investments. The most significant investment in this sector has been in the China–Zambia Friendship farm located to the west of the city of Lusaka, which dates from the early 1990s (Bastholm and Kragelund 2007).[3] In Zambia food in these estates is so far grown for the local market, although a potential Chinese investment in growing *Jatropha* trees to produce biofuels on 2 million acres is also now generating controversy, as there is concern that such projects may displace local farmers and food production.

Given its potential for exports, linkages and technological development, manufacturing is a key sector in economic development and poverty reduction, and growing Asian investment offers potential to achieve these objectives. Investment in this sector can be seen in such companies as Gourock Plastics, Zambezi Paper Mills, and Tata Motor Assembly in Ndola, and Sakiza Spinning in Kitwe. However, the largest proportion of investment in this sector is by the Chinese in the Chambishi MFEZ in Copperbelt Province (Hampwaye 2008). As noted earlier, the Chinese are building seven of these zones across Africa and this 'multi-facility high-tech' manufacturing zone in the north of the country is 'the first of its kind in Africa' (Edinger 2007, cited in Davies 2008). The targeted investment package to complete this industrial park is US$800 million in total (Hampwaye 2008). As Hönke (2009, p. 282) notes, 'Zambia…has become a core country in China's search for energy and industrial resources in Africa'.

The Zambian MFEZ is anchored by a US$200 million copper smelter, but is also meant to manufacture 'TV's, mobile phones and other electronic items' (CCS 22 June 2007, cited in Kaplinsky 2008,

p. 7). While estimates vary, some suggest, once the zone has been completed, it will house up to sixty Chinese companies, employing 60,000 people (Davies 2008; Ndulo 2008). The division between local and Chinese labour use is as yet uninvestigated. Recent estimates of the number of jobs created thus far put it at 3,500.

The siting of the MFEZ in Chambishi in Northern Zambia is significant as the province contains most of the country's mineral reserves, and is in close proximity to the DRC, where, as noted earlier, Chinese companies have signed multi-billion-dollar resource (copper and cobalt) deals. The copper smelter in the zone will provide a secure source of supply of this key strategic industrial mineral to China, in addition to reducing transportation costs as copper cathodes, or large sheets of copper, are cheaper to transport than ore. The MFEZ is an integral part of the 'go out' strategy, and an attempt to extend and embed Chinese-centred GPNs.

There is some dispute as to whether Zambian companies and other foreign investors may be located in the zone, with the Chinese government claiming it is only for Chinese investors, and the Zambian government taking the opposite position. Which of these claims is correct is important in understanding the operation of sovereignty in the zones and whether they will serve as Chinese enclaves of resource extraction and local market exploitation, or springboards for Zambian companies to export and develop locally centred GPNs, as in Mauritius' export processing zones (Brautigam 2009). As of 2009, it was only Chinese companies involved in copper production and processing which were operational in the zone (fieldnotes 2009).

The Chinese are also building another Multi-facility Economic 'sub-zone' in Lusaka. This development was announced by the Zambian President and the Chinese Minister of Commerce. In his speech the Zambian President argued that the zone would have extensive linkages with the rest of the Zambian economy as investors would source products and services locally – 'our raw materials will now have the chance to enjoy value addition' (quoted in *China Daily* 2009). The Malaysians, Japanese and Indians are also to invest in MFEZs in Lusaka, and feasibility studies have already been carried out (see, for example, JICA and RoZ 2007).

In contrast to other initiatives, such as the Zambia–Malawi–Mozambique Growth Triangle or the proposed 'Triangle of Hope' MFEZ in Lusaka, which is being planned by a Malaysian company, the Chambishi zone is already operational because it is not dependent on attracting footloose private investment, but is being set up and run by a state-owned company which won one of the spots in the Chinese government competition to set up and run overseas economic zones around the world (Brautigam 2009; interview with MFEZ Manager, ZDA August 2009; ZMM-GT Coordinating Secretariat 2003). This then represents a new form of globalization in which the Chinese state, in cooperation with state-owned companies, may catalyse additional entrepreneurial and private corporate investment.

Helping Zambia reinvigorate its moribund manufacturing sector is one way in which China can achieve access to resources through consent. However, the construction of these SEZs also offers potential for job creation and technology and knowledge transfer from Chinese managers and workers to their Zambian counterparts, and vice versa. While some claim that the 'Chinese model of development has come to Africa' (Davies 2008), and Broadman and Isik (2007) argue Chinese investment is propelling African trade into cutting-edge transnational networks, there would appear to be relatively little evidence of that in Zambia at the moment, although the new zone is meant to be 'high-tech' (*African Business*, 2008). However, the extent to which activities such as mobile phone assembly, or copper smelting for that matter, can be considered high-tech is open to question. These operations are low-skill and no research and development is being conducted in the MFEZ. Indeed, some argue that this is in reality a 'pseudo-economic zone' (Michel, Beuret and Woods 2009) which is merely designed to lock in tax breaks for Chinese companies in their resource extraction operations. Given the current profile of companies active in the zone, this would appear plausible as they are all subsidiaries of the Chinese Non-Ferrous Metals Corporation engaged in resource extraction and processing. This may change over time, and there is a social imperative for there to be economic diversification, given the scale of resistance and conflict around the operations of this zone. However, while Kaplinsky (2008) argues that the competitive displacement pressures generated by China are deindustrializing in effect for Africa, Brautigam (2009) argues that the Chinese government's promotion of offshoring of labour-intensive and polluting elements of GPNs does offer potential for Africa to industrialize. The two positions are not incommensurable, however. Deindustrialization in labour-intensive light manufacturing such as clothing would appear to be in evidence in much of Africa, while resource processing manufacturing is growing. There does not, as of yet, appear to be much evidence of the offshoring of labour-intensive assembly operations from China itself, particularly as the country still has its own massive 'reserve army of labour' in the interior and the government is attempting to spread economic development throughout the country.

The construction of the new Chinese economic zones arguably serves both political and economic logics. During the Zambian presidential election of 2006, the main opposition candidate drew on an explicitly racist anti-Chinese and nationalist register. When President Hu of China visited in 2007 he was greeted by protests from Zambian miners over wages and working conditions, and unemployed textile workers whose companies (including the Chinese joint venture mentioned earlier) had not been able to compete with Chinese imports. Paradoxically, the Copperbelt and Lusaka were the two regions of Zambia which experienced the most dramatic reductions in poverty during the recent commodity boom, and have also seen substantial resistance to the Chinese presence as these are the two regions of the country most affected by Chinese in-migration (see Carmody 2009b and Negi 2008).

Politically, the construction of the zone is beneficial to China as economic diversification may serve to diffuse some of the popular discontent over competition for jobs and market opportunities amongst the Zambian population. However, these zones are technically 'spaces of exception' where there are extended tax holidays and labour law enforcement is weak (confidential interview, Zambia–China Cooperation Zone, August 2009). According to an official at the UN Economic Commission for Africa, Chinese investors know they can 'come over here and do whatever they like' (interview, Lusaka, August 2009). Consequently, these zones may also generate other resistances over labour standards and regimes. Another perspective, however, is that these zones merely expand the terms and conditions of labour in the informal economy into the formal manufacturing sector,[4] creating a hybrid space, the (in)formal economy: new spaces of (Chinese) globalization.

Nature and Impacts of Asian-Owned Businesses

With some notable exceptions (e.g. Kragelund 2009), very little detailed empirical research has been undertaken on the nature and impacts of Asian-owned businesses in Africa. To that end, a survey of Asian-owned businesses was conducted in 2009. The survey was conducted by two research assistants, and for logistical reasons was undertaken in the Copperbelt and the capital city Lusaka, where Asian investment is concentrated. This regional focus captured both mining-related and urban manufacturing and service activities, but not agricultural investments. Firms were identified from lists provided by the ZDA, visited, and given a questionnaire. Sometimes repeat visits were required to pick up the completed survey. A total of twenty-seven firms, out of forty which were approached, ultimately responded (table 8.1). The majority of firms which responded were Chinese, but some 'Indian' companies, including long-standing ones, were also included. Interviews were then conducted with various stakeholders and Asian companies.

Retailing and manufacturing were the top two sectors in terms of the number of companies responding in the survey. The majority of

Table 8.1 Structure of Asian investment in selected companies in Zambia

Sector	Number	Selected products	Markets
Mining	2	Copper, copper balls, acid, copper cathodes	China, Zambia, South Africa, DRC, Zimbabwe
Manufacturing	12	Duvets, clothes, shoes, soft drinks, stationery, tissue, soap, sweets, motorbikes, *maheu* (soft drink), purified water, water-dispenser machines, blankets, concentrates, sugar, carbon dioxide, limestone, talcum powder, bed sheets, uniforms, cloth, biscuits	Zambia, Mozambique, DRC, South Africa, Namibia
Construction	1	Construction materials	Zambia
Service, i.e. Retailing, Wholesaling	9	Clothes, shoes, umbrellas, handbags, electrical goods and electronics, furniture, purified water, water-dispenser machines, shoe polish, cement, tiles	Zambia, Mozambique
Banking services	1	Banking services	Zambia
Hospital/clinic	2	Medical service	Zambia

Source: survey data 2009

Asian-owned companies in these two sectors are located in the capital city Lusaka, while investments in the mining sector are concentrated in Copperbelt Province. Table 8.1 further reveals that production from the companies located in Zambia is not only consumed locally, but also exported to neighbouring countries. However, extra-regional manufacturing exports were not reported. The pattern of investment then is clear, with refined minerals and raw materials being exported to China, while manufacturing, agricultural and trading investment is local/regional market-serving. This inter-sectoral division of labour is problematic given the limited potential for expansion based on regional markets.

For the twenty-seven companies that took part in the survey, the mean year of establishment was 1994, but the mode, or most common, year of establishment was 2004, showing a concentration of investment in the last number of years. Of the eleven retailers and traders and other service providers in the survey, the mean year of establishment was 1998. For the manufacturers, the mean year was 1989. However, this figure is skewed somewhat by very early Indian-owned businesses appearing from 1954. Both of the mining companies in the survey were established in 2004. Mean employment in the survey was 134 employees and the median, or the middle, value in the range was 48. The fact that the mean is so much higher than the median bespeaks the impact of the large employers in mining.

In terms of why companies or entrepreneurs chose to locate in Zambia, many traders and manufacturers noted the lack of an industrial base in the country and consequently that there was less competition than in China. In this way underdevelopment creates a competitive advantage for Chinese and Indian companies. As per capita incomes are similar in China and India to those in Africa, Asian products are well suited and priced to the market. In some cases Chinese companies mimic Western and Japanese brands – with names like 'Philibs' and 'Sunny' for radios, for example (Theroux 2003).

Many companies also noted that the structural adjustment policies of economic liberalization adopted in the 1990s had made the investment climate more favourable, through currency convertibility for example. Paradoxically then, as noted earlier – given the concern expressed in the Western media about China's 'march into Africa' – it was Western-sponsored liberalization in the 1990s which laid the groundwork for subsequent Asian investment. However, as would be expected, some of the textile manufacturers were struggling. 'When we acquired the business there were incentives for textile manufacturers. The main raw material was zero-rated duty wise' (survey return, 2009), but this is no longer the case and this textile manufacturer had reduced employment by 40 per cent over the previous three years.

Interestingly, the two healthcare providers in the survey noted that there was now excessive competition from other Chinese surgeries and private hospitals. Also, excess competition was noted in companies selling goods catering specifically for the Chinese market, such as self-named traditional Chinese traders. Consequently economic liberalization may have generated first-mover advantages for some Asian investors, but the market may have over-shot, specifically for Chinese traditional goods and remedies. It used to be that you only needed to invest US$50,000 to get a residence permit and tax incentives in Zambia, but in response to public unease the government has now raised the figure for availing of tax incentives to half a million US dollars (Kelly 2007). This is in effect a form of market restriction in response to popular pressure, but may also prevent 'excessive' competition.

Of the twenty-seven companies, eleven noted China as their primary source of inputs. Many of these were traders selling clothes, umbrellas and shoes, for example. Several companies noted that the booming mining sector has created demand for their products, although some also noted the impacts of the global recession: people 'didn't have money, like before'. There seemed to be relatively little training for workers and managers, although one mining company did note that 'hard-working staff were sent to Beijing for familiarization programmes'.

In terms of the difficulties of doing business in Zambia, many companies noted high tax rates and transportation costs, partly as a result of Zambia being landlocked. Others argued though that Zambia's central location and membership of the SADC was an advantage, making it a logical entry point or entrepôt for the region. Another company noted that 'There are no problems, that is why there are so many Asians doing business here', although other entrepreneurs expressed insecurity in relation to residence and employment permits and the potential for shake-downs by corrupt officials (confidential interview, Lusaka, August 2009).

As noted earlier, labour relations at Asian firms in Zambia have been controversial. An International Labour Organization official argued that 'Chinese companies have not shown themselves to be willing to observe the law of the land' (quoted in Carmody 2009b, p. 1202). Responses from the surveys shed light on this. A large mining company noted that 'hiring labour is expensive here compared to our country', even though some Chinese mining companies have reportedly been paying their contract staff as little as US$30 a month (Kurlantzick 2007). Nonetheless, high copper prices provided leverage for mineworkers' unions to get an agreement to convert casual and contract positions in the Chambishi mine into permanent ones (Lee 2009). The slump in the copper price in 2008 reduced this bargaining power, however.

Low wages feed into another business logic. Bob Jessop (2002) has noted that wages are contradictory in capitalist economies: as a cost to capital, but also a source of demand. However, the structure of demand may also be important in the hyper-competitive neoliberal context. A trading company in the survey noted that the fact that the majority of Zambians were poor was good for business as they wanted cheap goods (from China). There were, however, also other retailers in the survey selling flat-screen televisions to emergent middle-class consumers in Zambia.

Another interesting thing to emerge from the survey was some tension between Asian and South African investors, with one Asian company, which had undergone a major investment expansion to supply Shoprite, the South African retail chain, noting that its contract had been cancelled and that Shoprite was now favouring South African producers instead. Shoprite may have been responding to the South African government-sponsored campaign to source nationally: 'Proudly South African'.

Developmental Impacts of Asian Investment

The debate surrounding the developmental impact of the Asian investment in Zambia has not received substantial systematic attention. There are those who argue that this investment has created jobs for the local people, while those who oppose this investment argue that the jobs created so far are of poor quality and add little if anything towards raising the living standards of ordinary people: that Zambia's position in these global production and trade networks is unfavourable.

Undoubtedly, Asian investment in Zambia has created jobs for thousands of Zambians. According to the data from the ZDA, close to 10,000 jobs were created by Asian investment between 2000 and 2007 (ZDA 2008), although more recent estimates put the number created by Chinese investment alone at 15,000 (Nkolomba and Chambwa 2009). By 2007, the total invested during this period had accumulated to US$670.76 million: US$596.36 million from China and US$74.4 million from India (ZDA 2008). The number of jobs created by Chinese investment is more than three times as high as that created from the Indian investment during the same period (see table 8.2).

As table 8.2 shows, there are substantial differences in the capital intensity of Chinese versus Indian investment, largely as a result of major Chinese investments in the mineral extraction and processing sector. However, Chinese investment seems to exhibit a 'snowball effect'. With the construction of MFEZs by the Chinese in Chambishi and by the Chinese and the Malaysians in Lusaka, the manufacturing sector could outstrip the mining sector as an employer amongst Asian investments in Zambia. Pledged Chinese investment in manufacturing was US$583 million, which, if realized, would create 9,115 jobs (ZDA, cited in Nkolomba and Chambwa 2009). Much of this looks set to be in basic manufacturing, however, involving the processing and refining of minerals. This will in turn be dwarfed by the recently announced new mining agreements in terms of total investment.

Although the number of jobs created during this period fluctuated, the general trend was one of increase from 2000 to 2007 (see table 8.2). It can, therefore, be argued that these investment projects have contributed to local economic development in the specific areas where these projects are located, and towards overall national development. However, there are also downsides, such as the displacement of local businesses, and the fact that these new companies may outcompete local companies for bank loans. Small businesses in Zambia already have to pay exorbitant interest rates (de Luna Martinez 2007), while some Chinese companies can access state-subsidized credit, making them more competitive – through the Bank of China, which, as noted earlier, set up its first African branch in Zambia in 1997, for example (*Zambanker* 2008; Kragelund 2009).

The other side of the argument with respect to Chinese investment is that the jobs which have been created are not decent. One of those who strongly oppose this kind of investment is the leader of the main opposition party, the Patriotic Front (PF), Mr Michael Sata. Concern has also been raised over the safety of the workers in these companies, to the extent that the Zambian government had to close down a Chinese coal mining company in Southern Province of Zambia due to poor working conditions (McGreal 2007). As noted earlier, forty-nine miners were previously killed in an explosion at an explosives factory owned by the Chinese in Chambishi in 2007 (Carmody 2009b). This explosion was perhaps not surprising as the workforce for the plant

Table 8.2 Approved Indian and Chinese investment in Zambia – Zambian Development Agency data (various years)

Approved Asian investment in Zambia	US$m Chinese	US$m Indian	Number of jobs from Chinese investment	Number of jobs from Indian investment	Capital per job – Chinese investment	Capital per job – Indian investment
2000	13.7	1.3	1,308	118	$10,474	$11,016
2001	7.2	0.9	412	90	$17,476	$10,000
2002	20.7	0.3	400	48	$51,570	$6,250
2003	2.86	3.5	494	527	$5,789	$6,641
2004	14	0.9	1,400	215	$10,000	$4,186
2005	41.4	60.2	1,240	634	$33,387	$94,953
2006	209.5	6	1,227 (Chambishi copper smelter)	279	$170,741	$21,505
2007	287	1.3	960 (nickel smelter)	228	$298,958	$5,701
Total/average[a]	596.36	74.4	7,441	2,139	$80,145	$34,782

[a]The figures for capital per job are averages

was selected from casual workers who would gather outside the factory each morning. Needless to say, they did not have training in handling explosive materials and the plant was only designed for around twenty, rather than fifty, workers. The workers didn't have to give up their mobile phones, lighters or cigarettes, and there weren't separate areas for making dynamite and explosives (Michel, Beuret and Woods 2009). The company paid out to the families less than US$10,000 per worker killed. A month after the explosion, the development of the Chinese SEZ in Chambishi was announced.

Relations between Chinese companies and Zambian unions have been fraught. According to one union representative and member of Chambishi City Council:

> I've never seen such difficult negotiations. The Chinese like to keep changing the makeup of the delegation. It's a stalling tactic. They send people who don't have the authority to make decisions, and then replace them with more people with no decision-making power. And then if we do make any gains, they split up companies so that those gains no longer apply to most of the workers in them... If they start to feel put-upon, then they just lay off a load of people and turn to ununionized temporary workers. (Quoted in Michel, Beuret and Woods 2009, p. 239)

There have also been negative environmental impacts, and mineral resource extraction projects are, by definition, unsustainable. As Michael Klare (2008, p. 176) notes, 'when... the... copper is depleted, the... mining companies will just pick up their stakes and move elsewhere, leaving behind massive unemployment, broken promises and large, empty holes'.

Apart from the poor working conditions in these companies, the other complaint from those who oppose Asian investment is the fact that many Chinese workers have been recruited to go and work in Zambia. It has been reported that thousands of Chinese nationals are working there (McGreal 2007) and it is often argued that most of the jobs being done by Chinese can ably be done by Zambians. For example, the current bricklayers for the construction of the Sino-Zambian Friendship stadium are Chinese, while Zambians are confined to mixing cement (fieldnotes, Ndola, August 2009). However, it is evident that there are relatively more local workers employed in Chinese companies than in other countries, such as Sierra Leone for example (Carmody 2009a), but this is nonetheless an issue which has generated concern and resistance amongst Zambians, although less than there might be because of another axis of engagement. Journalists examining an issue of the *Post*, which is Zambia's largest independent newspaper, in June 2008 found that there were no fewer than thirty stories in it from the official Chinese government press agency (Michel, Beuret and Woods 2009), which employs around eight times more people than the best-known private press agency in the world, Reuters. This reporting may favourably influence public perceptions of China.

There are also other contradictions arising from greater Chinese involvement in Zambia. In the survey of Asian businesses, two of the main issues identified were currency instability and the desire to reduce taxes. The Zambian kwacha is a commodity currency, or one whose value tracks copper prices and exports. When copper prices go up, the kwacha goes up in value as well. As China is now the world's largest consumer of copper, its demand largely drives the copper price, which has fluctuated dramatically recently. The dramatic currency depreciation as the copper price fell in 2008 had substantial implications for the majority of Zambians by raising the cost of imports, and also affecting profit margins for Chinese traders, for example. Thus, increased dependence of the national economy on copper exports potentially undermines other axes of Chinese engagement as traders' profits may be reduced and prices for overseas inputs into the new economic zones may fluctuate, undermining production planning.

The Impacts of the Global Recession on Sino-Zambian Relations

Since mid-2008 the global economy has entered a period of profound turbulence. The extent and depth of the current global financial and economic crises are unknown; however, it is worthwhile interrogating the impacts of the crisis to examine the future prospects for Sino-Zambian economic relations. What then are the channels through which Zambia's economy is being affected by the current global crisis and what are the impacts on Asian investment and trade links likely to be?

Cali et al. (2008) identify two types of channels through which Africa was affected by the crisis: financial and real. The financial channels include flows into stock markets, bank lending and FDI. The real channels they identify are remittances, import and export volumes, terms of trade and aid.

Oil exporters and other mono-economies, such as Zambia, dependent on a single commodity which saw dramatic reductions in price, were adversely affected by the crisis. In November 2008, the Canadian mining company, First Quantum laid off 286 workers at its mine in Zambia, and there have been other closures and projects have been put on hold. Reportedly, 100 small-scale Chinese mine operators left Zambian mines as the copper price declined by 65 per cent in 2008 (Herbst and Mills 2009). However, this was offset by new large-scale investments by Chinese state-owned enterprises, as the Chinese government still has to recycle its massive foreign exchange reserve and is pursuing a 'counter-cyclical' policy both domestically and internationally (Davies 2009). The copper price recovered to approximately US$7,000 per ton by early 2010 and the momentum of the mining-led construction and service sector booms meant economic growth in Zambia remained relatively robust at 5 per cent for 2009 (RoZ 2009). Some even estimate economic growth at close to 7 per cent for the year.

The new Zambian President, Rupiah Banda, is confident that his country's new relationship with China will help the country ride out the crisis, and indeed the likely impact of the crisis will be further to deepen and entrench Zambian economic relations with Asia as opposed to Northern countries. The President of the African EXIM Bank has argued that one of the ways for African countries to insulate themselves from the effects of the crisis is to diversify their exports towards the Asian markets (Xinhua 2008). Thus the crisis may serve to reorient African economies further towards the still relatively fast-growing countries of East and South Asia. As noted earlier, China is now already Africa's second-largest trading partner and the largest for some countries like South Africa (*African Business* 2009; Radio Netherlands Worldwide 2009). South Africa exports 65 per cent of all the metal ores exported from Africa to China (Holslag et al. 2007).

While Arrighi (2007) refers to China's influence in the developing world as 'domination without hegemony', others see China losing influence. For example, when the DRC closed its border with Zambia to combat illegal mining and smuggling of minerals, some Chinese companies in Zambia, whose plants were designed to process ore from DRC, were brought close to bankruptcy (Michel, Beuret and Woods 2009). Reportedly, the Chinese government brought pressure to bear on both parties, but without an immediate resolution.

The Zambian economy remains heavily and increasingly dependent on copper exports. Indeed Chinese companies are taking the opportunity to purchase major mines, such as Luanshya, from European companies which have closed as a result of the global economic crisis. Chinese companies are thus positioning themselves strategically for the global economic upturn.

The rise of China is a world historic event which may be somewhat slowed down, but not stopped, by the current financial crisis, as its economy continues to grow rapidly. Consequently interaction between China and Zambia, and Africa more broadly, will continue to increase. Ten times as many Chinese entrepreneurs migrated to Africa in 2006 as in 2003 (Arrighi 2007), and while the pace of migration may moderate, it seems unlikely to be reversed. Migration is in part driven by the desire to access more land for cultivation, as was discussed in the previous chapter.

As discussed in the preceding chapters, the new scramble for Africa is primarily about getting access to increasingly scarce, and hence valuable, resources, and also markets. It is different from the first scramble in terms of the variety of actors and the fact that Asian companies are now playing a substantial role as compared to European ones. It also has distinctive features such as the development of SEZs. The final chapter of this book assesses the new scramble in historical context and examines whether or not it may be possible for Africans to assert more control over the destiny of their continent.

9 CAN AFRICANS UNSCRAMBLE THE CONTINENT?

There is a great variety of external actors involved in Africa today; both old and new, with varying motivations, who are interested in both the short and long-term benefits. There is thus no great sense in character-izing or understanding their actions as imperial. The contemporary world is far more complex than it was during the late nineteenth century and there is no serious comparison between the initial and the new scrambles, however inviting the label might be. (Melber and Southall 2009, p. xxii)

Asia is also much more important as a trading partner for Africa than Africa is for Asia. While China, India and Asia as a whole are beginning to dominate Africa's imports and exports, Africa in 2005 took only 2.55 per cent of China's exports and less than 2 per cent of Asia's exports, and represented but 3.45 per cent of China's imports and less than 2 per cent of Asia's imports. Nor is this figure increasing: the share of both imports and exports is less than it was in 1980, with the export share falling by over half. This reveals a pattern of unequal exchange and power, common for so long with Europe and North America. (Martin 2008, p. 126)

This book has described the drivers, actors, nature and impacts of the new scramble for African resources and markets. In this concluding chapter, the major themes of the book are brought together to assess the likely impacts on inter-state conflict and African political and economic development in the coming decades.

Scrambling to Conflict or Democracy? The United States and China in Africa

The original scramble for Africa was a military affair often involving conflict with indigenous African groups (Pakenham 1991). However, as noted earlier, it was largely consensual amongst the colonial powers as a result of the Congress of Berlin. Only in the case of Fashoda, in modern-day Sudan, did the two main powers involved, Britain and France, nearly come to blows. France conceded in this instance, partly to secure Britain's alliance against a rising Germany. There have been echoes of this more recently.

As Africa rose up Britain's foreign policy agenda towards the end of the last millennium, the British Foreign Secretary instituted a process to resolve disputes with Paris over Africa called the St Malo process, which led to more frequent bilateral meetings (Porteous 2008). As discussed earlier, the French are also making space for the increased American presence on the continent, and the Chinese and the Americans are now holding dialogues over Africa. Rather than Britain and France, it is now the US and China and their companies which compete most heavily in Africa, with many other emergent players and powers as well.

In Chinese government statements, there are often references to the need to guard against and cooperate with other developing countries against 'hegemonism'. This phraseology is obviously directed against the United States. However, as noted earlier, the Chinese government has spoken of the country's 'peaceful rise' as an objective in the international system. More recently it was felt that even this phrase was potentially too threatening and aggressive, and it has been replaced by the phrase 'peaceful development'.

The Chinese government is fully aware that it cannot compete against the United States militarily. In 2008 the United States spent 41.5 per cent of total global military expenditure – more than nearly the next thirty biggest military spenders in the world combined – and China was second, for the first time, at 5.8 per cent (Stockholm International Peace Research Institute 2010) as Chinese military expenditure has tripled in the last decade. Given these statistics, the Chinese have a strategy of 'asymmetric power projection', whereby they seek to compete primarily economically and politically, rather than militarily, with the US (Ramo 2004). Other powers are also dramatically increasing military spending, whether for competitive or defensive purposes. In 2009 India increased defence spending by more than a third, in part perhaps to guard against any Chinese attempt to restrict sea lane access (Patel 2009).

According to the Director of the Royal African Society in the United Kingdom, 'if it comes to a battle for the world's diminishing resources, the US may choose to fall back on its military might. So wary China is building a substantial ocean-going navy. In 2006 defence spending was increased by 15 per cent. Africa could be a battleground' (Dowden 2009, p. 487). However, other analysts point out that much of China's increased military spending is defensive. While military planners in the Pentagon worry about 'choke points' which might disrupt US trade – such as the Suez Canal through which much of the world's oil supply transits and which can be blocked by the sinking of a ship, as happened in 2004 for example – the Chinese arguably face a global 'choke space' as the United States has the world's only 'blue water' navy.[1]

What Richard Dowden's analysis neglects are the intense intercon-nections between the United States and Chinese economies, which make open conflict between the two highly unlikely. The Chinese are dependent on US FDI and markets for their goods, while the United States is dependent now on cheap industrial goods from China and the Chinese government recycling its massive foreign exchange reserves by buying United States government debt. Competition for African resources is a relatively minor concern compared to the importance of these flows. Consequently, economic globalization has reduced major inter-state conflicts, while promoting some other inter-state ones – particularly in Africa, as almost 70 per cent of all conflict-related deaths around the world from 1994 to 2003 occurred in SSA (United Nations Development Programme 2005). Thus any conflict between the US and China is likely to take a proxy form, as has happened already in the cases of Chad and Sudan, where they backed different sides in these overlapping conflicts.

Conflict is a double-edged sword in terms of geo-economic strate-gies. It may be simultaneously economically functional and dysfunc-tional for outside powers. As noted earlier, the conflict in Darfur gives Chinese companies a competitive advantage over Western ones in Sudan who are either unable to invest as a result of sanctions (American companies) or more likely to be subject to reputational risk and consumer boycotts (European and Japanese companies). However, if conflict becomes large-scale and geographically extensive, it can substantially disrupt trade. Consequently, both the United States and China, and other external powers, have a general common interest in the maintenance of conditions facilitative of African resource extraction, and the avoidance of uncontrolled conflict. While their companies may compete over specific sites, this common interest also creates incentives for cooperation, again making direct military confrontation in Africa unlikely. Sarah Raine (2009) argues that Africa is a space where the Americans and the Chinese can test the limits of conflict and cooperation.

According to an American diplomat in Congo-Brazzaville, the ambassador there has made competing with Chinese business interests his highest priority (Michel, Beuret and Woods 2009). Geo-economic competition with China is then likely to dominate American foreign policy in Africa, and neither major power has been shy of supporting autocrats, sometimes simultaneously, where their interests dictate. Western and Chinese support for autocrats may generate other conflicts, however.

According to Tom Porteous (2008, p. 129):

> across Africa, counterterrorism concerns led to a deepening of the relationships between Western and African security and intelligence agencies. This in turn has resulted in a distinct militarization of the West's approach to African states, which served to strengthen the very groups whose actions and lack of accountability had been the cause of so much conflict and destabilization in Africa in the past.

As has been recounted during the course of this book, there are new conflicts being sparked by this militaristic approach – in Niger, for example – which does not sit easily with another arm of Western policy on the continent – democracy promotion.

The Chinese government position is that Africa, like China itself, is not yet ready for liberal multi-party democracy and that pushing this philosophy has resulted in increased conflict. There would appear to be empirical support for this proposition. For example, the disputed Kenyan elections of 2007 resulted in over 1,500 people being killed, largely as a result of ethnic conflict as different groups backed different parties. Raila Odinga, the current Prime Minister, secured 98 per cent of the Luo vote for example (Collier 2009). For one Chinese author, 'fortunately, the scurrilous machinations of the West, which have caused so much tension within African nations, have been foiled, and the "waves of democratization on the continent have started to weaken since 1995"' (Wu 2006, pp. 40 and 46, quoted in Michel and Beuret 2009, p. 70). The noted Oxford development economist Paul Collier also calls democracy promotion in very low-income countries 'democrazy' (Collier 2009).

It would appear that democracy must be internally driven to be sustainable, although this does not mean that authoritarian governments should be supported. As this book has described, Western and other powers have once again become increasingly tolerant of autocrats in Africa in order to secure resource access and 'security'. A veneer of democracy is maintained, however. For example, President Paul Kagame in Rwanda won 93 per cent of the vote in the election in 2010. All of his opposition at the poll were affiliated with, or supportive of, his party. There are 'opposition' parties in the government, for example, while the real opposition was harassed and arrested on charges of 'genocide denial' prior to the election. Consequently, authoritarian states are being strengthened as a result of the new scramble. However, some might argue that there is a potential upside to this. The East Asian, and in particular Chinese, experience has shown authoritarian governments are sometimes compatible with economic development. As China's governance impact increases in Africa, what are the likely outcomes?

Chinese Power and African Political Economy

As the only developing country with a permanent seat at the United Nations Security Council China has a particular structural power which enables it to help shape global rules and regimes. This exceptionalism is manifest in discourse. For example, the biggest geopolitical grouping of developing countries is referred to as the 'G77 and China'. China is obviously first amongst unequals in this group and the other developing country groupings to which it belongs. China's ability to lead in this context is partly because there are important coincidences of interest between it and other BRICs in seeking to move away from a unipolar world dominated by the United States (Ribeiro 2009).

China brings political competitive advantages to its relations with African states. The avowed policy of 'non-interference' in African government or governance is particularly attractive to incumbent political elites. Consequently, external support for authoritarian regimes from China looks likely to remain firmly in place.

The Chinese state has been described as ruthlessly developmental as its legitimacy is dependent on economic growth. While Ramo (2004) argues that there is a Beijing Consensus on economic policy which disavows static comparative advantage in favour of developing countries leapfrogging into higher-technology economic activities, in Africa there is as yet little evidence of this. While certain features of the Chinese economic model, such as SEZs, are being transferred, the nature of 'the' African state remains intact and the notion of China as a model is more as an alternative to Western prescriptions, rather than as a coherent set of policies.

Rather than prescribing a particular set of economic reforms, the Chinese are tolerant of a 'flexeconomy' approach, as long as African countries remain open to Chinese trade and investment.[2] Politically, the Consensus as ingested by African state elites is that you can do whatever you like, as long these conditions are met and you support Beijing at international fora. In some cases, T-55 tank assembly plants serve Chinese interests, whereas multi-facility SEZs work better in other countries. Flexigemony in Africa then is first and foremost about economics and the politics required to support China's continued economic ascent. Such a socio-political configuration is unlikely to promote economic transformation in Africa. What are the possibilities in this context for moving beyond autocracy to more representative and developmental governance?

The answer to this question depends crucially on the class structure of African societies and how this evolves. Many African states are authoritarian, either of the soft or hard variety, and the elites collude with foreign interests to accumulate wealth for themselves to the detriment of local populations. So-called 'donor countries' pressure African governments to open up their markets and trade, and make noises about democracy, while in practice often turning a blind eye to human rights abuses. In the rich countries, working and middle classes have been key to holding the state accountable; however, in Africa these social classes have been underdeveloped.

The neo-colonial post-independence era saw the emergence of different class strata in African society. The majority of the population continued to rely on agriculture for subsistence, but urbanization also gave rise to middle and working classes and an underemployed 'lumpen proletariat' in the informal sector. As economies were weak, the 'best and the brightest' often went into politics, where the monetary rewards could be vast. Kenya's parliamentarians are reportedly the highest-paid in the world. Given the high stakes involved in maintaining political power in this context, often only the most ruthless politicians survive. As Paul Collier (2009) has argued, many African politicians might not be the kind of people your parents would like you to invite home for tea, but they would beat you at poker.

Increased Asian investment has led to growing formal sector employment in some countries in mining, agriculture and infrastructure in particular, but it is doubtful that these employment changes will fundamentally alter the class structure of African society, partly because many Chinese companies often bring over their own workers. Also there has been very little growth in technical, administrative and professional employment – the 'intermediate classes' – except perhaps in South Africa, where there is a growing black middle class. Rather, Africa is still, for the most part, characterized by a class gulf between the politically connected elites and the impoverished masses. Under a liberal trade and capital regime, only if labour costs rise substantially in China and elsewhere in Asia and there is massive offshoring of labour-intensive manufacturing and services might a forceful industrial working class, which could keep the state accountable, develop. For the moment, however, the new scramble for Africa is largely replicating previous patterns of enclave-led growth on the continent. By giving rentier states access to new revenue streams, it is also reinforcing the power of incumbent and often authoritarian regimes, although there are also progressive dimensions to it. What about the likely impacts of the new scramble on economic development?

Power, Development and Economic Structure

As discussed in chapter 1, the current development fashion is for integration into the global economy. Very few people would now disagree that Africa needs to be integrated. However, the questions are what the terms of integration are, and how increased Asian and American involvement, investment and trade, in particular, on the continent are affecting the prospects for a more strategic integration.

As has been argued over the last half-century in the political economy literature, underdevelopment is a relational phenomenon and process. As some parts of the world become rich, others are underdeveloped by processes of combined and uneven development, such as unequal trade and capital flows. Some places serve as resource colonies for others as they industrialize. For example, as a result of the huge differentials in purchasing power, the average command of the inhabitants of the core or rich countries of the global economy over the human and natural resources of SSA is approximately sixty times more than the other way around (Arrighi 2003, cited in Payne 2005), and it is well known that several planets would be required for all of the earth's population to consume at North American rates.

Some more mainstream work acknowledges power inequality. For example, in his most recent book, Jeffrey Sachs has acknowledged that colonialism was deeply unhelpful to African development, and the need to move beyond a violent world order where nation states 'scramble for markets, power and resources' (2008, p. 3). However, for Sachs, many low-income countries in SSA are stuck in a 'poverty trap' in which they are simply too poor to grow.

Where the majority of people are poor, savings rates, of necessity, will be low. Also, rich Africans tend to offshore their capital to other continents. Low investment means that these countries remain stuck in what economists call a factor-driven growth stage based on cheap labour, land or natural resources, rather than deriving growth from investment or innovation which requires highly educated workers, technology, capital and infrastructure. Absent substantial foreign investment, which has been scarce outside of the resource sector, this is the pattern in much of Africa. However, the question which must be asked is: how have these traps been constructed and how are they reproduced through time?

Underdevelopment is related to inequality at a global scale. In fact, we might think of underdevelopment as the primary manifestation of global inequality. The scale of this inequality is vast. The richest 500 people in the world have a combined income greater than the poorest 416 million (United Nations Development Programme 2005; Lines 2008), and the 3 richest people have assets worth more than the poorest 600 million people earn in a year. While roughly half of the world's population lives on less than the equivalent of US$2 a day – in terms of what it would buy you in the United States – some financial traders are, until recently at least, paid up to a billion dollars a year (Blake, Barber and LaFranco April/May 2006). The former head of ExxonMobil, the world's largest private-sector company by market valuation, earned US$686 million during his tenure (Maass 2009).

In the 'new economic geography' theories discussed earlier, greater openness and infrastructural investment will lead to development as markets overcome the barriers of 'natural' geography. However, global poverty is the outcome of power inequality (Oyen 2004). This power inequality is not fundamentally rooted in physical geography – although it partly has its genesis in this – but in differential agent positions in largely unregulated markets. Power inequality is socially reproduced through social structures to the benefit of existing power holders. Overcoming underdevelopment in Africa will require power redistribution and conflict resolution, not a reshaping of its physical geography.

Economic geographers refer to 'rounds of restructuring' in which the nature of economies changes as old industries and infrastructures are closed and new ones created (Lovering 1989). Africa is currently undergoing an intensified round of economic restructuring driven largely by the growth of Asia and increasing global resource scarcity, and advances in technology, particularly the rapid diffusion of mobile phones, although the extent to which these are substantively changing the broader developmental landscape is open to question (Carmody 2010). Nonetheless, this round of economic restructuring is significant.

Kaplinsky and Farooki (2009) see the current round of economic restructuring in Africa as a period of 'punctuated equilibrium', in which, after a period of relative stability – or in Africa's case, stable decline – conditions change to a new, in this case hopefully more positive, equilibrium. As China is now the world's second-biggest economy, and India will be perhaps the third-largest by 2035, the authors argue that their growth will disrupt and change previous patterns of economic development on the continent.

In a widely cited article Acemoglu, Johnson and Robinson (2001) argue that the nature of European colonialism in Africa largely influenced post-colonial patterns of development. Their argument is that, where there were substantial numbers of European settlers, different institutions, such as secure property rights, were put in place. In contrast, they argue, where there were few settlers, more extractive institutions were developed and these patterns continued in the post-colonial period – although other scholars have disputed this deterministic interpretation of history (Austin 2008). Current patterns of BRIC investment, trade and migration are different from previous European ones, and it remains to be seen exactly what types of institutions will result from this increased 'inter-regionalism' or interconnection between Asia and Africa, in particular. However, the emergence of new economic powers in Africa has opened up more policy space – flexeconomy.

The genius of Deng Xiaoping in China was to realize the power of markets and also the need to constrain them. His reform programme was inspired by a desire not to repeat the past disasters of the Cultural Revolution and the so-called 'Great Leap Forward' from which he had suffered personally. He was also a pragmatist, arguing that the path across the river is found by groping for the stones.

According to the head of one of the largest African multinational banks, the Togo-based Ecobank, 'Africa is where China was twenty years ago' (*African Banker* 2008). However, this thinking has the classic failings of the a-historical 'stages of development model', as twenty years ago China did not have to compete with China,[3] and Africa's economy is already highly liberalized, unlike China's even today. Consequently, there is much more limited scope in the current global economic system or regime, which favours free markets, to engage in strategic industrial policy interventions in order to develop and grow 'infant industries' and foster learning-by-doing. Rather, there is a danger that African countries will be trapped in a mercantilist cycle with China: exporting raw materials and importing manufactures (Kurlantzick 2007).

There are certain states in Africa which have attempted to foster economic growth as part of their regime survival strategy, such as Uganda, whereas in others the regime has destroyed the economy to stay in power, as in Zimbabwe. There have been a variety of problems with potentially more developmental states in Africa, however.

Uganda achieved relatively rapid economic growth, based on following the precepts of the World Bank and the IMF, during the 1990s. While poverty arguably reduced, there was no structural transformation of the economy as it remained heavily dependent on agriculture in particular. Uganda also boosted its economic growth through the plundering of the DRC, as described earlier, and substantial oil reserves have also been discovered. It remains to be seen whether the 'curse of the black gold' will manifest itself there too.

The new scramble has, however, also brought some concrete economic benefits to Africa. Rates of economic growth have dramatically improved over the dismal 1980s and early 1990s. Some new jobs have been created in mining, infrastructure and, on a more limited scale, in manufacturing investment. Higher growth and tax revenues mean more money is available for state legitimation expenditure, as in Angola, but the importance of enclaves, of either the mineral, manufacturing or agricultural types, is also being reinforced. Enclave development is problematic because states can access revenues from these without being more broadly accountable to their populations through tax bargains (Leonard and Strauss 2003).

Infrastructure is a key constraint on manufacturing development in Africa. Around 40 per cent of Africans live in countries that are landlocked (Broadman 2007a) and, as a result of poor infrastructure, one Chinese firm in South Africa finds that sending products to Angola is as expensive as shipping them to China. While there are currently major infrastructure projects being put in place across the continent, it is important that new transport infrastructure which is put in place does not simply run from the interior to the coast in order to facilitate natural resource extraction and manufactured imports, as during the colonial period. While the new scramble is reintegrating Africa into the global economy and reducing 'distance' in the World Bank schema, the quality of trade is important. Intra-African trade only accounts for about 8 per cent of the continent's total trade, but is much more technology-intensive than extra-regional trade and consequently should be promoted in order to foster technological development and upgrading (Kaplinsky and Farooki 2009). Also, Chinese infrastructure companies often import up to 70 per cent of the labour from China to work on projects, reducing the impact on unemployment in African countries (Rocha 2006).

While it is thought in Western policy circles that best practice is to untie aid, so that recipients do not have to purchase designated products and services from the donor country, India and China adopt a different approach by often integrating lines of credit with resource extraction deals. Consequently, the trade–aid–investment 'vectors' of economic engagement are linked and coordinated in ways arguably reminiscent of colonial rule (Kaplinsky and Farooki 2009). However, it should be noted that lines of credit, even when they are at somewhat concessional interest rates, do not constitute aid; only the interest rate reduction below market rates in this instance constitutes aid (Brautigam 2009).

African consumers are often now able to access cheap Asian imported manufactured products. 'Thanks to affordable Chinese manufacturing, millions of Africans are able to buy their first piece of high-tec electronic equipment' (Dowden 2009, p. 492), whether it be a mobile phone or a radio. However in Osikango, Namibia, Chinese traders sell a carton of 300 shoes for US$100 (Kaplinsky, McCormick and Morris 2006), which no local producer can hope to compete with. 'Even in Angola's war-torn region of Huambo, five Chinese retailers have, since their arrival in 2000, managed to carve out a position that has effectively closed down established suppliers and retailers' (Alden 2005, p. 157). Thus the gains from both trade and production are largely kept within ethnic business networks, rather than diffusing through local populations.

Faster economic growth in Africa has attracted increased investment, even outside of the traditional mineral resource extraction area. Whereas in 2004 there were only two investment funds that invested primarily in Africa, by 2007 there were more than a dozen (Dowden 2009). Africa also has the fastest growth rate for use of mobile phones in the world. As other markets have become saturated for these products, much of Africa is a 'frontier' – perhaps the last major largely untapped market. However, for the most part, these phones are not developed or manufactured in Africa, and usage by itself has limited capacity to raise productivity.

In much of the recent literature there has also been an emphasis on how Africa can 'move up the value chain' into higher-value agro-processing, mineral beneficiation and manufacturing (Cramer 1999). It is undoubtedly correct that this needs to happen, but the challenges of achieving this are stark. China is now outcompeting even its regional neighbours – with the partial exception of Vietnam in labour-intensive manufactures – leading to a spatial reconcentration of manufacturing value chains in that country (Yusuf, Naabeshima and Perkins 2007). Indeed, China is now the world's leading exporter of high technology, meaning that it is now able to 'sell all along the line', a feature of previous economic hegemonies such as the US and Britain at different points in their history (Balogh 1963).

Citing work by Hidalgo, Barabasi and Haussman, the World Bank (2009) in its *World Development Report* – discussed in detail earlier – also argues that 'diversifying an economy is no easy task' and that the 'current export structure of a country determines how easy it will be to diversify its production base over higher-value products' (p. 263). It is argued that 'the main goal of any regional integration process should thus be to promote sound export-led growth. Indeed, the success factor of regional integration is "open regionalism"' (p. 264). However, if economic diversification is difficult, such a policy will often lock in the existing economic patterns in Africa, as the growth impulses are externally rather than domestically determined. According to the renowned economist Robert Wade (2003), development is about establishing a creative synergy between internal and external impulses.

There may be more scope for Africa in areas complementary to Chinese growth, such as in agro-processing and minerals. Agro-processing also offers somewhat limited potential for value addition by its nature. Africa then confronts an economically full world, at the same time as demand for its natural resources is increasing to satisfy the (generally) growing global economy. There is then a particular path dependence to the commodity chains which were put in place during colonialism. This path dependence and the resource- and agro-based structures of African colonial economies created global commodity chains which constrain the ability to diversify economies.

Mineral processing is notoriously capital-intensive, with few linkages and multiplier effects, and therefore will not result in structural transformation, unless the mineral rents can be harvested and sown. Thus, in contrast to what is often assumed, it is possible to industrialize resource-based economies. As Kaplinsky and Farooki (2009, p. 23) argue, 'either Africa can remain a simple source of materials, providing little else but basic ores and oil, or it can become a source of knowledge for the resource sector. This high road is a path trodden by the USA in the 19th Century and by Australia and Norway in recent decades where the National System of Innovation was oriented to making the most of the commodity resources (Wright and Czelusta 2004).' This will depend on renegotiation of, or scrapping, the transnational contract of extroversion.

Some scholars have argued that African governments, through the AU, or NEPAD which is now an official programme of that organization, should undertake collective bargaining and have common standards in their dealings with outside companies and other actors. The AU and NEPAD seek to take advantage of the opportunities offered by globalization while minimizing its adverse effects (Soderbaum 2007). For example, some have suggested that resource access agreements, for fish for example, should be negotiated collectively by African countries to prevent under-bidding and a 'race to the bottom'. In Peru the President ordered that certain types of fish should only be caught for human consumption and not for fishmeal, which is exported (Leyton 2000). Such an approach could, in theory, be adopted across Africa.

African governments should adopt a strategic approach to foreign investment, by selectively continuing to promote it while maximizing local benefits, as China has. Given the extent of sunk costs in new mining investments and MFEZs, African governments will potentially have greater bargaining power with the Chinese and other major investors. In one case the ZDA (n.d.) has found evidence of linkages between foreign and domestic firms, and African governments should attempt to nurture such extra-regional export linkages among Asian firms, in addition to helping develop small and medium-sized indigenous businesses which can feed into global supply chains.

Small-scale investments which displace local entrepreneurs should be discouraged, as profits may be expatriated and fewer local staff hired, while large-scale investments, such as the copper smelter in the Zambian MFEZ, which represent additional investment, should be encouraged. China in the initial stages of its market-led reforms imposed conditions, such as the necessity of having local joint-venture partners, on foreign investors (Breslin 2007). The huge increases in foreign investment which parts of Africa have witnessed of late (Zambia achieved an inflow of US$1.3 billion in 2007 (interview with Manager, ZDA, August 2009)) allow greater latitude to impose these types of conditions.[4]

Such an approach will require the construction of a policy that is more autonomous from China and also the World Bank. Indeed, according to a manager at Chambishi Copper Mine, the Chinese President told managers there on his visit in 2007 that they had to 'take away less, and give back, contribute more' (quoted in Haglund 2008, p. 568), suggesting an openness to greater regulation. Informally, the Chinese say they are open to discussing such proposals, but African officials do not raise them (Keet 2010), perhaps because their material interests are well served by the current configuration of relations, or because they have been habituated to free market thinking after decades of SAPs, or a combination of the two.

However, the World Bank (2009b) continues to press for further government divestment from the mining sector, and details on Chinese loans to African governments are often kept secret. Movements for transparency therefore assume a critical importance in Africa's developmental future. However, it must be mass socio-political movements which carry a more assertive, transformational agenda. How likely is this? The fundamental issue is the vast power inequalities between external and African actors and between the masses and political elites within Africa. Consequently the nature of and struggles over the African state are of central importance.

Conclusion: The New Scramble in Perspective

> The New Scramble presents both opportunities and threats for African economic development, but which of these is predominant will depend on social and political struggles. It appears to be largely reinforcing the resource-based nature of African economies and authoritarian states. For example, while there was a near balance between manufactures and primary exports to China from Africa in 2001, by 2008 84 per cent of African exports to China were primary commodities. (UNCTAD 2010)

The political economy of colonialism was centred on resource extraction, and historically most Africans have benefited very little from their resources. The Asian footprint in Africa to date has been heavily based on natural resources, and capital accumulation in the primary sector tends to be more conflictual. As many African currencies are unconvertible, natural resources serve as substitute currencies – a source of sovereignty (Nordstrom 2007) – and the majority of Africans have benefited little from them.

In an effort to attract foreign investment under World Bank and IMF-sponsored programmes of economic liberalization and structural adjustment, African governments have set very low mineral royalty rates, as noted in the Zambian case discussed earlier, for example. In other cases, such as in Ghana – which is often hailed for reviving its mining industry, particularly in gold – mining only accounts for about 3 per cent of total tax revenue (IMF 2005, cited in Prichard 2009). In Guinea, local communities are only expected to receive 0.4 per cent of tax revenues arising out of a new aluminium smelter (Labonne 2009, cited in Prichard 2009). These examples show how previous resource-extractive and exploitative patterns are being replicated in the current era.

Western dominance in Africa in the 1980s and 1990s was associated with falling commodity prices and conflict. For example, in 1989 the United States withdrew from the International Coffee Agreement and the price of coffee plummeted. In response Rwandan farmers pulled up hundreds of thousands of trees and their children out of school (Chossudovsky 1997), and the resulting poverty was implicated in the subsequent genocide of 1994. This was the initial phase of the reassertion of Western dominance on the continent. Then the US stopped supporting some of the autocrats whom it had previously backed, such as Siad Barre in Somalia, launching that country into decades of civil war. Higher commodity prices driven by Asian demand and renewed support for autocratic governments is likely to reduce the number of failed states in Africa, but also to promote resistance in particular resource-rich locales where people are not being seen to benefit proportionately: new point, as opposed to diffuse, conflicts. As global resource scarcity bites in the context of constrained supply, geo-economic competition between multinational companies and their home countries will become even more acute, in some cases potentially leading to new proxy conflicts.

As some authors have noted, there are fundamental differences between the first and current scrambles for Africa. The current scramble has emerged in a context in which African states are juridically or legally sovereign, and consequently there is greater potential for them to bargain with major powers and multinational resource companies over conditions of access – so it has increased the power of political elites in resource-rich states (Vines et al. 2009). Indeed, contrary to popular perception and much academic writing (e.g. Strange 1996), globalization has not necessarily reduced the power of poor Third World states.

In 2008 the President of Angola argued that 'globalization naturally makes us see the need to diversify international relations and to accept the principle of competition, which has in a dynamic manner replaced the petrified concept of zones of influence that used to characterise the world' (quoted in Vines et al. 2009, p. 56). The new scramble, in contrast to the contest between the old colonial powers, can be likened to a three-legged race in which outside powers are tied to African state elites – but they are not necessarily tied to them permanently, given the greater diversity of potential partners.

The fact that African states are juridically independent has other impacts. While labour practices in Asian firms in Africa have been controversial, they do not perhaps compare to the brutality of colonialism, in which mothers in Portuguese Mozambique were forced to leave their new-borns in boxes until they had picked a certain amount of cotton (Hanlon 1996), people in Congo were executed, or porters had their feet tarred in British Tanganyika to stop them wearing through (Schraeder 2000).

However, it is different from the previous scramble for Africa because there is also relatively small-scale but still significant – particularly Chinese – investment taking place in manufacturing, unlike during the colonial era. Manufacturing investment offers potential for economic diversification, particularly if African nodes can be inserted into GPNs for export over the longer term. To date, however, there would appear to be little evidence of this from the survey reported earlier. Current Asian investment fits with an extractive rather than a productive and transformative pattern of globalization. This must be changed through policies of embedding foreign investment and linking it to domestic companies so that they too can grow and expand into overseas markets. Whether such a goal can be realized will depend importantly on relations with China.

The Chinese 'march into Africa' is, however, still a relatively recent phenomenon and faces challenges of both economic and social embedding. For example, over roughly the last decade there were fourteen Chinese manufacturers which set up operations in South Africa. Yet by 2008 all of these had closed down. According to Richard Dowden (2009), this was because the Chinese business model and labour regime did not work in a country with strong trade unions and labour laws.

The difference between the first and the second scrambles is the difference between colonialism and globalization. It is the difference between direct territorial control and juridical independence in the era of what sociologist Manuel Castells calls the 'space [and time] of flows' (Castells 2009). However, this should not obscure the similarities. Both were largely economic in motivation – particularly in the desire to gain access to resources to sustain and grow national (post-)industrial advantage. Both the colonial occupation and the new scramble are being largely conducted by private, and in some cases state-owned, companies. The French often granted near-sovereignty to their concessionary companies operating in Africa. There are echoes of this in the Chinese SEZs being set up across the continent, although national laws still apply selectively, so these are now 'graduated sovereignties' (Ong 2006).

The era of exclusive economic spaces, outside of SEZs or mineral concessions, is over, although the latter may be cheaper forms of quasi-sovereignty focused on resource extraction without having to pay colonial administration costs. Perhaps then it may be more accurate to refer to the current round of increased interest and investment in Africa as the Scramble in Africa, rather than the Scramble for Africa. The scramble in Africa is largely about achieving secure access to natural resources, and building the alliances and security cooperation arrangements which will facilitate and sustain this.

This Scramble in Africa is in any event an outcome of the policies of economic liberalization and globalization promoted by Western governments and the institutions they largely control: the World Bank, the IMF and, to a lesser extent, the World Trade Organization. It was these institutions and Western governments which encouraged or indeed required India, Brazil and other developing countries to liberalize their economies in exchange for loans. The dramatic increases in economic growth which were unleashed in some of these countries, then, have generated massively increased demand for natural resources.

The Chinese followed a somewhat different path, as they did not adopt a completely free market approach to their development, judiciously mixing state and market mechanisms to achieve the desired results, but they were certainly encouraged by the Western powers to open their economy to FDI and to liberalize their trade.

Different rising and established powers have, however, pursued a multiplicity of strategies and modes of penetration and integration into African economies (Perrot and Malaquais 2009) but China is now undoubtedly the most influential country in Africa, as it is currently the biggest provider of loans to the continent, even outstripping the World Bank. However, the perception that the Chinese government is directing all axes of engagement with Africa from above, for example, is misplaced, as individual companies and entrepreneurs may also pursue their own strategies, independent of their home governments.

Speaking from his own perspective, a Western mining executive said: 'the horse [Africa] has bolted but we can still talk to the rider [China]' (quoted in Dowden 2009, p. 504). Thus, it would appear that there is an awareness amongst both private-sector and, increasingly, public-sector actors that China must be engaged with in and by Africa. London School of Economics Politics Professor Christopher Alden has also noted that, while China has an Africa strategy, Africa does not have a China strategy, and that there is an urgent need to develop this (Alden 2005; Cheru and Calais 2010). However, China prefers to deal individually with African countries through FOCAC rather than with the AU.

What is sometimes neglected, however, is that African political elites already have a China strategy, which is to use it as a counterweight to Western conditionality and thereby bolster their own rule. There is thus an implicit 'liberal' bargain between them and China. African governments do not, for the most part, impose regulations on Chinese investment, while the Chinese government does not impose political conditions on African state elites. As a manager from the Zambia–China Mulungushi Textile Factory noted, echoing theories of dependency: 'instead of winning the confidence of the employees, the Chinese action was to win the politicians' confidence' (quoted in Brooks 2010, p. 130). Western governments are now also contemplating reducing conditionality on their aid in order to compete with China (Isaac 2010).

As access to resources becomes an increasingly strategic priority for the United States and Europe, and competition with China intensifies, there is likely to be even less external pressure on African governments in relation to 'governance' issues. The head of the European Investment Bank has also argued that the bank should lower its standards on the environment and social issues in order to compete with the Chinese in Africa, for example (Bosshard 2008). While President Obama pointedly snubbed Nigeria as a destination on his first official trip to Africa, in favour of more democratic Ghana, so-called *realpolitik* – in which countries pursue their interests with few scruples – continues to dominate practice, if not discourse and pronouncements. This is not a promising development for the continent.

It is important to remember though that there is diversity amongst African states and that they are not just vehicles of personal enrichment for elites, but continue to provide services for the citizens, even if often at very low levels. Ordinary people may also benefit from new job opportunities, in the infrastructure, construction and mineral extraction sectors in particular, and from cheap Chinese imports. However, as others such as Ian Taylor (2007) have argued, the overall structure of African political economy is likely to remain largely intact.

Pliny the Elder wrote that there was always something new out of Africa. This may be true, but another aphorism may be more appropriate in this context – *plus ça change, plus c'est la même chose* (the more things change, the more they stay the same). Ultimately it is Africans, in collaboration and in conflict with each other, and with outside powers, who will determine whether resource dependence and authoritarianism on the continent can be overcome.

NOTES

1 The New Scramble, Geography and Development

1 There are two trades in the world today that kill people – the (Northern-dominated) arms trade and the (Southern-dominated) drugs trade. The fact that one is legal and the other is illegal reflects the global distribution of power.
2 'For goodness sakes this is the 21st century. We've got to get over what happened 50, 100, 200 years ago and let's make some money for everybody. That's the best way to create new energy and growth in Africa' (quoted in Nevin 2010, p. 24).

2 Old Economic Power Interests and Strategies in Africa

1 Relations appeared to improve somewhat in 2010 when the French President Sarkozy visited Rwanda. He has a history of controversy on the continent, however, particularly after one speech in which he said that Africa's challenge was 'to enter into a greater extent into history', echoing the opinion of the famous British historian Lord Dacre (Hugh Trevor-Roper) in the 1960s that Africa's history was one of 'barbarous gyrations' – so far from the truth it is not worthy of further comment.
2 It should be noted that, as only a minority of people in Africa speak English or French as their first language, speaking of Francophone or Anglophone Africa is a misnomer and really a geopolitical statement about spheres of influence.
3 Not all members of the EU use the euro as their currency.
4 China, perhaps not coincidentally, also had its own 'Year of Africa' in 2006.
5 William Clinton, in conversation, Dublin, August 2003.

6   There is also a religious scramble for Africa, but this is the subject of
    another book. Evangelical religions appear to be gaining, particularly as
    the Pope on a visit to Africa claimed condoms aggravate the problems of
    HIV/AIDs and that African people are 'living in fear of spirits, of malign
    and threatening powers. In their bewilderment they end up even condemn-
    ing street children and the elderly as alleged sorcerers' (quoted in Patel
    2009, p. 97).
7   Comment at 'Beyond the BRICs' workshop, University of Manchester,
    July 2010.
8   Diamonds from this field were subsequently auctioned at Harare's
    International airport in 2010. Some buyers from India and elsewhere flew
    in on executive jets and immediately left with their new purchases. The
    major US-based diamond trading group Rapaport has, however, banned
    its members from trading in these stones.
9   Interview, Durban, South Africa, August 2010.

3   Chinese Interests and Strategies in Africa

1   There is some dispute as to when this strategy became official policy. It
    was formalized in the early 2000s, but was in informal operation from the
    mid- to late 1990s.
2   Peace is, of course, a relative rather than an absolute term. The colonial
    labour regime generated violent resistance in Zambia and there have been
    many urban riots over food price increases, for example.
3   This report, undertaken in 2000, carried out a comprehensive review of
    UN peacekeeping operations with a view to how they could be improved.

4   Other New Economic Power Interests and Relations with Africa

1   This company was formed from the merger of Arcelor and Mittal in 2006
    and is now headquartered in Luxembourg, but Lakshimi Mittal is the
    chairman of the board. This then is an example of transnational capital in
    terms of its ownership, management and corporate operations, but with
    strong Indian connections and associations.
2   The pH scale measures how acidic or alkaline a liquid is and ranges from
    0 to 14. Pure water has a pH of 7.

5   Driving the Global Economy: West African and Sahelian Oil

1   Ethiopia is another key state for the Chinese in Africa, given its popula-
    tion, strategic location and site as the headquarters of the AU, although
    without substantial oil deposits. The Chinese embassy in the capital of
    Ethiopia is the second-biggest in the world after the one in New Delhi,
    although it was India which became the single largest foreign investor in

Ethiopia in November 2008, with a stock of US$4 billion in private-sector investment (Mawdsley and McCann 2010).

2   As climate change may compromise African agriculture, it may make the continent's economies even more resource-dependent. Furthermore, the pace of climate change may accelerate as an estimated 25 per cent of the world's undiscovered oil and gas are thought to lie under the Arctic Ocean, which is being opened up to exploration as the ice cap melts (Boyes 2010).

3   Mugabe's government arrested a planeload of mercenaries destined for Equatorial Guinea to overthrow Obiang in 2004. Obiang repaid this debt in oil (Clarke 2008).

4   Brazil and Portugal have also provided US$1.8 billion and US$1.4 billion credit lines, respectively, to Angola.

6   Powering and Connecting the Global Economy through Conflict: Uranium and Coltan

1   Sovereign wealth funds, which invest government money, often derived from natural resources and often investing overseas, play an increasingly important role in the global economy.

2   These large mammals also suffer in other conflict zones. According to Care for the Wild, between 6,000 and 12,000 elephants a year are killed in Sudan, Chad, CAR and Congo-Brazzaville, largely to supply the Chinese market with ivory (Michel, Beuret and Woods 2009).

3   Artisanal miners are often exposed to major health risks – through the use of mercury to mine gold, for example. Some estimates suggest that up to 3 tonnes of toxic waste are produced in mining enough gold to make an ordinary gold wedding ring. In Congo the major international conglomerate Anglo-Gold Ashanti has admitted to paying protection money to rebel groups, whereas in Ghana it is reportedly company policy to shoot artisanal miners on sight if they infringe on company property (Amankwah and Amin-Sackey 2006).

7   Furnishing and Feeding the World? Timber, Biofuels, Plants, Food and Fisheries

1   Not all biofuels grown in Africa are necessarily exported, however. While it is often foreign companies which are involved, Malawi already had a bioethanol programme in 1982 and now produces 18 million litres a year (Peskette, Slater et al. 2007). Zimbabwe is meant to be developing a national biodiesel programme which could contribute up to 10 per cent of its diesel consumption (Amigun, Sigamoney and von Blottnitz 2006), and the development of biofuels may stimulate new industries around processing.

2   In 2005 Africa's net imports of rice, wheat and maize reached 55 million tons, a source of substantial debt, although there have also been successes in increasing food crop production in SSA, partly as a result of UN programmes. For example, the production of sorghum and sweet potatoes has doubled since 1990, showing that, with the right conditions and interventions, developmental successes in Africa are possible. Recently, Malawi has had notable success in improving its maize yields by providing subsidized inputs – such as fertilizer to farmers (see Denning et al. 2009).

3   When European colonists arrived in parts of West Africa they encountered forest islands, which they assumed were the remnants of previously existing forests which had been cut away. In fact, local communities had planted these forest islands to provide fruit, fodder and other services (Fairhead and Leach 1996).

4   This kind of reward would appear to be relatively common practice, with the Chinese building a multi-million-dollar mansion for the Sudanese President, who is wanted by the ICC for crimes against humanity. In Zimbabwe, the Chinese supplied roof tiles for Robert Mugabe's new mansion, which is the largest private residence in Africa.

5   It should be noted, however, that Chinese companies are also sometimes involved in environmental improvements. For example the CNPC built a sewage treatment plant on the Nile and now over a million people there have access to purified water (He 2010).

6   This is Professor Abdi Samatar's assessment (in conversation, December 2009). Quoted with permission.

7   This lack of respect for Somali people's lives is also evidenced by opinion pieces in the *Washington Post* with headlines like 'Kill the Pirates' (Minter and Volman 2009), and the innocent civilians killed by US cruise missile strikes in Somalia are merely 'collateral damage' for some – 'non-people' to use John Pilger's (2002) phrase.

8   There are, however, some efforts to restrict these practices internationally through the Convention on Biological Diversity and the International Treaty for Plant Genetic Resources which disallows the patenting of sixty-four species (Food and Agriculture Organization 2004, cited in Thompson 2009).

8   The Asian Scramble for Investment and Markets: Evidence and Impacts in Zambia

1   As noted earlier, this is, strictly speaking, now a British-headquartered company, as that is where its primary stock market listing now is, but its origins and management are largely Indian.

2   According to the CCS (2006, p. 7), the success of China's companies, particularly state-owned enterprises (SOEs), can be attributed to several factors: cost competitiveness in overall bidding price; access to cheap capital through Chinese state-owned banks; access to skilled low-cost

labour; access to cheap building materials through supply chains from China; and political support from the Chinese government channelled through Chinese embassies and Economic and Commercial Councils in the respective African countries.

3   The other Chinese investments of importance in the agricultural sector, according to Bastholm and Kragelund (2007, pp. 23–4), include: the Jhonken Estates and the Jhonken Friendship Farm. Together the farms mainly produce wheat, eggs, beef and pork for sale. None of the farms export any products, which, according to the managers of the Friendship Farm and Jhonken Estates, is because Zambia has a deficient production of agricultural food and they estimate that the situation will keep them from exporting for another five to ten years due to the domestic market conditions.

4   We are grateful to Dr Jamie Cross for this point.

9   Can Africans Unscramble the Continent?

1   A blue water navy, which used to be the preserve of the British, is capable of projecting power anywhere in the world.

2   I am grateful to Joseph Stiglitz for this point.

3   I am very grateful to a referee for this point.

4   In Zambia there are signs that the government is moving away from the policy of attracting overseas investment at any cost, as tax incentives for investments under half a million US dollars were recently abolished and there is a recognition of the need to learn from Asia in targeting specific sectors for investment promotion.

BIBLIOGRAPHY

Abrahamsen, R. (2000). *Disciplining Democracy: Development Discourse and Good Governance in Africa*. London and New York: Zed Books.

Abrahamsen, R. (2005). 'Blair's Africa: the politics of securitization and fear'. *Alternatives* 30(1): 55–80.

Acemoglu, D., S. Johnson and J. Robinson (2001). 'The colonial origins of comparative development: an empirical investigation'. *American Economic Review* 91(5): 1369–1401.

Adebajo, A., A. Adedeji and C. Landsberg (2007). 'Introduction'. *South Africa in Africa: The Post-Apartheid Era*, ed. A. Adebajo, A. Adedeji and C. Landsberg. Durban: University of KwaZulu-Natal Press.

Africa Research Bulletin (2006). 16 Feb. – 15 March.

African Banker (2008). 'Star interview: Arnold Ekpe – Africa is where China was 20 years ago'. 4th quarter: 18–25.

African Business (2008). 'Country file: Zambia: economic ties with China grow stronger'. 336(Nov.): 70.

African Business (2009). 'African Economic Review, 2009'. 349: 17–31.

African Development Bank (2003). *African Development Report 2003*. Oxford: Oxford University Press.

Africathegoodnews (2010, 19 April). 'Turkey seeks to regain foothold in Africa'. Retrieved 15 August, from www.africagoodnews.com/trade-and-investment/turkey-seeks-to-regain-foothold-in-africa.html.

Agnew, J. (2005). *Hegemony: The New Shape of Global Power*. Philadelphia: Temple University Press.

Ahmed, M. (2005). 'Market access and liberalisation in the fish trade'. Paper presented at the ICTSD Workshop 'Untangling Fisheries and Trade: Towards Priorities for Action'. Geneva, ICTSD.

Alden, C. (2005). 'Leveraging the dragon: toward 'An Africa that can say no'. *YaleGlobal Online Magazine*. Retrieved 18 Sept. 2009, from http://yaleglobal.yale.edu/content/leveraging-dragon-toward-africa-can-say-no.

Alden, C. (2007). *China in Africa: Partner, Competitor or Hegemon?* London, Zed Books.

Alden, C. (2008). 'Africa without Europeans'. *China Returns to Africa: A Rising Power and a Continent Embrace*, ed. C. Alden, D. Large and R. S. de Oliveira. London: Hurst.

Alder, J., and U. Sumaila (2004). 'Western Africa: a fish basket of Europe past and present'. *Journal of Environment and Development* 13(2): 156–78.

Amankwah, R., and R. K. Anim-Sackey (2006). 'Fostering cooperation between small- and large-scale gold-miners in West Africa', *Small-Scale Mining, Rural Subsistence and Poverty in West Africa*, ed. G. Hilson. Warwickshire: Practical Action.

Amigun, B., R. Sigamoney and H. von Blottnitz (2006). 'Commercialisation of biofuel industry in Africa: a review'. *Renewable and Sustainable Energy Reviews* 12: 690–711.

Amin, S. (1976). *Unequal Development: An Essay on the Social Formations of Peripheral Capitalism.* Hassocks, UK: Harvester Press.

Amsden, A. (1994). 'Why isn't the whole world experimenting with the East Asian model to develop? Review of the East Asian Miracle'. *World Development* 22(4): 627–33.

Anonymous (2005). 'World business leaders laud Africa growth prospects'. *Business Times* [Tanzania] 22 July, p. 1.

Anonymous (2009). 'KBR pleads guilty in Bonny Island bribes case'. *Rigzone* 2 Nov. 2009. Retrieved 15 Jan. 2010, from www.rigzone.com.

Arestis, P., and A. Caner (2009). 'Financial liberalization and the geography of poverty'. *Cambridge Journal of Regions, Economy and Society* 2: 229–44.

Areva (2009). 'Areva and Niger: a sustainable partnership'. Retrieved 6 Oct., from http://niger.areva.com/scripts/niger_home/publigen/content/templates/ Show.asp?P=74&L=EN#ancre6.

Armstrong, C., U. Sumaila, et al. (2004). 'Benefits and costs of the Namibianisation policy', *Namibia's Fisheries: Ecological, Economic and Social Aspects*, ed. U. Sumaila, D. Boyer, M. Skogen and S. Steinshamn. Amsterdam: Eburon.

Arnold, G. (2009). *The New Scramble for Africa.* London: North-South Books.

Arrighi, G. (2007). *Adam Smith in Beijing: Lineages of the Twenty-First Century.* New York and London: Verso.

Asche, H. (2008). 'Preserving Africa's economic policy space in trade negotiations', *Negotiating Regions: The EU, Africa and the EPAs*, ed. H. Asche and U. Engel. Leipzig: Leipziger Universitätsverlag.

Asche, H., and U. Engel (2008). 'Preface', *Negotiating Regions: The EU, Africa and EPAs*, ed. H. Asche and U. Engel. Leipzig: Leipziger Universitätsverlag.

AsiaPulse News (2008). 'India seeks African diamonds: Ramesh to visit Angola, Namibia', *AsiaPulse News*. Retrieved 1 Dec. 2010, from www. highbeam.com/doc/1G1-176976148.html.

Austin, G. (2008). 'The "reversal of fortune" thesis and the compression of history: perspectives from African and comparative economic history'. *Journal of International Development* 20(8): 996–1027.

Balogh, T. (1963). *Unequal Partners.* Oxford: Blackwell.

Banister, J. (2005). *Manufacturing Employment and Compensation in China.* Washington, DC: United States Department of Labor.

Barkawi, T. (2006). *Globalization and War.* Lanham, MD: Rowman and Littlefield.

Barma, N., and E. Ratner (2006). 'Chinese illiberalism'. *Democracy* 2: 56–68.

Bartels, L. E. A. (2007). *Policy Coherence for Development and the Effects of EU Fisheries Policies on Development in West Africa.* Brussels: European Parliament.

Basedau, M. (2005). 'Context matters – rethinking the resource curse in Sub-Saharan Africa'. *Working Papers: Global and Area Studies.* German Overseas Institute. Responsible Institute: Institute of African Affairs 1.

Bastholm, A., and P. Kragelund (2007). 'State-driven Chinese investment in Zambia: combining strategic interests and profits'. Mimeo.

Batidzirai, B., A. P. C. Faaij, et al. (2006). 'Biomass and bioenergy supply from Mozambique'. *Energy for Sustainable Development* 10(1): 54–81.

Bauman, Z. (1998). *Globalization: The Human Consequences.* New York: Columbia University Press.

Bayart, J. F. (1993). *The State in Africa: The Politics of the Belly.* London: Longman.

BBC (2009). 'Madagascar leader axes land deal'. Retrieved 10 Nov., from http://newsvote.bbc.co.uk.

Bellamy, A., and P. Williams (2004). 'What future for peace operations? Brahimi and beyond'. *International Peacekeeping* 11(1): 183–212.

Bello, W. (2009). *The Food Wars.* London: Verso.

Benza, B. (2010). Botswana and India in diamond trade deal-report. Mmegionline. Retrieved 1 Dec. 2010, from www.mmegi.bw/index. php?sid=4&aid=15&dir=2010/January/Friday8.

Bergsten, C. F. (2008). *Zhang bu Zhongguo: Meiguo zhi ku tou shi Zhongguo jue qi* (China: The Balance Sheet. What the World Needs to Know Now about the Emerging Superpower). Beijing: Zhongguo fa zhan chu ban she.

Bhattacharya, S. (2010). 'Engaging Africa: India's interests in the African continent, past and present'. *The Rise of China and India in Africa*, ed. F. Cheru and C. Obi. London and Uppsala: Zed Books and Nordiska Afrikainstitutet.

Becker, D. G., and R. L. Sklar (1999). *Postimperialism and World Politics.* Westport, CT: Praeger.

Blair, T. (2008). 'Faith and globalisation lecture'. From http://tonyblairoffice. org/2008/04/speech-on-faith-globalisation.html.

Blake, R., A. D. Barber and R. LaFranco (2006). 'The Trader Monthly 100: earn, baby, earn'. Retrieved 27 Oct. 2009, from www.trade2win.com/ boards/foyer/19392-trader-monthly-top-100-traders-list-2005-a.html.

Blank, M. (2009). 'Hugging with tactical arms: what motivates China to export weapons?' BA thesis, Ann Arbor: University of Michigan.

Block, R. (1997). 'As Zaire's war wages, foreign businesses scramble for inroads'. *Wall Street Journal* 14 April.

Bloom, D., and J. Sachs (1998). *Geography, Demography, and Economic Growth in Africa.* Cambridge, MA: Harvard University, Harvard Institute for International Development.

Boddinger, D. (2007). 'Boosting biofuel crops could threaten food security'. *The Lancet* 370: 923–4.

Bond, P. (2006). *Looting Africa: The Economics of Exploitation.* London: Zed Books.

Bond, P., and Zapiro (2006). *Talk Left, Walk Right: South Africa's Frustrated Global Reforms.* Scottsville, South Africa: University of KwaZulu-Natal Press.

Bosshard, P. (2008). 'China's environmental footprint in Africa'. *Pambazuka News* 376. Retrieved 1 Dec. 2010, from www.pambazuka.org/en/category/comment/48442.

Boyes, R. (2010). *Meltdown Iceland: How the Global Financial Crisis Bankrupted an Entire Country.* London, Berlin and New York: Bloomsbury.

BP (2005). 'Statistical review of world energy'. Retrieved 1 Dec. 2010, from www.bp.com/liveassets/bp_internet/globalbp/globalbp_uk_english/publications/energy_reviews_2005/STAGING/local_assets/downloads/pdf/statistical_review_of_world_energy_full_report_2005.pdf.

Braeckman, C. (1999). 'Partition poses as protection'. *Le Monde Diplomatique* (Paris). Retrieved 3 Mar. 2010, from http://mondediplo.com/1999/10/08congo.

Brautigam, D. (2009). *Dragon's Gift: The Real Story of China in Africa.* Oxford and New York: Oxford University Press.

Breslin, S. (2007). *China and the Global Political Economy.* Basingstoke and New York: Palgrave Macmillan.

Broadman, H. (2007). 'Connecting Asia and Africa'. *Finance and Development* 44(2). Retrieved 1 Dec. 2010, from www.relooney.info/00_New_2600.pdf.

Broadman, H. G., and G. Isik (2007). *Africa's Silk Road: China and India's New Economic Frontier.* Washington, DC: World Bank.

Bush, C., and J. Seeds (2008). 'Apocalypse found: coltan, cell phones and the crisis in the Congo'. *The Bear Deluxe Magazine* 19 April. Retrieved 1 Dec. 2010, from www.commondreams.org/print/29016.

Bush, R. (2007). *Poverty and Neoliberalism: Persistence and Reproduction in the Global South.* London: Pluto.

Buur, L., S. Jensen and F. Stepputat (eds) (2007). 'The security–development nexus'. *The Security–Development Nexus: Expressions of Sovereignty and Securitization in Southern Africa,* ed. L. Buur, S. Jensen and F. Stepputat. Pretoria: HSRC Press.

Cali, M., I. Mass and D. W. te Velde (2008). 'The global financial crisis: financial flows to developing countries set to fall by one quarter'. Retrieved 15 February 2011, from www.odi.org.uk/resources/download/2523.pdf.

Callaghy, T. M. (1979). 'State formation and absolutism in comparative perspective: seventeenth century France and Mobutu Sese Seko's Zaïre. Ph.D. thesis, University of California, Berkeley.

Campaign Against Arms Trade (2003). 'Fanning the flames: how UK arms sales fuel conflict'. Retrieved 1 Dec. 2010, from www.caat.org.uk/campaigns/fantheflames/FtF_6page_briefing_pdf.

Campbell, H. (2008). 'Remilitarisation of African societies: analysis of the planning behind proposed US Africa Command'. *International Journal of Africa Renaissance Studies* 3(1): 6–34.

Carlson, A. (2006). 'More than just saying no: China's evolving approach to sovereignty and intervention'. *New Directions in the Study of China's Foreign Policy*, ed. A. Johnston and R. Ross. Stanford, CA: Stanford University Press.

Carmody, P. (2007). *Neoliberalism, Civil Society and Security in Africa.* Basingstoke and New York: Palgrave Macmillan.

Carmody, P. (2009a). 'Cruciform sovereignty, matrix governance and the scramble for Africa's oil: interpretations from Chad and Sudan'. *Political Geography* 28: 353–61.

Carmody, P. (2009b). 'An Asian-driven economic recovery in Africa? The Zambian case'. *World Development*, 37(7): 1197–207.

Carmody, P. (2010). *Globalization in Africa: Recolonization or Renaissance?* Boulder, CO: Lynne Rienner Publishers.

Carmody P., and G. Elder (2008). 'The globalization–AIDS–poverty syndrome in Africa', *Current Politics and Economics of Africa*, ed. F. Columbus. New York: Nova.

Carmody, P., and F. Owusu (2007). 'Competing hegemons? Chinese vs. American geoeconomic strategies in Africa'. *Political Geography* 26(5): 504–24.

Carmody, P., and I. Taylor (2010). 'Flexigemony and force in China's resource diplomacy in Africa'. *Geopolitics* 15(3): 496–515.

Carrier, J., and D. E. Miller (1998). *Virtualism: A New Political Economy.* Oxford and New York: Berg.

Castells, M. (1998). *End of Millennium.* Malden, MA: Blackwell.

Castells, M. (2009). *The Power of Identity.* Malden, MA: Wiley-Blackwell.

CBS (2003). 'The Kuwait of Africa'. *Sixty Minutes*, 16 Nov. Retrieved 21 April 2005, from web.lexis-nexis.com..

CCS (2006). *China's Interest and Activity in Africa's Construction and Infrastructure Sectors.* Stellenbosch: CCS.

Chambers, R. (2005). *Ideas for Development.* London and Sterling, VA: Earthscan.

Chang, H.-J. (2008). *Bad Samaritans: The Myth of Free Trade and the Secret History of Capitalism.* New York: Bloomsbury Press.

Cheru, F. (1989). *The Silent Revolution in Africa: Debt, Development, and Democracy.* Harare, London and Atlantic Highlands, NJ: Anvil and Zed Books.

Cheru, F. (2002) *African Renaissance: Roadmaps to the Challenge of Globalisation.* London: Zed Books.

Cheru, F., and M. Calais (2010). 'Countering "new" imperialisms: what role for the New Partnership for Africa Development?' *The Rise of China and India in Africa*, ed. F. Cheru and C. Obi. London and Uppsala: Zed Books and Nordiska Afrikainstitutet.

Cheru, F., and C. Obi (2010). 'Introduction – Africa in the twenty-first century: strategic and development challenges', *The Rise of China and India in Africa*, ed. F. Cheru and C. Obi. London and Uppsala: Zed Books and Nordiska Afrikainstitutet.

Chipungu, S. (1992). 'Accumulation from within: the Boma class and the Native Treasury in colonial Zambia'. *Guardians in their Time: Experiences of Zambians under Colonial Rule, 1890–1964*, ed. Chipungu. London: Macmillan.

Chossudovsky, M. (1997). *The Globalisation of Poverty: Impacts of IMF and World Bank Reforms*. Penang, Malaysia: Third World Network.

Chossudovsky, M. (2002). *War and Globalisation: The Truth behind September 11*. Shanty Bay, Ont.: Global Outlook.

Clapham, C. S. (1996). *Africa and the International System: The Politics of State Survival*. Cambridge and New York: Cambridge University Press.

Clapham, C. (2007). 'Fitting China In', *China Returns to Africa: A Rising Power and a Continent Embrace*, ed. C. Alden, D. Large and R. S. de Oliveira. London: Hurst.

Clark, J. (2002a). 'Introduction'. *The African Stakes of the Congo War*. Basingstoke and New York: Palgrave Macmillan.

Clark, J. (2002b). 'Museveni's adventure in the Congo War: Uganda's Vietnam'. *The African Stakes in the Congo War*. Basingstoke and New York: Palgrave Macmillan.

Clarke, D. (2008). *Crude Continent: The Struggle for Africa's Oil Prize*. London: Profile Books.

Clinton, B. (2004). *My Life*. New York: Knopf.

Cochrane, J. (2008). 'Miracle or menace?' *Development Asia: A Publication of the Asian Development Bank* 1. Retrieved 1 Dec. 2010, from http://development.asia/issue01/feature-01.asp.

Coe, N. M., P. Dicken and M. Hess (2008). 'Global production networks: realizing the potential'. *Journal of Economic Geography* 8(3): 271–95.

Coe, N. M., M. Hess, H. Yeung, P. Dicken and J. Henderson (2004). '"Globalizing" regional development: a global production networks perspective'. *Transactions of the Institute of British Geographers* 29(4): 468–84.

Collier, P. (2007). *The Bottom Billion*. Oxford and New York: Oxford University Press.

Collier, P. (2009). *Wars, Guns, and Votes: Democracy in Dangerous Places*. New York: Harper.

Commission for Africa (2005). *Our Common Interest: Report of the Commission for Africa*. London: Commission for Africa.

Congressional Record (2001). *Proceedings and Debates of the 107th Congress, First Session*. Vol. CXLVII, Part 8, 12–25 June. Washington, DC: Government Printing Office.

Cooper, R. (2003). *The Breaking of Nations: Order and Chaos in the Twenty-first Century*. London: Atlantic Books.

Copson, R. (2005). 'The Global Fund and PEPFAR in U.S. international AIDS policy: implications for Africa'. Paper presented for the annual meeting of the African Studies Association, Washington, DC, 17–20 Nov.

Copson, R. (2007). *The United States in Africa: Bush Policy and Beyond*. London and Cape Town: Zed Books and David Phillips.

Corbridge, S., and J. Harriss (2000). *Reinventing India: Liberalization, Hindu Nationalism and Popular Democracy*. Cambridge, UK, and Malden, MA: Polity.

Cox, R. W. (1987). *Production, Power and World Order: Social Forces in the Making of History*. New York: Columbia University Press.

Craig, D., and P. Porter (2006). *Development beyond Neoliberalism: Governance, Poverty Reduction and Political Economy*. London: Routledge.

Cramer, C. (1999). 'Can Africa industrialize by processing primary commodities? The case of Mozambican cashew nuts'. *World Development* 27(7): 1247–66.

Cramer, C. (2006). *Civil War is Not a Stupid Thing*. London: Hurst.

Crosoer, D., L. van Sittert and S. Ponte (2006). 'The integration of South African fisheries into the global economy: past, present and future'. *Marine Policy* 30(1): 18–29.

Curtis, M. (2009) *Web of Deceit: Britain's Real Role in the World*. London: Vintage.

Daniel, J., and N. Bhengu (2009). 'South Africa in Africa: still a formidable player', *A New Scramble for Africa? Imperialism, Investment and Development*, ed. R. Southall and H. Melber. Durban: University of KwaZulu-Natal Press.

Daniel, J., and J. Lutchman (2006). 'South Africa in Africa: scrambling for energy', *State of the Nation: South Africa 2005–6*, ed. Buhlungu et al. Cape Town: Human Sciences Research Council Press.

Davies, M. (2008). 'Special economic zones: China's developmental model comes to Africa'. *China into Africa: Trade, Aid and Influence*, ed. R. Rothberg. Washington, DC: Brookings Institution.

Davies, M. (2009). 'China's new risk model for capital investment in Africa'. *China Business Frontier* Aug.: 1–4.

Dawes, N. (2008). 'India's African inroads'. *Mail and Guardian* (South Africa) 12 April. Retrieved 19 Jan. 2009, from www.mg.co.za//articlePage.aspx?articleid=336688&area=/insight/insight_africa.

De Luna Martinez, J. (2007). 'Financial services: dealing with limited and unequal access'. *Services Trade and Development: The Experience of Zambia*, ed. A. Mattoo and L. Payton. Basingstoke and New York: Palgrave Macmillan for the World Bank.

de Sardan, J. P. O. (1999). 'A moral economy of corruption in Africa'. *Journal of Modern African Studies* 37(1): 25–52.

Denning, G., P. Kabambe, P. Sanchez et al. (2009). 'Input subsidies to improve smallholder maize productivity in Malawi: toward an African green revolution'. *PLoS Biology* 7(1): 2–10.

Diamond, J. M. (1997). *Guns, Germs and Steel: The Fates of Human Societies.* New York: W. W. Norton & Co.

Diop, B. B. (2010). 'La vie en %$! Why is France still propping up Africa's dictators?' *Foreign Policy* (July/Aug.). Retrieved 1 Dec. 2010, from www.foreignpolicy.com/articles/2010/06/21/la_vie_en.

Dobler, G. (2008). 'From Scotch whisky to Chinese sneakers: international commodity flows and new trade networks in Oshikango, Namibia'. *Africa* 78: 410–32.

Dowden, R. (2009). *Africa: Altered States, Ordinary Miracles.* New York: PublicAffairs.

Downey, J. (2010). 'Irish troops will train Somali soldiers'. *Sunday Independent* (Dublin) 28 Feb. Retrieved 1 Dec. 2010, from www.independent.ie/world-news/irish-troops-will-train-somali-soldiers-2083597.html.

Downs, E. (2007). 'The fact and the fiction of Sino-African energy relations'. *China Security* 3(3): 42–68.

Dubosse, N. (2010). 'Chinese development assistance to Africa: aid, trade and debt', *Chinese and African Perspectives on China in Africa*, ed. A. Harneit-Sievers, S. Marks and S. Naidu. Cape Town, Nairobi, Dakar and Oxford: Pambazuka Press.

Dumas, C., and D. Choylevam (2006). *The Bill from the China Shop: How Asia's Savings Glut Threatens the World Economy.* London: Profile Books.

Dunkley, G. (2004). *Free Trade: Myth, Reality, and Alternatives.* London and New York: Zed Books.

Dunn, K. C. (2001). 'Imagining Mobutu's Zaire: the production and consumption of identity in international relations'. *Millennium – Journal of International Studies* 30(2): 235–58.

Easterly, W. (2000). *The Lost Decades: Developing Countries' Stagnation in Spite of Policy Reform 1980–1998.* Washington, DC: Developmental Research Group, World Bank.

Eckert, P. (2008). 'U.S. report links China arms sales to Darfur carnage'. Reuters.

Economist (2007). 'African governance: it's better to be out to sea', 27 Sept.: 46.

Economist (2010). 'Oil, glorious oil: the country's breakneck growth is slowly benefiting the masses' 28 Jan.

Economist Intelligence Unit (2005). *Country Report June 2005: Zimbabwe.* London: EIU.

Edinger, H. (2007). 'Hu's agenda'. *China Monitor* 15 Feb.

Eisenman, J. (2007). 'China's post-Cold War strategy in Africa: examining Beijing's methods and objectives', *China and the Developing World: Beijing's Strategy for the Twenty-First Century*, ed. J. Eisenman, E. Heginbotham and D. Mitchell. London and New York: M. E. Sharpe.

Eisenman, J., E. Heginbotham and D. Mitchell (2007). 'Introduction'. *China and the Developing World: Beijing's Strategy for the Twenty-First Century*, ed.. J. Eisenman, E. Heginbotham and D. Mitchell. New York and London: M. E. Sharpe.

El-Tom, A. (2003). 'The Black Book of Sudan: imbalance of power and wealth in Sudan'. *Journal of African National Affairs* 1(2): 25–35.

emii.com (2008). 'Brazil's Petrobras may operate in Ghana'. From www.emii.com/article.aspx?ArticleID=1917168.

Environmental Justice Foundation (2009). 'Pirate fishing – the scourge of West Africa'. Retrieved 10 Nov. 2009, from www.ejfoundation.org/page275.html.

Erlinder, P. (2009). 'The real authors of the Congo crimes. Nkunda has been arrested but who will arrest Kagame?' *Global Research* 2 Feb.

Essick, K. (2001). 'Guns, money and cell phones'. *The Industry Standard Magazine* 11 June. Retrieved 1 Dec. 2010, from www.globalissues.org/article/42/guns-money-and-cell-phones.

EU NAVFOR: Somalia (2010). 'About MSCHOA and OP ATALANTA'. Retrieved 1 Dec. 2010, from www.mschoa.org/Pages/About.aspx.

European Commission (2005). 'EU strategy for Africa – towards a Euro-African pact to accelerate Africa's development' (SEC(2005)1255). Retrieved 1 Dec. 2010, from http://eur-lex.europa.eu/smartapi/cgi/sga_doc?.

Fairhead, J., and M. Leach (1996). *Misreading the African Landscape: Society and Ecology in a Forest–Savanna Mosaic.* Cambridge and New York: Cambridge University Press.

Ferguson, J. (2006). *Global Shadows: Africa in the Neoliberal World Order.* Durham, NC: Duke University Press.

Ferrett, G. (2007). 'Biofuels "crime against humanity"'. Retrieved 7 Mar. 2008, from http://news/bbc.co.uk/2/hi/americas/7065061.stm.

Fick, D. (2006). *Africa: Continent of Economic Opportunities.* Johannesburg: STE Publishers.

Finch, J. (2007a). 'Russia and China battle over AfricanrUranium'. StockInterview.com. Retrieved 6 Oct. 2009, from www.stockinterview.com.

Finch, J. (2007b, 20 July). 'Tuareg rebels threaten uranium mining in Niger'. From http://seekingalpha.com/article/41746-tuareg-rebels-threaten-uranium-mining-in-niger.

Fitzgerald, M. (2008). 'Zambia becomes shorthand for what can go wrong'. *Irish Times* 8 Aug.

Food and Agriculture Organization (2004). International Treaty on Plant Genetic Resources for Food and Agriculture. Rome: Food and Agriculture Organization.

Fraser, A., and J. Lungu (2007). *For Whom the Windfalls? Winners and Losers in the Privatisation of Zambia's Copper Mines.* Lusaka: Civil Society Trade Network of Zambia.

Freemantle, S., and J. Stevens (2009). Economics: Africa: BRIC and Africa: Tectonic shifts tie BRIC and Africa's economic destinies, Standard Bank. Retrieved 1 Dec. 2010, from www.blog.standardbank.com/blog/standard-bank-team/2009/10/tectonic-shifts-tie-bric-and-africa-s-economic-destinies.

French, P., and S. Chambers (2010). *Oil on Water: Tankers, Pirates and the Rise of China.* London: Zed Books.

Frynas, J. G., and M. Paulo (2007). 'A new scramble for African oil? Historical, political, and business perspectives'. *African Affairs* 106(423): 229–51.

Fung, B. (2010). 'The geopolitics of the iPhone'. *Foreign Policy* 28 June.

Gamora, G., and K. Mathews (2010). 'Ethio-China relations: challenges and prospects', *Chinese and African Perspectives on China in Africa*, ed. A. Harneit-Sievers, S. Marks and S. Naidu. Cape Town, Nairobi, Dakar and Oxford: Pambazuka Press.

Ghazvinian, J. (2007). *Untapped: The Scramble for Africa's Oil*. London: Harcourt.

Gibbon, P. (1996) 'Structural adjustment and structural change in sub-Saharan Africa: some provisional conclusions'. *Development and Change* 27: 751–84.

Gill, S. (2003). *Power and Resistance in the New World Order*. Basingstoke and New York: Palgrave Macmillan.

Glennerster, R. (2009). *Africa's Turn?* ed. E. Miguel. Boston: Boston Review.

Glennie, J. (2008). *The Trouble with Aid: Why Less Could Mean More for Africa*. London: Zed Books.

Glosny, M. A. (2007). 'Stabilizing the backyard: recent developments in China's policy toward Southeast Asia'. *China and the Developing World: Bejing's Strategy for the Twenty-First* Century, ed. J. Eisenman, E. Heginbotham and D. Mitchell. London and New York: M. E. Sharpe.

Goodison, P. (2007). 'The future of Africa's trade with Europe: "new" EU trade policy'. *Review of African Political Economy* 34(111): 139–51.

Gorez, B. (2000). 'Pink gold, muddy waters'. *Samudra* 25(April): 27–30.

Gorilla Journal (2001). 'Falling coltan prices'. Retrieved 1 Dec. 2010, from www.berggorilla.org.

Graham, M. (2011, forthcoming). 'Time machines and virtual portals: the spatialities of the digital divide'. *Progress in Human Geography*.

Greenpeace (2009). 'Robbing West Africa'. Retrieved 10 Nov. 2009, from www.greenpeace.org.

Grieco, J. M., and G. J. Ikenberry (2003). *State Power and World Markets: The International Political Economy*. New York: W.W. Norton & Co.

Grimmett, R. F. (2009). 'Conventional arms transfers to the developing nations, 2001–2008'. Retrieved 1 Dec. 2010, from www.fas.org/sgp/crs/weapons/R40796.pdf.

Guijin, L. (2004). *China–Africa Relations: Equality, Cooperation and Mutual Development*. Pretoria: China–Africa Relations, Institute for Security Studies, South Africa.

Hampwaye, G. (2008). 'Decentralization, local economic development and urban agriculture in Zambia'. Ph.D. dissertation, Johannesburg, University of the Witwatersrand.

Hanlon, J. (1996). *Peace without Profit: How the IMF Blocks Rebuilding in Mozambique*. Portsmouth, NH: Heinemann.

Harvey, D. (2003). *The New Imperialism*. Oxford and New York: Oxford University Press.

Hassan, M. O. (2009). 'Somalia's new order: filthy rich pirates'. *Brisbane Times.* Retrieved 1 Dec. 2010, from http://odaycabdille.org/en/index. php?option=com_content&view=article&id=1607:somalias-new-order-filthy-rich-pirates&catid=2:news&itemid=18.

Hattingh, S. (2007). 'South Africa's role in Nigeria and the Nigerian elections'. *MRzine a project of Monthly Review.* Retrieved 27 Nov. 2009, from http://mrzine.monthlyreview.org/2007/hattingh260607.html.

Hayes, K., and R. Burge (2003). *Coltan Mining in the Democratic Republic of Congo: How Tantalum-Using Industries Can Commit to the Reconstruction of the DRC.* Cambridge: Fauna & Flora International.

He, W. (2010). 'The Darfur issue and China's role'. *Chinese and African Perspectives on China in Africa,* ed. A. Harneit-Sievers, S. Marks and S. Naidu. Cape Town, Nairobi, Dakar and Oxford: Pambazuka Books.

Herald, The (2006) 'Zimbabwe: Zimplats nets operating profit of US$25.4 million'. 2 August 2006. Retrieved 9 Aug. 2006, from http://allafrica.com/stories/200608020249.html.

Herbst, J., and G. Mills (2009). 'Commodity flux and China's Africa strategy'. *China Brief: A Journal of Analysis and Information* 10(2): 4–6.

Hills, A. (2006). 'Trojan Horses? USAID, counter-terrorism and Africa's police'. *Third World Quarterly* 27(4): 629–43.

Holden, P. (2009). *In Search of Structural Power: EU Aid Policy as a Global Political Instrument.* Farnham, Surrey: Ashgate.

Holmberg, J. (2005). 'Natural resources in sub-Saharan Africa: assets and vulnerabilities: a contribution to the Swedish Government White Paper on Africa commissioned by the Nordic Africa Institute'. Brussels. Retrieved 1 Dec. 2010, from www.sweden.gov.se/content/1/c6/08/35/07/1b807683.pdf.

Holslag, J. (2007). 'New scramble for Africa: exit Europe?' *VUB Asian note.*

Honahan, P. (2009). 'Developing countries and the slump'. Millennium Development Goals Lecture Series. Dublin, Trinity College.

Hönke, J. (2009). 'Extractive orders: transnational mining companies in the nineteenth and twenty-first centuries in the Central African Copperbelt'. *A New Scramble for Africa? Imperialism, Investment and Development,* ed. R. Southall and H. Melber. Durban: University of KwaZulu-Natal Press.

Hoogvelt, A. (2005). 'Postmodern intervention and human rights: report of the Commission for Africa'. *Review of African Political Economy* 32(106): 595–9.

Horne, G. (2009). 'Brazil in Africa – South Africa beware'. *Political Affairs Magazine.* Retrieved 8 Mar. 2010, from www.politicalaffairs.net.

Howden, D. (2008). 'Pirates seize massive oil tanker off Somali coast'. *Irish Independent* (Dublin) 17 Nov.: 30.

Hudson, J. (2007). 'South Africa's economic expansion into Africa: neocolonialism or development?' *South Africa in Africa: The Post-Apartheid Era,* ed. A. Adebajo, A. Adedeji and C. Landsberg. Durban: University of KwaZulu-Natal Press.

Humphreys, M., J. Sachs and J. Stiglitz (eds.) (2007). *Escaping the Resource Curse.* New York: Columbia University Press.

Ikhuoria, E. (2010). 'The impact of Chinese imports on Nigerian traders'. *Chinese and African Perspectives on China in Africa*, ed. A. Harneit-Sievers, S. Marks and S. Naidu. Cape Town, Nairobi, Dakar and Oxford: Pambazuka Press.

IllegalLoggingInfo (2010). 'China to push for sustainable logging overseas: China issues guidelines for sustainable forest plantations abroad'. Retrieved 15 Apr. 2010, from www.illegal-logging.info/item_single.php?it_id= 2056&it=news.

Ilnyckyj, M. (2007). 'The legality and sustainability of European Union fisheries policy in West Africa'. *MIT International Review* Spring. Retrieved 1 Dec. 2010, from http://web.mit.edu/mitir/2007/spring/fisheries.html.

IMF (2005). 'Ghana: statistical appendix'. Retrieved 1 Dec. 2010, from www. imf.org/external/pubs/ft/scr/2005/cr05286.pdf.

IMF (2009). 'Direction of trade statistics'. Retrieved from www.imf.org.

India Brand Equity Foundation (2010a). 'Mauritius contributes largest FDI'. Retrieved 19 April 2010, from www.ibef.org.

India Brand Equity Foundation (2010b). 'Govt approves plan of IIDF'. Retrieved 19 April 2010, from www.ibef.org.

India Brand Equity Foundation (2010c). 'Nextcell forms JV with African firm'. Retrieved 19 April 2010, from www.ibef.org.

India News (2006). 'President Mwanawasa commissions Tata Zambia assembly plant'. 3(3): 7.

Indian High Commission (2009). 'India–Zambia relations'. Retrieved 24 Aug. 2009, from www.hcizambia.com/pdf/zambia.pdf.

Institute for the Analysis of Global Security (2004). 'The future of oil'. Retrieved 1 Dec. 2010, from www.iags.org/futureofoil.html.

International Telecommunications Union (2007). 'Africa 2004 special report mobile Africa'. Retrieved 1 Dec. 2010, from www.itu.int/itunews/ manager/display.asp?lang=en&year=2004&issue=05&ipage-africa Mobile&ext=html.

International Trade Centre (2008). *International Trade Statistics 2001–2005*. Geneva: UNCTAD and WTO.

International Trade Centre (2010). 'Trade map'. Retrieved 6 Jan. 2009, from www.trademap.org/tradestat/Country_SelProductCountry_TS.aspx.

Isaac, E. (2010). 'The West's retreat and China's advance in Angola'. *Chinese and African Perspectives on China in Africa*, ed. A. Harneit-Sievers, S. Marks and S. Naidu. Cape Town, Nairobi, Dakar and Oxford: Pambazuka Press.

Jauch, H. (2004). 'No justice for the poor: a reflection on the deportation of Bangladeshi workers at Ramatex'. *The Namibian* (Windhoek) 17 Sept.

Jenkins, S. (2007). 'Africa is being torn apart – proof of continents on the move'. *Science in Africa*. Retrieved 1 Dec. 2010, from www.scienceinafrica. co.za/2007/february/continents.htm.

Jessop, B. (2002). *The Future of the Capitalist State*. Cambridge and Malden, MA: Polity.

Jiang, W. (2008). 'China's emerging strategic partnerships in Africa'. *China into Africa: Trade, Aid and Influence*, ed. R. Rotberg. Washington, DC: Brookings Institution Press.

Joll, J. (1983). *Europe since 1870: An International History*. Harmondsworth, Middlesex, and New York: Penguin Books.

Jomo K. S., and J. Baudot (2007). 'Preface'. *Flat World, Big Gaps: Economic Liberalization, Globalization, Poverty and Inequality*, ed. K. S. Jomo and J. Baudot. London: Zed Books.

Jonne, B. (2008). 'The inclusion of the "Singapore issues" in the EPAs: a resurgence of ancient Roman negotiation tactics in contemporary EC–ACP relations?' *Negotiating Regions: The EU, Africa and the EPAs*, ed. H. Asche and U. Engel. Leipzig: Leipziger Universitätsverlag.

Joseph, R. (1999). 'The reconfiguration of power in late 20th century Africa'. *State, Conflict and Democracy in Africa*, ed. Joseph. Boulder, CO: Lynne Rienner Publishers.

Junger, S. (2007). 'Enter China, the giant'. *Vanity Fair* July: 126–38.

Kabemba, C. (2010). 'The dragon is not green enough: the potential environmental impact of Chinese investment in the DRC'. *Chinese and African Perspectives on China in Africa*, ed. A. Harneit-Sievers, S. Marks and S. Naidu. Cape Town, Nairobi, Dakar and Oxford: Pambazuka.

Kabwe, W. (2007). 'Crédit chinois'. *Le Potential* 19 Sept.

Kaczynski, V. M., and D. L. Fluharty (2002). 'European policies in West Africa: who benefits from fisheries agreements?' *Marine Policy* 26: 76–93.

Kanbur, R., and A. Venables (2007). 'Spatial disparities and economic development'. *Global Inequality: Patterns and Explanations*, ed. D. Held and A. Kaya. Cambridge: Polity.

Kaplinsky, R. (2005). *Globalization, Poverty and Inequality*. Cambridge: Polity.

Kaplinsky, R. (2006). 'Revisiting the revisited terms of trade: will China make a difference?' *World Development* 34(6): 981–95.

Kaplinsky, R. (2008). 'What does the rise of China do for industrialisation in Sub-Saharan Africa?' *Review of African Political Economy* 35(115): 7–22.

Kaplinsky, R., and M. Farooki (2009). *Africa's Cooperation with New and Emerging Development Partners: Options for Africa's Development: Report Prepared for The Office of the Special Advisor on Africa, Department of Economic and Social Affairs*. New York: United Nations.

Kaplinsky, R., D. McCormick and M. Morris (2006). *The Impact of China on Sub-Saharan Africa*. London: DFID China Office, UK Department for International Development.

Kaplinsky, R., and J. Readman (2000). *Globalization and Upgrading: What Can (and Cannot) Be Learned from International Trade Statistics in the Wood Furniture Sector?* Brighton: University of Brighton, and Institute of Development Studies, University of Sussex.

Kashi, E., and M. Watts (2008). *Curse of the Black Gold: 50 Years of Oil in the Niger Delta*. Brooklyn, NY: PowerHouse Books.

Katzensteiner, W. (2002) 'State Department briefing, 18 November'. Retrieved 19 June 2005, from web.lexis-nexis.com.

Keet, D. (2010). 'South–South strategic bases for Africa to engage China'. *The Rise of China and India in Africa*, ed. F. Cheru and C. Obi. London and Uppsala: Zed Books and Nordiska Afrikainstitutet.

Kennan, J. (2009). *The Dark Sahara: America's War on Terror in Africa*. London: Pluto.

Kennedy, P. M. (1987). *The Rise and Fall of the Great Powers: Economic Change and Military Conflict from 1500 to 2000*. New York: Random House.

Kenny, B., and C. Mather (2008). 'Milking the region? South African capital and Zambia's dairy industry'. *African Sociological Review* 12(1): 55–66.

Kfir, I. (2008). 'The challenge that is AFRICOM'. *Joint Force Quarterly* (49): 110–13.

Klare, M. (2008). *Rising Powers, Shrinking Planet: How Scarce Energy is Creating a New World Order*. Oxford: One World.

Klein, N. (2005). 'A noose, not a bracelet'. *The Guardian*, 10 June. Retrieved 20 June 2005, from www.guardian.co.uk/print/0,3858,5212562–103390,00. html.

Knaup, H. (2008). 'Africa becoming a biofuel battleground: Western companies are pushing to acquire vast stretches of African land to meet the world's biofuel needs'. *Business Week* 8 Sept.

Kolnes, S. (2008). 'Biofuel Africa says ActionAid is wrong about biofuels in Ghana'. *Ghana Business News* 16 July.

Koyome, M., and J. Clark (2002). 'The economic impact of the Congo War'. *The African Stakes of the Congo War*, ed. J. Clark. Basingstoke and New York: Palgrave Macmillan.

Kragelund, P. (2009). 'Knocking on a wide-open door: Chinese investments in Africa'. *Review of African Political Economy* (122): 479–97.

Krugman, P. R. (1991). *Geography and Trade*. Leuven, Belgium, and Cambridge, MA: Leuven University Press and MIT Press.

Kurlantzick, J. (2007). *Charm Offensive: How China's Soft Power is Transforming the World*. New Haven and London: Yale University Press.

La Lettre du Continent (2008). 'Base militaire chinoise au Congo-K'. 543 (19 June).

Labonne, B. (2009). 'Harnessing mining for poverty reduction, especially in Africa'. *National Resources Forum* 26: 69–73.

Lake, A., C. T. Whitman, P. Lyman and S. Morrison (2006). *More than Humanitarianism: A Strategic U.S. Approach toward Africa – Report of an Independent Task Force*. New York: Council on Foreign Relations.

Lalji, N. (2007). 'The resource curse revised: conflict and coltan in the Congo'. *Harvard International Review* 31 Dec. Retrieved 1 Dec. 2010, from http:// hir.harvard.edu/economics-of-national-security/the-resource-curse-revised? page=0,2.

Lambert, D. (2008). 'Making the past present: historical wrongs and demands for reparations'. *Geographies of Globalisation: A Demanding World*, ed. C. Barnett, J. A. Robinson and R. Gillian. London: SAGE.

Landsberg, C. (2002). 'The impossible neutrality: South Africa's policy in the Congo War'. *The African Stakes of the Congo War*, ed. J. Clark. Basingstoke and New York: Palgrave Macmillan.

Landsberg, C., and F. Kornegay (1999). 'From dilemma to detente: Pretoria's policy options on the DRC and Great Lakes'. *Policy Brief 11*. Johannesburg: Centre for Policy Studies.

Lanteigne, M. (2009). *Chinese Foreign Policy: An Introduction*. New York: Routledge.

Larmer, M., and A. Fraser (2007). 'Of cabbages and King Cobra: populist politics and Zambia's 2006 election'. *African Affairs* 106(425): 611–37.

Le Billon, P. (2004). 'The geopolitical economy of resource wars'. *Geopolitics* 9(1): 1–28.

Le Billon, P. (2008). 'Diamond wars? Conflict diamonds and geographies of resource wars'. *Annals of the Association of American Geographers* 98(2): 345–72.

Lee, M. (2006). 'The 21st century scramble for Africa'. *Journal of Contemporary African Studies* 24(3): 303–29.

Lee, M. (2009). 'Trade relations between the European Union and Sub-Saharan Africa under the Cotonou Agreement'. *A New Scramble for Africa? Imperialism, Investment and Development*, ed. R. Southall and H. Melber. Durban: University of KwaZulu-Natal Press.

Lensink, R. (1996). *Structural Adjustment in Sub-Saharan Africa*. London and New York: Longman.

Leonard, D. K., and S. Strauss (2003). *Africa's Stalled Development: International Causes and Cures*. Boulder, CO: Lynne Rienner Publishers.

Leonard, M. (2008). *What Does China Think?* New York: PublicAffairs.

Leyton, M. (2000). 'Peru: sardines and mackerel species for "direct human consumption" only'. *Intrafish*. Retrieved 6 Mar. 2010, from www.intrafish.no.

Lieberthal, K. (1992). 'The fragmented authoritarianism model and its limitations'. *Bureaucracy, Politics, and Decision Making in Post-Mao China*, ed. L. Kenneth and D. M. Lampton. Berkeley: University of California Press.

Lines, T. (2008). *Making Poverty: A History*. London: Zed Books.

Lipietz, A. (1987). *Mirages and Miracles: The Crisis in Global Fordism*. London: Verso.

Liu, H. (2010). 'China's development cooperation with Africa: historical and cultural perspectives'. *The Rise of China and India in Africa*, ed. F. Cheru and C. Obi. London and Uppsala: Zed Books and Nordiska Afrikainstitutet.

Lockwood, M. (2005). *The State They're In: An Agenda for International Action on Poverty in Africa*. Bourton-on-Dunsmore, Warwickshire: ITDG Publishing.

Longman, T. (2002). 'The complex reasons for Rwanda's engagement in Congo'. *The African Stakes of the Congo War*, ed. J. Clark. Basingstoke and New York: Palgrave Macmillan.

Lough, R. (2009). 'Criminal gangs plunder Madagascar forests'. *Mail and Guardian Online* 19 Nov. Retrieved 1 Dec. 2010, from www.mg.co.za/article/2009-11-29-criminal-gangs-plunder-madagascar-forests.

Lovelock, J. (2009). *The Vanishing Face of Gaia: A Final Warning*. New York: Basic Books.

Lovering, J. (1989). 'The restructuring debate'. *Models in Geography: The Political Economy Perspective*, ed. R. Peet and N. Thrift. London: Unwin Hyman.

Lyman, P. N., and P. Dorff (2007). *Beyond Humanitarianism: What You Need to Know about Africa and Why It Matters*. New York: Council on Foreign Relations / Foreign Affairs.

Lyons, M., and A. Brown (2010). 'Has mercantilism reduced urban poverty in SSA? Perception of boom, bust, and the China–Africa trade in Lomé and Bamako'. *World Development* 38(5): 771–82.

Maass, P. (2009). *Crude World: The Violent Twilight of Oil*. London: Allen Lane.

MacGaffey, J., R. Bazenguissa-Ganga, et al. (2000). *Congo-Paris: Transnational Traders on the Margins of the Law*. London and Bloomington: International African Institute in association with James Currey, Indiana University Press.

Mamdani, M. (1996). *Citizen and Subject: Contemporary Africa and the Legacy of Late Colonialism*. Kampala, Cape Town, London: Fountain Publishers, David Philip, James Currey.

Mandelson, P. (2005). 'EPAs: progressive trade policy into practice. ACP–EU Joint Parliamentary Assembly'. From http://europa.eu/rapid/pressReleaseAction.do?reference=SPEECH/.

Mangcu, X. (2009). *The Democratic Moment*. Sunnyside, South Africa: Jacana.

Manning, P. (1982). *Slavery, Colonialism, and Economic Growth in Dahomey, 1640–1960*. Cambridge and New York: Cambridge University Press.

Mantz, J. (2008). 'Improvisational economies: coltan production in the eastern Congo'. *Social Anthropology* 16(1): 34–50.

Mao, Y. (2007). 'China's interests and strategy in the Middle East and the Arab world. *China and the Developing World: Beijing's Strategy for the Twenty-First Century*, ed J. Eisenman, E. Heginbotham and D. Mitchell. London and New York: M. E. Sharpe.

Marchal, R. (2006). 'Chad/Darfur: how two crises merge'. *Review of African Political Economy* 109: 467–82.

Marginaganti, A., E. Sheppard and J. Zhang (2009). 'Where is the geography? World Bank's WDR 2009'. *Economic and Political Weekly* 44(29): 45–51.

Marriage, Z. (2010). 'Many conflicts, one peace'. *The Political Economy of Africa*, ed. V. Padayachee. London: Routledge.

Martin, W. (2008). 'South Africa's subimperial futures: Washington Consensus, Bandung Consensus, or Peoples' Consensus?' *African Sociological Review* 12(1): 124–34.

Marysse, S., and S. Geenen (2009). 'Win-win or unequal exchange? The case of the Sino-Congolese cooperation agreements'. *Journal of Modern African Studies* 47(3): 371–96.

Massey, S., and R. May (2009). 'Oil and War in Chad'. *A New Scramble for Africa? Imperialism, Investment and Development*, ed. R. Southall and H. Melber. Durban: University of KwaZulu-Natal Press.

Mathews, J. A. (2007). 'Biofuels: what a biopact between North and South could achieve'. *Energy Policy* 35(7): 3550–70.

Mawdsley, E. (2008). 'Fu Manchu versus Dr Livingstone in the Dark Continent? How British broadsheet newspapers represent China, Africa and the West'. *Political Geography* 27(5): 509–29.

Mawdsley, E. (2010). 'The Non-DAC donors and the changing landscape of foreign aid: the (in)significance of India's development cooperation with Kenya'. *Journal of Eastern African Studies* 10(1): 361–79.

Mawdsley, E., and G. McCann (2010). 'The elephant in the corner? Reviewing India–Africa relations in the new millennium'. *Geography Compass* 4(2): 81–93.

Mayer, J., and P. Fajarnes (2005). *Tripling Africa's Primary Export: What? How? Where?* Geneva: UNCTAD.

Mbaye, S. (2010). 'Matching China's activities with Africa's needs'. *Chinese and African Perspectives on China in Africa*, ed. A. Harneit-Sievers, S. Marks and S. Naidu. Cape Town, Nairobi, Dakar and Oxford: Pambazuka Press.

McCann, G. (2010a). '"Diaspora", political economy and Indian investment in Kenya'. *India in Africa: Changing Geographies of Power*, ed. E. Mawdsley and G. McCann. Cape Town, Nairobi, Dakar and Oxford: Fahamu Books and Pambazuka.

McCann, G. (2010b). 'Ties that bind or binds that tie: India's contemporary African engagements and the political economy of Kenya'. *Review of African Political Economy* 27(126): 465–82.

McCormick, D. (2008). 'China and India as Africa's new donors: the impact of aid on development'. *Review of African Political Economy* 115: 73–92.

McFarland, S. (2009). 'The Caspian connection: Russian & Chinese arms supplies to Sudan'. Paper presented at the annual ISA–ABRI Joint International Meeting. Rio de Janeiro, Brazil. 22 July.

McFate, S. (2008). 'Briefing – US Africa command: next step or next stumble?' *African Affairs* 107(426): 111–20.

McGown, J. (2003). *Biodiversity Mystery Theatre*. Washington, DC: Edmonds Institute.

McGreal, C. (2007). 'Thanks, China, now go home: buy-up of Zambia revives old colonial fears'. *The Guardian*. In *China into Africa: Trade, Aid and Influence*, ed. R. Rotberg. Washington, DC: Brookings Institution Press.

McLister, I. (2009). 'Enemies of the human race'. *Trinity News* (Dublin) December.

Melber, H. (2009). 'Global trade regimes and multi-polarity: the US and Chinese scramble for African resources and markets'. *The New Scramble for Africa: Imperialism, Investment and Development*, ed. R. Southall and H. Melber. Durban: University of KwaZulu-Natal Press.

Melber, H., and R. Southall (2009). 'A new scramble for Africa?' *A New Scramble for Africa? Imperialism, Investment and Development*, ed.. R. Southall and H. Melber. Durban: University of KwaZulu-Natal Press.

Meredith, M. (2005). *The Fate of Africa: From the Hopes of Freedom to the Heart of Despair – A History of Fifty Years of Independence*. New York: Public Affairs.

Meyn, M. (2008). 'EPAs – a preliminary review'. *Negotiating Regions: The EU, Africa and EPAs*, ed. H. Asche and U. Engel. Leipzig: Leipziger Universitätsverlag.

Michel, S., M. Beuret and P. Woods (2009). *China Safari: On the Trail of China's Expansion in Africa*. New York: Nation Books.

Miller, D., E. Nel and G. Hampwaye (2008). 'Malls in Zambia: racialised retail expansion and South African foreign investors in Zambia'. *African Sociological Review* 12(1): 35–54.

Miller, D., O. Oloyede and R. Saunders (2008). 'South African corporations and post-apartheid expansion in Africa'. *African Sociological Review* 12(1): 1–19.

Milner, C., O. Morrissey and E. Zgovu (2008). 'Adjustment implications of bilateral trade liberalisation under EPAs: some evidence for Africa'. *Negotiating Regions: The EU, Africa and the EPA*, ed.. H. Asche and U. Engel. Leipzig: Leipziger Universitätsverlag.

Minter, W., and D. Volman (2009). 'Piracy and Washington: the Somalia crossroads'. *In These Times*. From http://towardfreedom.com.

Mohan, G., and M. Power (2008). 'New African choices? The politics of Chinese engagement'. *Review of African Political Economy* 115: 23–42.

Monama, M. (2009). Black CEOs thin on ground. *Fin24.com*. Retrieved 1 Dec. 2010, from www.fin24.com/Business/Black-CEOs-thin-on-ground-20090621.

Montague, D. (2002). 'Stolen goods: coltan and conflict in the DRC'. *SAIS Review* 22(1): 103–18.

Moore, D., and S. Mawowa (2010). 'Mbimbos, Zvipmuzis and "primitive accumulation" in Zimbabwe's violent mineral economy'. *The Political Economy of Africa*, ed. V. Padayachee. London: Routledge.

Morato, T. (2006). 'Fishing down the deep'. *Fish and Fisheries* 7(1): 24–34.

Moseley, W. G., and L. Gray (2008). *Hanging by a Thread: Cotton, Globalization, and Poverty in Africa*. Athens, OH, and Uppsala: Ohio University Press and Nordic Africa Institute.

Moyo, D. (2009). *Dead Aid: Why Aid Is Not Working and How There Is a Better Way for Africa*. New York: Farrar, Straus and Giroux.

Muneku, A., and G. Koyi (2007). 'The social economic impact of Asian FDI in Zambia: a case of Chinese and Indian investments in the extractive industry in Zambia (1997–2007)'. Report submitted to the Friedrich Ebert Stiftung, Zambia.

Naidu, S. (2008). 'India's growing Africa strategy'. *Review of African Political Economy* 35(115): 116–28.

Naidu, S. (2009). 'India's engagements in Africa: self-interest or mutual partnership?' *A New Scramble for Africa? Imperialism, Investment and Development*, ed. R. Southall and H. Melber. Durban: University of KwaZulu-Natal Press.

Naidu, S. (2010). 'India's African relations: in the shadow of China?' *The Rise of China and India in Africa*, ed. F. Cheru and C. Obi. London and Uppsala: Zed Books and Nordiska Afrikainstitutet.

Naidu, S., and J. Lutchman (2005). 'Understanding South Africa's engagement in the region: has the leopard changed its spots?' Paper presented to 'Stability, Poverty Reduction, and South African Trade and Investment in Southern Africa' conference. 29–30 March.

National Bureau of Statistics of China (2010). 'China statistical yearbook 2009'. Retrieved 16 April 2010, from www.stats.gov.cn/tjsj/ndsj/2009/indexeh.htm.

National Council for Construction (2009). 'Registered contractors and gradings'. Unpublished paper. Lusaka: National Council for Construction.

Naude, W. (2009). 'Geography, transport and Africa's proximity gap'. *Journal of Transport Geography* 17(1): 1–9.

Ndulo, M. 'Chinese investments in Africa: a case study of Zambia'. *Crouching Tiger, Hidden Dragon? Africa and China*, ed. K. Apoiah and S. Naidu. Durban: University of KwaZulu-Natal Press.

Negi, R. 'Beyond the "Chinese scramble": the political economy of anti-China sentiment in Zambia'. *African Geographical Review* 27: 41–63.

Neimark, B., and R. Schroeder (2009). 'Hotspot discourse in Africa: making space for bioprospecting in Madagascar'. *African Geographical Review* 28: 43–69.

Nelson, J. (2008). 'Consumers must stop forest destruction'. Retrieved 2 March 2010, from http://news.bbc.co.uk.

Nest, M. W., and F. Grignon (2006). *The Democratic Republic of Congo: Economic Dimensions of War and Peace*. Boulder, CO: Lynne Rienner Publishers.

Nevin, T. (2004). 'Under construction: Africa's economic highway to Brazil'. *African Business* April. Retrieved 1 Dec. 2010, from http://africasia.com/africanbusiness/ab/php?ID=320&back_month=28#.

Nevin, T. (2010). 'Agoa's many happy returns'. *African Business* 1 Aug. 367.

Nkolomba, M., and Z. Chambwa (2009). 'Chinese create 15,000 jobs for Zambia'. Retrieved 17 Jan. 2010, from www.thelusakapaper.com/?p-76.

Nkrumah, Kwame (1965). *Neo-Colonialism: The Last Stage of Imperialism*. London: Nelson.

Nolan, P. (2009). *Crossroads: The End of Wild Capitalism and the Future of Humanity*. London: Marshall Cavendish Business.

Nordstrom, C. (2007). *Global Outlaws: Crime, Money, and Power in the Contemporary World*. Berkeley: University of California Press.

Nye, J. S. (2004). *Soft Power: The Means to Success in World Politics*. New York: Public Affairs.

Nye, J. S. (2008). 'Security and smart power'. *American Behavioral Scientist* 51(9): 1351–6.

Obi, C. (2009). 'Scrambling for oil in West Africa?' *A New Scramble for Africa? Imperialism, Investment and Development*, ed. R. Southall and H. Melber. Durban: University of KwaZulu-Natal Press.

Obi, C. (2010). 'African oil in the energy security calculations of China and India'. *The Rise of China and India in Africa*, ed. F. Cheru and C. Obi. London and Uppsala: Zed Books and Nordiska Afrikainstitutet.

Odularu, G. O. (2008). 'Nigeria–US trade relations in the non-oil sector'. *Dissertation.com*. Retrieved 6 Jan. 2010.

Ogier, T. (2009). 'Out of Brazil and into Africa'. *Latin Trade*. Retrieved 23 Mar. 2010, from http://latintrade.com.

Ohmae, K. (1995). *The End of the Nation State*. New York: Free Press.

Okeke, C. N. (2008). 'The second scramble for Africa's oil and mineral resources: blessing or curse?' *International Lawyer* 43(1): 193–209.

Oliveira, R. S. de (2007). *Oil and Politics in the Gulf of Guinea*. New York: Columbia University Press.

Ong, A. (2006). *Neoliberalism as Exception: Mutations in Citizenship and Sovereignty*. Durham, NC: Duke University Press.

O'Rourke, K. (2009). 'Power and plenty in 2030'. *International Integration Institute Working Paper 298*. Dublin: Trinity College Dublin. Retrieved 1 Dec. 2010, from www.tcd.ie/iiis/documents/discussion/pdfs/iiisdp298.pdf.

Overseas Development Institute (2007). *The Costs to the ACP of Exporting to the EU under the GSP*. Leipzig: Leipziger Universitätsverlag.

Oyen, E. (2004). 'Poverty production: a different approach to poverty understanding. *Advances in Sociological Knowledge over Half a Century*, ed. N. Genov. Wiesbaden: Verlag für Sozialwissenschaften.

Pachauri, R. K., and A. Reisinger (eds.) (2007). *Fourth Assessment Report*. Geneva: Intergovernmental Panel on Climate Change.

Pakenham, T. (1991). *The Scramble for Africa, 1876–1912*. New York: Random House.

Palloti, A. (2004). 'SADC: a development community without a development policy?' *Review of African Political Economy* 101: 513–31.

Pan, E. (2006). 'China, Africa and oil'. Council on Foreign Relations. Retrieved 1 Dec. 2010, from www.cfr.org/publication/9557/china_africa_and_oil.html.

Patel, R. (2009). *The Value of Nothing: How to Reshape Market Society and Redefine Democracy*. New York: Picador.

Patnaik, U. (2008). 'Imperialism, resources and food security with reference to the Indian experience'. *Human Geography: A New Radical Journal* 1(1). Retrieved 1 Mar. 2010, from www.hugeog.com/index.php?option= com_content&view=article&id=77:imperialism-resources-and-food-security-with-reference-to-the-indian-experience-&catid=34:hgissues1 &Itemid=64.

Patterson, A. S. (2006). *The Politics of AIDS in Africa*. Boulder, CO: Lynne Rienner Publishers.

Pauly, D. (2006). 'Major trends in small-scale marine fisheries, with emphasis on developing countries, and some implications for the social sciences'. *Maritime Studies* 4(2): 7–22.

Payne, A. (2005). *The Global Politics of Unequal Development*. Basingstoke and New York: Palgrave Macmillan.

Peck, J., and A. Tickell (2002). 'Neoliberalizing space'. *Antipode* 34(3): 380–404.

Perrot, S., and D. Malaquais (2009). 'Afrique, la globalisation par les Suds'. *Politique Africaine* 113: 5–27.

Perry, A. (2007). 'Africa's oil dreams'. *Time*: 24–31.

Peskette, L., R. Slater et al. (2007). *Biofuels, Agriculture and Poverty Reduction*. London: Overseas Development Institute.

Phillips, L. (2009). 'The European roots of Somali piracy'. *euobserver.com*. Retrieved 26 Feb., from http://euobserver.com.

Phillips, M. (2007). *The Africa Book: A Journey Through Every Country in the Continent*. London: Lonely Planet Publications.

Phillips, R., and S. Talty (2010). *A Captain's Duty: Somali Pirates, Navy Seals, and Dangerous Days at Sea*. New York: Hyperion.

Pilger, J. (2002). *The New Rulers of the World*. London: Verso.

Ploch, L. (2007). *Africa Command: U.S. Strategic Interests and the Role of the US Military in Africa*. Washington, DC: Congressional Research Service.

Polanyi, K. (1944). *The Great Transformation*. New York and Toronto: Farrar & Rinehart.

Ponte, S. (2008). 'Greener than thou: the political economy of fish ecolabeling and its local manifestations in South Africa'. *World Development* 36(1): 159–75.

Ponte, S., J. Raakjaer and L. Campling (2007). 'Swimming upstream: market access for African fish exports in the context of WTO and EU negotiations and regulation'. *Development Policy Review* 25(1): 113–38.

Ponte, S., and L. van Sittert (2007). 'The chimera of redistribution in post-apartheid South Africa: "Black economic empowerment" (BEE) in industrial fisheries'. *African Affairs* 106(424): 437–62.

Porteous, T. (2008). *Britain in Africa*. London, New York and Pietermaritzburg, South Africa: Zed Books and University of KwaZulu-Natal Press.

Powell, C. (1992). 'US forces: challenges ahead'. *Foreign Affairs* Winter. Retrieved 1 Dec. 2010, from www.cfr.org/publication/7508/us_forces.html.

Pradhan, J. (2008). 'Indian direct investment in developing countries: emerging trends and development impacts'. Munich Personal PePEc archive. Retrieved 1 Dec. 2010, from http://mpra.ub.uni-muenchen.de/12323.

Prahalad, C. K. (2005). *The Fortune at the Bottom of the Pyramid*. Upper Saddle River, NJ: Wharton School Publishing.

Prichard, W. (2009). 'The mining boom in Sub-Saharan Africa: continuity, change and policy implications'. *A New Scramble for Africa? Imperialism, Investment and Development*, ed. R. Southall and H. Melber. Durban: University of KwaZulu-Natal Press.

Prunier, G. (2009). *Africa's World War: Congo, the Rwandan Genocide, and the Making of a Continental Catastrophe.* Oxford and New York: Oxford University Press.

Public Broadcasting Service (1999). *Frontline: The Triumph of Evil.*

Radio Netherlands Worldwide (2009). 'China becomes South Africa's biggest trading partner. *www.rnw.nl.* Retrieved 21 March 2010.

Raine, S. (2009). *China's African Challenges.* Abingdon, Oxon, and New York: Routledge for the International Institute for Strategic Studies.

Ramo, J. (2004). *The Beijing Consensus.* London: Foreign Policy Centre.

Renton, D., D. Seddon, et al. (2007). *The Congo: Plunder and Resistance.* London and New York: Zed Books.

Republic of Zambia (2006). 'Levy commissions bus, truck plant'. 8 Sept. Retrieved 6 Jan. 2009, from www.statehouse.gov.zm.

Republic of Zambia (2009). *Letter of Intent, Memorandum of Economic and Financial Policies, and Technical Memorandum of Understanding to the International Monetary Fund.* Retrieved 1 Dec. 2010, from www.imf.org.

Reuters (2006). 'French jets fire on Central African Republic rebels'. *Reuters AlertNet.* 30 Nov.

Reuters (2007). 'India says June qtr FDI inflows rise to $4.9 billion'. *Reuters.* 17 Aug.

Ribeiro, C. (2009a). 'Brazil's new African policy'. *World Affairs: The Journal of International Issues* 13(1). Retrieved 5 Mar. 2010, from www.indianjournals. com/ijor.aspx?target=ijor:wa&volume=13&issue=1&article=004.

Ribeiro, C. (2009b). 'La politique africaine du Brésil et le gouvernement Lula'. *Politique Africaine* 113: 71–91.

Ribeiro, D. (2010). 'Disappearing forests, disappearing hope: Mozambique'. *Chinese and African Perspectives on China in Africa,* ed. A. Harneit-Sievers, S. Marks and S. Naidu. Cape Town, Nairobi, Dakar and Oxford: Pambazuka Press.

Rich, B. (1994). *Mortgaging the Earth: The World Bank, Environmental Impoverishment and the Crisis of Development.* Boston: Beacon Press.

Ritzer, G. (2010). *Globalization: A Basic Text.* Malden, MA: Wiley-Blackwell.

Roberts, A. (2006). *The Wonga Coup: Guns, Thugs, and a Ruthless Determination to Create Mayhem in an Oil-Rich Corner of Africa.* New York: PublicAffairs.

Rocha, J. (2006). 'Managing natural resource wealth: African strategies for China'. *The New Sinosphere: China in Africa,* ed. L. Wild and D. Mepham. London: Institute for Public Policy Research.

Rodney, W. (1972). *How Europe Underdeveloped Africa.* London: Bogle-L'Ouverture Publications.

Royce, E. (2002). 'African oil: a priority for US national security and African development'. Symposium by the Institute for Advanced Strategic and Political Studies. Retrieved 1 Dec. 2010, from www.iasps.org/strategic/africawhitepaper.pdf.

Rueschemeyer, D., E. Huber, et al. (1992). *Capitalist Development and Democracy.* Chicago: University of Chicago Press.

Rundell, S. (2009). 'China's long game in Africa'. *African Business* 356: 30–2.

Runge, C. F., and B. Senauer (2007). 'How biofuels could starve the poor'. *Foreign Affairs* 86(3): 41–53.

Rupiya, M., and R. Southall (2009). 'The militarisation of the new scramble in Africa'. *A New Scramble for Africa? Imperialism, Investment and Development*, ed. R. Southall and H. Melber. Durban: University of KwaZulu-Natal Press.

Ruppert, M. (1995). *Producing Hegemony: The Politics of Mass Production and American Global Power*. Cambridge and New York: Cambridge University Press.

Ruppert, M. (2005) 'Saudi Arabia, West Africa – next stop on the infinite war for oil'. Retrieved 19 June 2005, from www.fromthewilderness.com/free/ ww3/051503_saudi_africa.html.

Sachs, J. (2003). 'The strategic significance of global inequality'. *ECSP Report* 9: 27–35.

Sachs, J. (2005). *The End of Poverty: How We Can Make It Happen in Our Lifetime*. London: Penguin.

Sachs, J. (2008). *Commonwealth: Economics for a Crowded Planet*. London: Penguin.

Sachs, J. (2010). Address to the College Historical Society, Trinity College Dublin. 27 Jan.

Salkever, A. (2010). '$550 billion solar farm in the Sahara'. *Dailyfinance.com*. Retrieved 8 Mar. 2010, from www.dailyfinance.com/story/550-billion-solar-farm-in-the-sahara/19103451/.

Sanchez, D. (2008). 'Transnational telecommunications capital expanding from South Africa into Africa: adapting to African growth and South African transformation demands'. *African Sociological Review* 12(1): 105–23.

Sandbrook, R. (1993). *The Politics of Africa's Economic Recovery*. Cambridge and New York: Cambridge University Press.

Satgar, V. (2009). 'Global capitalism and the neo-liberalisation of Africa'. *A New Scramble for Africa? Imperialism, Investment and Development*, ed. R. Southall and H. Melber. Durban: University of KwaZulu-Natal Press.

Saunders, R. (2008). 'Crisis, capital, compromise: mining and empowerment in Zimbabwe'. *African Sociological Review* 12(1): 67–89.

Sauper, H. (2006). *Darwin's Nightmare*. Potential Films.

Schieg, E. (2008). 'Foreword: EPAs as development instruments – the view of German development policy'. *Negotiating Regions: The EU, Africa and the EPAs*, ed. H. Asche and U. Engel. Leipzig: Leipziger Universitätsverlag.

Schoeman, M. (2007). 'South Africa in Africa: behemoth, hegemon, partner or "just another kid on the block"?' *South Africa in Africa: The Post-Apartheid Era*, ed. A. Adebajo, A. Adedeji and C. Landsberg. Durban: University of KwaZulu-Natal Press.

Schraeder, P. J. (2000). *African Politics and Society: A Mosaic in Transformation*. Boston: Bedford / St Martin's.

Schroeder, R. (2008). 'South African capital in the land of Ujamaa: contested terrain in Tanzania'. *African Sociological Review* 12(1): 20–34.

Sen, K. (2007). 'Why did the elephant start to trot? India's growth acceleration re-examined'. *Economic and Political Weekly* 42(43): 37–47.

Servant, J.-C. (2003). 'The new Gulf oil states'. *Le Monde Diplomatique*, 8 Jan. Retrieved 21 June 2005, from www.globalpolicy.org/security/natres/oil/2003/0114angola.htm.

Shanghai Daily (2008). 'China buys share in Areva mining'. 9 Oct.

Shaw, M. (2000). *Theory of the Global State: Globality as Unfinished Revolution*. Cambridge and New York: Cambridge University Press.

Shaw, T. (2010). 'China, India and (South) Africa: what international relations in the second decade of the twenty-first century?' *The Rise of China and India in Africa*, ed. F. Cheru and C. Obi. London and Uppsala: Zed Books and Nordiska Afrikainstitutet.

Shaxson, N. (2007). *Poisoned Wells: The Dirty Politics of African Oil*. Basingstoke and New York: Palgrave Macmillan.

Sheppard, E. (2011, forthcoming). 'Geography, nature and the question of development'. *Dialogues in Human Geography*.

Shiva, V. (2000). *Stolen Harvest: The Hijacking of the Global Food Supply*. Cambridge, MA: South End Press.

Shiva, V. (2008). *Soil Not Oil: Environmental Justice in a Time of Climate Crisis*. Cambridge, MA: South End Press.

Singh, S. (2007). *India and West Africa: A Burgeoning Relationship*. London: Chatham House.

Slater, D. (2004). *Geopolitics and the Post-colonial: Rethinking North–South Relations*. Malden, MA, and Oxford: Blackwell.

Smeets, E., A. P. C. Faaij and I. Lewandowsky (2004*). A Quickscan of Global Bio-energy Potentials to 2050*. Utrecht: Utrecht University.

Soderbaum, F. (2007). 'African Union'. *Encyclopedia of Globalization*, ed. J. A. Scholte and R. Robertson. New York: MTM Publishing.

Southall, R. (2009). 'Scrambling for Africa: continuities and discontinuities with formal imperialism'. *A New Scramble for Africa? Imperialism, Investment and Development*, ed. R. Southall and H. Melber. Durban: University of KwaZulu-Natal Press.

Southall, R., and A. Comninos (2009). 'The scramble for Africa and the marginalization of African capitalism'. *A New Scramble for Africa? Imperialism, Investment and Development*, ed. R. Southall and H. Melber. Durban: University of KwaZulu-Natal Press.

Southall, R., and H. Melber (2009). 'Conclusion: towards a response'. *A New Scramble for Africa? Imperialism, Investment and Development*, ed. R. Southall and H. Melber. Durban: University of KwaZulu-Natal Press.

Standing, A. (2002). *Beyond the New Paternalism: Basic Security as Equality*. London: Verso.

Standing, A. (2009). 'The European Union and the international scramble for African fish'. *A New Scramble for Africa? Imperialism, Investment and*

Development, ed. R. Southall and H. Melber. Durban: University of KwaZulu-Natal Press.

State Failure Task Force Report (1999). *Phase II Findings*. Prepared by D. C. Esty, J. A. Goldstone, T. R. Gurr et al. Retrieved 1 Dec. 2010, from wwws. wilsoncenter.org/events/docs/Phase2.pdf.

Stavrianos, L. S. (1981). *Global Rift: The Third World Comes of Age*. New York: Morrow.

Stiglitz, J. (2006). *Making Globalization Work*. London: Penguin.

Stockholm International Peace Research Institute (2008). *SIPRI Yearbook 2008: Armaments, Disarmament and International Security*. Stockholm: Stockholm International Peace Research Institute.

Stockholm International Peace Research Institute (2010). 'Recent trends in military expenditure'. Retrieved 1 April 2010, from www.sipri.org.

Storey, A. (2008). 'Would the Lisbon Treaty entangle Ireland in a military alliance? Yes'. *Irish Times* (Dublin) 2 June, p. 12.

Strange, S. (1996). *The Retreat of the State: The Diffusion of Power in the World Economy*. New York: Cambridge University Press.

Strauss, J., and M. Saavedra (2009). 'Editors' introduction: China, Africa and Internationalisation'. *China and Africa: Emerging Patterns in Globalization and Development*, ed. J. Strauss and M. Saavedra, China Quarterly Special Issues n.s. 9. Cambridge: Cambridge University Press.

Sutcliffe, R. (2007). *A Converging or Diverging World? Flat World, Big Gaps: Economic Liberalization, Globalization, Poverty and Inequality*, ed. K. S. Jomo and J. Baudot. London: Zed Books.

Tabb, W. K. (2001). *The Amoral Elephant: Globalization and the Struggle for Social Justice in the Twenty-first Century*. New York: Monthly Review Press.

Tandon, N. (2007). 'Biopolitics, climate change and water security: impact, vulnerability and adaptation issues for women'. *Agenda* 73: 4–40.

Taylor, I. (1998). 'China's foreign policy towards Africa in the 1990s'. *Journal of Modern African Studies* 36(3): 443–60.

Taylor, I. (2005). '"Advice is judged by results, not by intentions": why Gordon Brown is wrong about Africa'. *International Affairs* 81(2): 299–310.

Taylor, I. (2006). *China and Africa: Engagement and Compromise*. London and New York: Routledge.

Taylor, I. (2007). 'Governance in Africa and Sino-African relations: contradictions or confluence?' *Politics* 27(3): 139–46.

Taylor, I. (2009). *China's New Role in Africa*. Boulder, CO: Lynne Rienner Publishers.

Tegera, A., S. Mikolo and D. Johnson (2002). 'The coltan phenomenon: how a rare mineral has changed the life of the population of war-torn North Kiru province in the East of the Democratic Republic of Congo'. Goma: Pole Institute. Retrieved from www.poleinstitute.org/documents/coltanglais02.pdf.

Teng, C.-c. (2007). 'Hegemony or partnership: China's strategy and diplomacy toward Latin America'. *China and the Developing World: Beijing's*

Strategy for the Twenty-First Century, ed. J. Eisenman, E. Heginbotham and D. Mitchell. London and New York: M. E. Sharpe.

Theroux, P. (2003). *Dark Star Safari: Overland from Cairo to Cape Town*. Boston: Houghton Mifflin.

Thompson, C. (2009). 'The scramble for genetic resources'. *A New Scramble for Africa? Imperialism, Investment and Development*, ed. R. Southall and H. Melber. Durban: University of KwaZulu-Natal Press.

Toulmin, C. (2009). *Climate Change in Africa*. London and New York: Zed Books in association with International African Institute, Royal African Society.

Trade Law Centre for Southern Africa (2009). 'The African trading relationship with Brazil'. Retrieved 12 Jan. 2010, from www.tralac.org/cause_data/images/1694/AfricanTradingRelationshipBrazil.pdf.

Trade Law Centre for Southern Africa (2010). 'China–Africa trade relationship'. Retrieved 23 April 2010, from www.tralac.org/cause_data/images/1694/china09.pdf.

Turner, T. (2002). 'Angola's role in the Congo War'. *The African Stakes of the Congo War*, ed. J. Clark. Basingstoke and New York: Palgrave Macmillan.

Turner, T. (2007). *The Congo Wars: Conflict, Myth, and Reality*. London and New York: Zed Books.

Turok, B. (2008). *From the Freedom Charter to Polokwane: The Evolution of ANC Economic Policy*. Cape Town, South Africa: New Agenda: South African Journal of Social and Economic Policy.

UNCTAD (2005). 'Case study on outward foreign direct investment by South African enterprises'. Paper produced by Trade and Development Board, Commission on Enterprise, Business Facilitation and Development for Expert Meeting on Enhancing Productive Capacity of Developing Country Firms through Internationalization. Geneva. 5–7 Dec.

UNCTAD (2007a). 'Statistics handbook'. Retrieved 17 Feb. 2010, from http://stats.unctad.org.

UNCTAD (2007b). *Asian Foreign Direct Investment in Africa: Towards a New Era of Cooperation among Developing Countries*. New York: United Nations.

UNCTAD (2010). *Economic Development in Africa: Report 2010 – South–South Cooperation: Africa and the New Forms of Development Partnership*. Geneva: United Nations.

UNDP (2005). *Human Development Report 2005: International Cooperation at a Crossroads: Aid, Trade and Security in an Unequal World*. Oxford: Oxford University Press.

UNDP (2006). *Human Development Report 2006: Beyond Scarcity – Power, Poverty and the Global Water Crisis*. Oxford and New York: Oxford University Press.

UNDP (2009). 'Africa–Brazil cooperation programme on social development'. Retrieved 16 April 2010, from www.undp-povertycentre.org.

United Nations Dept. of Economic and Social Affairs, and UNCTAD (2008). *World Economic Situation and Prospects 2009*. New York: United Nations.

United Nations Environment Programme (2007). *Environmental Impact Assessment of Trade Liberalization and Trade-Related Policies: A Country Study on the Fisheries Sector in Senegal.* Geneva: UNEP.

United States Central Intelligence Agency (2009). 'World factbook'. Retrieved 16 Dec. 2009, from www.cia.gov/library/publications/the-world-factbook.

United States Central Intelligence Agency (2010). *The CIA World Factbook.* New York: Skyhorse Pub.

van de Walle, N. (2001). *African Economies and the Politics of Permanent Crisis.* Cambridge and New York: Cambridge University Press.

van Dijk, M. P. (2009). 'Introduction: objectives and instruments for China's new presence in Africa'. *The New Presence of China in Africa*, ed. M. P. van Dijk. Amsterdam: Amsterdam University Press.

Vetter, T. (2008). 'Resource wars and information and communication technology'. *International Institute for Sustainable Development Commentary* April.

Vines, A. (2010). 'India's security concerns in the western Indian Ocean'. *India in Africa: Changing Geographies of Power*, ed. E. Mawdsley and G. McCann. Cape Town, Nairobi, Dakar and Oxford: Fahamu Books and Pambazuka Press.

Vines, A., and B. Oruitemeka (2008). 'India's engagement with the African Indian Ocean Rim states'. *Africa Programme Paper.* London: Chatham House.

Vines, A., L. Wong, M. Weimer and I. Campos (2009). *Thirst for African Oil: Asian National Oil Companies in Nigeria and Angola.* London: Chatham House.

Wade, R. (2003). *Governing the Market: Economic Theory and the Role of Government in East Asian Industrialization.* Princeton, NJ: Princeton University Press, 2nd edn.

Walt, V. (2008). 'The breadbasket of South Korea: Madagascar'. *Time* 23 Nov.

Wank, D. (1998). *Commodifying Chinese Communism: Business, Trust, and Politics in a South Coast City.* Cambridge and New York: Cambridge University Press.

Waters, M.-A., and M. Koppel (2009). *Capitalism and the Transformation of Africa: Reports from Equatorial Guinea.* New York, London, Montreal and Sydney: Pathfinder.

Watts, M. (2006). 'Empire of oil – capitalist dispossession and the scramble for Africa'. *Monthly Review – an Independent Socialist Magazine* 58(4): 1–17.

Watts, M. (2007). 'Petro-insurgency or criminal syndicate? Conflict and Violence in the Niger Delta'. *Review of African Political Economy* 114: 637–60.

Weisbrot, M., D. Baker and D. Rosnick (2007). 'The scorecard on development: 25 years of diminished progress'. *Flat World, Big Gaps: Economic*

Liberalization, Globalization, Poverty and Inequality, ed. K. S. Jomo and J. Baudot. London: Zed Books.

Wendt, A. (1999). *Social Theory of International Politics*. Cambridge and New York: Cambridge University Press.

White, H., and T. Killick (2001). *African Poverty at the Millennium: Causes, Complexities, and Challenges*. Washington, DC: World Bank.

Wolpe, H. (1975). 'The theory of internal colonialism: the South African case'. *Beyond the Sociology of Development: Economy and Society in Latin America and Africa*, ed. I. Oxaal, T. Barnett and D. Booth. London and Boston: Routledge & Paul.

World Bank (2009a). *Reshaping Economic Geography: World Development Report 2009*. Washington, DC: World Bank.

World Bank (2009b). *Converting Zambia's Resources into Sustainable Development: Results of an Assessment Using the Extractive Industries Value Chain*. Discussion note for review and comment. Washington, DC: Government of Zambia.

World Bank (2010). 'Poverty analysis'. Retrieved from http://web.worldbank.org.

World Conservation Union (2001). 'Coltan mining in World Heritage sites in the Democratic Republic of Congo : updated summary'. 23 April. Retrieved 1 Dec. 2010, from http://tierra.rediris.es/coltan/coltanenvir.pdf.

Wright, G., and J. Czelusta (2004). 'The myth of the resource curse'. *Challenge* 47(2): 6–38.

Wu, Y. (2006). *China and Africa, 1956–2006*. Beijing: China Intercontinental Press.

Xinhua (2008). 'Global financial crisis hitting African economies'. Retrieved 1 Dec. 2010, from news.xinhuanet.com/english/2008-10/31/content_10283347.htm.

Yager, T. (2005). 'The minerals industry of Mozambique'. *United States Geological Survey Mineral Yearbook 2005*. Washington, DC: United States Government.

Yardley, J. (2004). 'China faces stiff challenge to create work'. *International Herald Tribune*.

Yates, D. A. (2009). *The French Oil Industry and the Corps des mines in Africa*. Trenton, NJ: Africa World Press.

Yepe, M. (2008). 'Roosevelt vs. Churchill'. *Political Affairs: Marxist Thought Online* March April. Retrieved 21 Feb. 2010, from www.politicalaffairs.net/article/view/6550/1/319/playlist.../playlist.xml.

Yi-Chong, X. (2008). 'China and the United States in Africa: coming conflict or commercial coexistence?' *Australian Journal of International Affairs* 62(1): 16–37.

Yusuf, S., K. Naabeshima and D. Perkins (2007). 'China and India reshape global industrial geography'. *Dancing with Giants: China, India and the Global Economy*, ed. A. Winters and S. Yusuf. Washington, DC: World Bank and Institute for Policy Studies.

Zambanker (2008). 'BOC regulatory capital swells by 1000%'. Dec.: 1.

Zambia Consolidated Copper Mines, I. H. (2005). *Preparation of Phase 2 of A Consolidated Environmental Management Plan, Task Reports (Task II–VI)*. Lusaka: Zambia Consolidated Copper Mines, Industrial Holdings.

ZDA (2008). *The Economic Impact of Direct Investment on the Zambian Economy*. Lusaka: ZDA.

ZDA (n.d.). 'Approved Chinese and Indian investment in Zambia'. Unpublished paper. Lusaka: ZDA.

Zeilig, L. (2002). 'Crisis in Zimbabwe'. *International Socialism* 2(93): 75–96.

Zhang Li (2003). 'Some reflections on international intervention'. *International Intervention and State Sovereignty*. Beijing: China Reform Forum.

Zhao, M. (2006). 'External liberalization and the evolution of China's exchange system: an empirical approach'. *World Bank China Research Paper 4*. Retrieved 1 Dec. 2010, from http://siteresources.worldbank.org/INDIAEXTN/Resources/events/359987-1149066764594/Paper_MinZhao.pdf.

Zhao, Q. (1996). *Interpreting Chinese Foreign Policy*. New York: Oxford University Press.

Zhi, Y., and J. Bai (2010). 'The Global Environmental Institute: regulating the ecological impact of Chinese overseas enterprises'. *Chinese and African Perspectives on China in Africa*, ed. A. Harneit-Sievers, S. Marks and S. Naidu. Cape Town, Nairobi, Dakar and Oxford: Pambazuka Press.

Zimplats (n.d.). 'The history of Zimplats'. Retrieved 31 July 2005, from www.zimplats.com/about/about.htm.

ZMM-GT (Zambia-Malawi-Mozambique Growth Triangle) Coordinating Secretariat (2003). *Zambia-Malawi-Mozambique Growth Triangle: Private Sector – Public Sector Partnership for Sub-regional Development*. Nairobi: African Centre for Economic Growth.

Zoellinck, R. (2009). 'Foreword'. *Reshaping Economic Geography: World Development Report 2009*. Washington, DC: World Bank.

Zweig, D. (2002). *Internationalizing China: Domestic Interests and Global Linkages*. Ithaca, NY: Cornell University Press.

INDEX

Page numbers in *italic* refer to tables.